Land-locked States of Africa and Asia

# Land-locked States of Africa and Asia

*Edited by*

Dick Hodder, Sarah J. Lloyd and
Keith McLachlan

FRANK CASS
LONDON • PORTLAND, OR

First published in 1998 in Great Britain by
FRANK CASS PUBLISHERS
Newbury House, 900 Eastern Avenue
London, IG2 7HH

and in the United States of America by
FRANK CASS PUBLISHERS
c/o ISBS, 5804 N.E. Hassalo Street
Portland, Oregon 97213-3644

*Website* http://www.frankcass.com

British Library Cataloguing in Publication Data

Land-locked states of Africa and Asia
1. Landlocked states 2. Landlocked states – Economic aspects
3. Access to the sea (International law) 4. Landlocked state
– International cooperation
I. Hodder, Dick II. Lloyd, Sarah J. III. McLachlan, K.S.
(Keith Stanley), 1937–
33.9'5

ISBN 0714 64829 9
ISBN 0714 64371 8

Library of Congress Cataloging-in-Publication Data

Land-locked states of Africa and Asia / edited by Dick Hodder, Sarah
J. Lloyd and Keith McLachlan.
  p.  cm.
"Geopolitics and international boundaries, volume 2, number 1,
summer 1997, special issue ..."–Galley.
  Includes index.
  ISBN 0-7146-4829-9 (hardcover).  ISBN 0-7146-4371-8 (pbk.)
  1. Access to the sea (International law) 2. Landlocked states
–Africa. 3. Landlocked states–Asia. I. Hodder, Dick. II. Lloyd,
Sarah J. III. McLachlan, I.S. (Keith Stanley) IV. Geopolitics and
international boundaries. v. 2, no. 1, summer 1997 (Special issue)
KZA1375.L36   1997
341.4'44--dc21                                              97-38217
                                                                CIP

This group of studies first appeared in a Special Issue on
'Land-locked States of Africa and Asia' in
*Geopolitics and International Boundaries* 2/1 (Summer 1997)
published by Frank Cass.

*Printed in Great Britain by Antony Rowe Ltd., Chippenham, Wilts*

In honour of Ieuan Ll. Griffiths

# Contents

Introduction      **Keith McLachlan**   1

The Experience of Land-lockedness in Africa    **Ieuan Ll. Griffiths**   12

Chad: Power Vacuum or Geopolitical Focus    **George Joffé**   25

Land-locked Niger and its Alternative Seaport Access    **Ali Djimba**   40

Land-lockedness and Dependency on
Coastal Countries: The Case of Ethiopia    **Wuhib Muluneh**   56

African Land and Access Corridors    **Ieuan Ll. Griffiths**   69

Afghanistan: the Geopolitics of a Buffer State    **Keith McLachlan**   82

Land-locked Central Asia: Implications
for the Future    **Sarah J. Lloyd**   97

Mongolia: Looking to the Sea    **Alan Sanders**   134

Land-locked Laos: Dilemmas of Development
at the Edge of the World    **Jonathan Rigg**   153

Transit Arrangements between Nepal and India:
A Study in International Law    **Surya P. Subedi**   175

Resolving the Problems of Land-lockedness    **Martin Ira Glassner**   197

Conclusions    **Dick Hodder**   209

Index    221

# Introduction

## KEITH McLACHLAN

Land-lockedness is the condition of having no access to the open sea and is one that affects some 44 countries. More states still struggle to preserve their independence in the face of restricted openings to the sea via corridors or constrained seaboards. Given the violence surrounding the creation of improved outlets to the sea, as in the case of Iraq in the invasion of Kuwait in August 1990, and the elimination of existing corridors, as in the case of Ethiopia's loss of Eritrea in 1993, the subject has an interest that will not be gainsaid. Yet there are few major studies of the subject *per se* with the honourable exception of Professor Ira Glassner (see his contribution).[1]

The present volume is, it is hoped, a useful addition to the literature dealing with the problems of land-lockedness, access and communications. It is the product of two separate conferences held at the Geopolitics & International Boundaries Research Centre (GRC) in the School of Oriental & African Studies (SOAS) with the addition of several specially commissioned articles. The editors have taken the liberty of harmonising spellings, place-names and the styles of referencing but have otherwise left author's contributions in their original form.

Africa was the home of the majority of land-locked states arising from the original 'scramble for Africa'. The nature of colonial boundaries reflected both the pattern of colonial occupation, particularly after the Berlin Africa Conference in 1884, and intra-colonial boundaries where independent states were former administrative districts of larger colonial entities, as in the case of French West Africa and French Equatorial Africa.[2] Colonialism also played a role in creating straight-line boundaries, though this, as in the case of Zaire, did not preclude openings to the sea. Ethiopia is a late land-locked state which was a result of the independence of Eritrea in May 1993.

There has been a rapid increase in recent years in the number of states that are land-locked, that is, have no direct access to the sea. The break up of the USSR and the political emancipation of its former territories in Caucasia, Transcaucasia and Central Asia was the cause in 1991–92 of the sudden expansion in land-lockedness (see Table 1).

The events following the independence of the states of the former USSR once more raise questions concerning the viability of land-locked countries

TABLE 1

| Country | Date of Independence | Area (sq. km.) | Population (1994 est.) | GDP (1993 est.) |
|---|---|---|---|---|
| Afghanistan | 19 August 1919 | 647,500 | 16,903,400 | NA |
| Andorra | 1278 | 450 | 63,930 | $760 mn |
| Armenia | 23 September 1991 | 29,800 | 3,521,517 | $7.1 bn |
| Austria | 12 November 1918 | 83,850 | 7,954,974 | $134.4 bn |
| Azerbaijan | 30 August 1991 | 86,600 | 7,684,456 | $15.5 bn |
| Belarus | 25 August 1991 | 207,600 | 10,404,862 | $61 bn |
| Bhutan | 8 August 1949 | 47,000 | 716,380 | $500 mn |
| Bolivia | 6 August 1825 | 1,098,580 | 7,719,445 | $15.8 bn |
| Bosnia & Herzegovina | April 1992 | 51,233 | 4,651,485 | NA |
| Botswana | 30 September 1966 | 600,370 | 1,359,352 | $6 bn |
| Burkina | 5 August 1960 | 274,200 | 10,134,661 | $7 bn |
| Burundi | 1 July 1962 | 27,830 | 6,124,747 | $6 bn |
| Central African Republic | 13 August 1960 | 622,980 | 3,142,182 | $2.5 bn |
| Chad | 11 August 1960 | 1,284,000 | 5,466,771 | $2.7 bn |
| Czech Republic | 1 January 1993 | 78,703 | 10,408,280 | $75 bn |
| Ethiopia | at least 2,000 years | 1,127,127 | 54,927,108 | $22.7 bn |
| Hungary | 1001 | 93,030 | 10,319,113 | $57 bn |
| Kazakhstan | 16 December 1991 | 2,717,300 | 17,267,554 | $60.3 bn |
| Kyrygzstan | 31 August 1991 | 198,500 | 4,698,108 | $11.3 bn |
| Laos | 19 July 1949 | 236,800 | 4,701,654 | $4.1 bn |
| Lesotho | 4 October 1966 | 30,350 | 1,944,493 | $2.8 bn |
| Liechenstein | 23 January 1719 | 160 | 30,281 | $630 mn |
| Luxemburg | 1839 | 2,586 | 401,900 | $8.7 bn |
| Macedonia | 17 September 1991 | 25,333 | 2,213,785 | $2.2 bn |
| Malawi | 6 July 1964 | 118,480 | 9,732,409 | $6 bn |
| Mali | 22 September 1960 | 1,024,000 | 9,112,950 | $5.8 bn |
| Moldova | 27 August 1991 | 33,700 | 4,473,033 | $16.3 bn |
| Mongolia | 13 March 1921 | 1,565,000 | 2,429,762 | $2.8 bn |
| Nepal | 1768 | 140,800 | 21,041,527 | $20.5 bn |
| Niger | 3 August 1960 | 1,267,000 | 8,971,605 | $5.4 bn |
| Paraguay | 14 May 1811 | 406,750 | 5,213,772 | $15.2 bn |
| Rwanda | 1 July 1962 | 26,340 | 8,373,963 | $6.8 bn |
| San Marino | 301 AD (by tradition) | 60 | 24,091 | $370 mn (1992 est.) |
| Slovakia | 1 January 1993 | 48,845 | 5,403,505 | $31 bn |
| Slovenia | 25 June 1991 | 20,296 | 1,972,227 | $15 bn |
| Swaziland | 6 September 1968 | 17,360 | 936,369 | $2.3 bn |
| Switzerland | 1 August 1291 | 41,290 | 7,040,119 | $149.1 bn |
| Tajikistan | 9 September 1991 | 143,100 | 5,995,469 | $6.9 bn |
| Turkmenistan | 27 October 1991 | 488,100 | 3,995,122 | $13 bn |
| Uganda | 9 October 1962 | 236,040 | 19,121,934 | $24.1 bn |
| Uzbekistan | 1 September 1991 | 447,400 | 22,608,866 | $53.7 bn |
| Vatican City | 11 February 1929 | .44 | 821 | NA |
| Zambia | 24 October 1964 | 752,610 | 9,188,190 | $7.3 bn |
| Zimbabwe | 18 April 1980 | 390,580 | 10,975,078 | $15.9 bn |

*Source:* GRC, SOAS, 1996

as truly autonomous nation-states. It has long been an axiom that movements for the creation of new states rarely succeed where the area contested has no outlet to the sea.[3] Contemporary Russia makes no secret of its determination to control Azerbaijan and the Central Asian states over matters such as the export of oil and natural gas by pipeline, rejecting all routes that omitted transit through its territory.[4] It is appropriate timing, therefore, that a new examination is given to the overall difficulty of land-locked states as essayed in this volume.

Since Africa was the birthplace of serious studies of the nature of land-locked states, this volume begins its regional coverage with an analysis of the experience of land-lockedness in Africa. The point is well made that 'Given the large but compact continental landmass of Africa, its division into fifty-two independent states, more than any other continent,[5] *some* land-locked states are to be expected. Add that Africa was partitioned by alien imperial powers...it is inevitable that there are *many* African land-locked states'. The balkanisation process, seen as an unnecessary and short-sighted concomitant of de-colonisation, is a recurring theme in the study of land-lockedness, as in West Africa where natural resource endowment is poor and the colonial experience of development largely negative. The coming of the railways in this area was late in the colonial period and did little to change the status of the area from being a colonial backwater.

The situation in East Africa was mixed, the British territories along the Mombasa-Kampala railway benefiting early from improved communications. Quite the opposite occurred in Rwanda and Burundi, where no modern transport system connected the territories to the sea. The development of other East African territories for the export of agricultural goods and copper is examined, with special concern for the growth of Rhodesian communications systems with their advantages and shortcomings. The growth of rail and other transport networks in Africa as a means of overcoming the difficulties of land-lockedness where distance of some countries from the sea is very considerable. The case of Zambia, is an instance of the conflict between legal regimes for land-locked states and the brutality of realpolitik. Eleven of the land-locked states of Africa are small, remote, economically and politically weak, underdeveloped and dependent. Land-lockedness, with very few countries being excepted, makes so much worse the constraints – particularly affecting external trade – on economic, political and social development in Africa.

The case of Chad demonstrates the problems of access for land-locked states within a context of international law and contemporary political realities. The Cairo Declaration of 1964 on the sanctity of colonial boundaries has been useful but far from fully followed as the case of the Aozou Strip between Libya and Chad demonstrates. The very valid point is made that many of the states of Africa face severe difficulties in constructing themselves as nation-states and that land-lockedness has further complicated matters. This is especially so where the regime in any case lacks political legitimacy.

The pre-colonial Chad shows the extent to which Chad's land-lockedness arose from the later accidents of history. Chad, before the French occupation, was part of a series of broader zones of human settlement – the nomadic north on the rim on the Sahara and its great mountain systems of Tibesti and Ennedi and adjacent to them the settled groups of Kanouri and Kamadja together with Arab tribal peoples. A detailed break down of these major agglomerations illustrates the oddness of the human patchwork, part of which was encompassed by the political entity that became Chad. The elements of fusion through alliance and inter-marriage are offset by patterns of conflict in religion, folk history – especially the incidence of slaving in the south – and tribal affiliation.

French colonial rule established itself piecemeal but eventually a set of borders was set up, largely serving French internal administrative needs within their new African territories. The emergence of Chad's borders exhibits just how imprecise the entire French exercise was in practice. There was, however, an irony in that the poorly constructed boundaries of the east and west were to throw up no immediate problems with neighbours while the northern boundary with Libya, apparently set in legal tablets of stone in the 1919 Franco-Italian agreement, caused decades of border conflict and military activity. The legal progress of the Aozou dispute is documented leading to the settlement at the International Court of Justice in 1994.

During French colonial rule the division of Chad into the southern zone, where educational and developmental activities were concentrated, and a Muslim zone, where colonial intrusion and economic investment was relatively small, deeply divided the Chad region. The disposition of power at the end of the colonial period was inverted, with the former powerful Muslim sultanates secondary to the richer south. The readjustments this occasioned after independence, including the civil wars, are discussed, with their ramifications of foreign (French and Libyan) intervention. The resulting economic prostration of Chad and its precarious internal political imbalances are summarised as products of the French colonial intervention. This sorry story is not proposed by the writer as the outcome of Chad's land-locked position, but rather as the expression of a political legacy of a centrally disposed state at the mercy of badly defined and unsettled frontiers.

Niger is a country which is technically classified as land-locked but which, by virtue of its location on the River Niger, has an economically dubious physical if not political avenue to the Atlantic Seaboard of West

Africa. Niger is hampered by the inherent problems of high transport costs for imports and exports because it is a large country without a fully developed internal transport system and suffers from all the difficulties faced by a struggling third world economy. The dependency problem is acute. Adjacent states with sea ports are bound with Niger in a series of transit agreements going back to the Treaty of Versailles in 1919, none of which is implemented securely or even-handedly from the point of view of Niger, which remains either a supplicant for better arrangements at the official level or a victim of the extortions of local trading chiefs who manage the informal sector. But the practicalities are that language differences, inharmonious currency and banking systems and inefficiency characterise the transportation network linking Niger to the outside world. A prime example of this difficulty is the new highway built with World Bank assistance, which links all the main cities in Niger to Cotonou in Benin but which is closed because Benin-Niger governments wish to exploit their monopoly of rail lines along the same route. Under-development is a product of the international division of labour, though the evidence he presents also indicates that internal policies deeply exacerbate whatever comparative disadvantages, including those of land-lockedness, plague Niger from outside.

Ethiopia is among the most recent of states to become land-locked. The country is learning to cope with its new dependency on its coastal neighbours of Eritrea and Djibouti. The conclusion must be that, despite the development of the port of Assab in Eritrea and the modernisation of transit facilities in Djibouti, Ethiopia's external trade will remain geared to stability and growth in the littoral states. The formation of a regional economic co-operation agreement with Djibouti and Eritrea provides a formal basis for future trade integration; political harmony and understanding will also be required if Ethiopia is not to suffer from the difficulties of land-lockedness.

The constraints on countries that suffer from limitations of access through land corridors to the open sea is a parallel consideration to full land-lockedness. Corridors are seen in two forms – first, those which currently exist that in configuration are long and narrow and, second, relict corridors. Corridors were constructed in both colonial times and following independence, the colonial legacy being far more effective and sustainable than successor lines of access.

The corridor of access to the sea for Zaire along the Congo was established in 1885 and survives to the present with a 35km Atlantic coastline. The history of this corridor is examined as an example of a successful attempt to off-set land-lockedness. A second instance is of the Caprivi Strip which connects the Zambesi River with northern Namibia. The Caprivi Strip is portrayed as 'a sore thumb on the political map of Africa.'.

Less obvious corridors also exist, principally the 'road north' between the Transvaal and the Kalahari, which was Cecil Rhodes' strategic corridor to the Cape. Other 'relict' land corridors are identified, including the two German-French constructs for access to the Obangui and Congo rivers from the German colony of Kamerun. The Anglo-Belgian arrangement for access for a British Cape-Cairo rail link between Lakes Tanganyika and Edward was short-lived while the Mahgi strip gave Belgian access to Lake Albert until the 1915 adjustment left the entire west shore of the lake in Belgian hands.

In the post-colonial era attempts to set up access corridors to the sea for land-locked states were well-intentioned but poorly based. The Ethiopian corridor through Eritrea worked for the period 1936–93 until Eritrea became independent. Malawi's claims to the Niassa corridor gained no support and the same fate overcame the Ugandan attempt in the 1970s to force a corridor through to the sea across Tanzanian territory. The Beira rail corridor for Zimbabwe to Mutare (Umtali) functions without needing any transfer of sovereignty, while the Swaziland to Kosi corridor proposed by South Africa in the 1980s never came into being at all.

The appeal of access corridors both for Africa and elsewhere is enduring as a solution to the problem of land-lockedness, despite the bad experience of African states in the twentieth century. Russian claims to access to the Black Sea keep access corridors a live issue in contemporary international politics.

Afghanistan is both land-locked and is a topographic divide. It acted as a buffer zone[6] between Russia, Great Britain and the Persian Gulf. This paper examines Afghanistan as a land-locked state and a buffer in the 'great game' of international geopolitics. The hypothesis presented is that Afghanistan is a mountain fortress, which the Russians, Persians and British were never able to control. The country may be seen as a zone from which rival great powers sought to exclude each other. Afghanistan was therefore in many ways a classic buffer-state throughout much of the nineteenth century. The conclusion must be that the 'tyranny of terrain remains a stubborn reality'[7] in Afghanistan. It is an area which repels rather than attracts. Its strategic significance is as a negative zone where external powers intrigue but find it difficult to put down roots.

The linkage between land-lockedness and the role of Afghanistan as a buffer-state can be seen as the result of special circumstances in which the application of the concept of buffer-state is reinforced by the national territory being land-locked. Afghanistan's designation as the 'Switzerland of the East'[8] is the analogy which gives support to this contention. At the same time, being land-locked, Afghanistan was created as the inevitable client to Russian and British patrons. Without transit routes through Russia and India, Afghanistan became isolationist and without flexibility in the management of its own affairs. There is also the interesting notion that land-lockedness gave Afghanistan no choice in selecting its allies. States other than Great Britain and Russia might be courted as allies by the Afghans but, without a territorial base, were at a disadvantage.[9] Being land-locked, Afghanistan was at the mercy of conspiracy, treaty or tacit arrangement between the neighbours for which it was a buffer-state.

The five new states of Central Asia – Kazakhstan, Turkmenistan, Uzbekistan, Tajikistan and Kyrgyzstan – , despite their wealth in hydrocarbon and other natural resources (or perhaps because of it), were ill-prepared for independence. The development of trade in Central Asia in relation to the transport infrastructure and the need for the regional states to create other outlets is vital if they are to escape the persistent economic and political influence of Russia.

Central Asia largely remains tied in to the imperial/communist Russian economy. The distortions this introduced remain central including the effects of Soviet developments in agriculture and industry. The structure of the oil sector and the alignment of the export system from a land-locked province to a scarcely better served Soviet centre add to the Central Asian problem. How the regional states will overcome their twin difficulties of tight linkage to an inefficient and restrictive Russian transportation network in which Moscow has monopolist power is to be seen within the context of the new pipeline route options other than those through Russia – Black Sea, Turkey, Iran, Afghanistan and China. Until such alternative export lines are constructed with the help of a forceful third party, the Central Asian states will remain dependent on Russia.

Interestingly, Iran is well placed to act as transit route for Central Asia, situated at the centre of south-west Asia and, in its Caspian provinces, linking the Middle East zone to Central Asia and Transcaucasia. It has for centuries played an important role in moulding the history of the Caspian Basin and is seen as crucially placed in determining the future of the region. Russia and the OECD states have yet to come to terms with Iran or to accommodate to the new geography of the Caspian region, which now includes Central Asia and much of Transcaucasia bordering Iran. Iran is misconstrued by Western governments as a cordon between the Caspian Basin and the warm waters of the Persian Gulf/Indian Ocean, limiting the options open for evacuating the hydrocarbon and other wealth of the Caspian Basin.[10]

It is clear from the debate on Caspian oil disposals that Iran can play a major logistical role for the land-locked states of Central Asia. During World War II Iran became an important Allied supply route to the USSR. The route used was that of the Trans-Iranian railway and the largely parallel road system. A secondary axis now also exists between Bandar Abbas and Messhed and thence to the USSR via Sarakhs to Marv or via Quchan to Central Asia. This route must still be a favoured gateway for the Caspian states to the south. By distance, however, the direct line down eastern Iran remains a potential axis for transportation development. New transport-communications links through Messhed-Birjand to Chah Bahar also offer short and potentially useful north-south access though Iran.[11]

Mongolia has been a form of independent land-locked state since 1924, but only under a liberal constitution since 1992. Mongolia was bypassed by modern developments through its isolation by the adjacent powers – Russia and China in their imperial and more recent guises. There is a notable lack of all-weather roads and useful waterways, leaving the crucial rail network to carry 90 per cent of national freight. The evolution of trade with China and Soviet Russia, opened up the country through the improvement of the rail system as a means of overcoming land-lockedness – the Ulan Bator line as the key element in the 1960s and the growth of land links with China in the 1980s. The inclusion of preferential treatment for Mongolia in the 1991 PRC-Mongolia transit agreement to Tianjin's Xingang international port was based on Mongolia's special needs as a land-locked state. There is some irony in the fact that 'hundreds of millions of dollars worth of aid' has been put into Mongolia's infrastructure to help overcome its land-locked situation while many of Africa's land-locked states languish with little help to overcome similar and possibly more pressing problems.

The case of Laos, as Southeast Asia's only land-locked state became independent from France in 1954.[12] The problems of overland transport in Laos have been exacerbated by its land-lockedness. Laos may be depicted as having undergone rapid political and economic change in which improvements in transport links to neighbouring countries and to the open sea have been pivotal. The comparative weakness of Laos vis-à-vis Vietnam and Thailand has led to a situation where, 'successful economic development...is contingent upon maintaining improved relations with Bangkok and Hanoi'.

The growth of international transport connections has absorbed no less than 20 per cent of total national investment funds yet Laos remains poorly served by links, much of its northern areas being effectively cut off from the world during the wet season. Meanwhile, there are problems of mountainous terrain, low population density and a legacy of damage from the Vietnam war.

While some efforts are being made, for example, to upgrade port and navigation facilities on the River Mekong, progress is very slow and expensive for this poor nation. The position is made worse by the intransigent attitude of Laos's neighbours. Thailand in particular may be seen as using the border and Laos's land-lockedness as a political tool – obstructing innocent passage of goods through tightening border controls and imposing what amounted to a wide ranging blockage against exports to and imports from Laos. The consequence of Thai policies was a realignment of export routes through Vietnam, aided by new investment in roads that were more expensive and circuitous than the Thai route. The pattern for the future is aptly positive, with a Lao deputy prime minister tellingly asserting recently that Laos hoped to be a link between adjacent states rather than a victim of its land-locked position. The Laos example illustrates how a policy of practising good relations with neighbours, even under provocation, is one way of defeating the dangers and isolation of Semple's 'central' countries' syndrome.[13]

International law is unkind to land-locked states. The problems faced by Nepal in its transit arrangements with India developed as a 'cold war' between the two states and the gradual closing down of Nepal's access through India to the sea. The Indian authorities curtailed Nepal's transit trade and Nepal has claimed that India violated international law in imposing a virtual economic blockade against it. The signature of a memorandum of understanding on trade and transit was signed between the two states in June 1990 ending the confrontation but leaving important questions of international law unresolved. Certainly, Nepal was forced to make major concessions to its larger neighbour, including accepting constraints on its acquisition of arms from China, foregoing defence dealings with China and granting privileges in law to Indian citizens. Additionally, it might be questioned whether, first, the agreement of 1990 need be renewed by India at its expiry, and, second, if India will feel obliged under international law to grant only one access point for Nepali goods in transit or indeed any access by right at all.

The nature of the Indo-Nepali relationship in historical, political and legal terms is defined by disputes. It is the legal side which is given stress, however, with the burden of the debate lying in the domain of the perspective of the Indian-Nepali transit dispute. The Barcelona Convention on Freedom of Transit is the starting point with key relevance of its provisions to the issue between India and Nepal. The provisions of other international agreements are also inspected, especially the 1982 Convention on the Law of the Sea. The weight of authorities supports the view that access to the sea is guaranteed by customary international law.

The claim by India that it was required to make a single transit point for Nepal under international law, rather that the fifteen which were used before the 1987 rift in relations, is dubious and there are authorities who believe that India's position has 'no legal basis'. By 1991 India appeared to have granted a restitution of the full *status quo ante* the 1987 crisis transit access to Nepal. The 1991 Transit Treaty also specifically accepted that 'Nepal as a land-locked country needs access to and from the Sea to promote its international trade'. The 1991 Treaty is less than ideal, none the less, since it takes full account of neither the 1982 Convention on the Law of the Sea nor UNCLOS III. India gained transit reciprocity from Nepal and other concessions entirely unwarranted under international law, leading to the conclusion that, in practice, right favours the strong.

It is concluded[14] that the academic community liaises but little with the UN and national authorities responsible for day-to-day management of problems of land-lockedness. Similarly, all the problems of land-locked states are political at heart and can only be solved by political means. Five approaches to transit difficulties can be offered – (1) elaboration of international conventions and UN-sponsored agreements, (2) intensified general economic growth which furnishes greater trade for all, (3) improved transit arrangements, (4) expanded facilities in the transit states to create capacity and demand for extra trade flows from the interior states, and (5) adoption of regional trade pacts which overarch local constraint on transit from land-locked states.

The scope for improved transit arrangements is a key area for useful progress. In summary, the point can be made that 'The rights and claims of land-locked states, therefore, are likely to become more, not less, prominent as we approach the end of the twentieth century.' Judging by the materials relating to both theory and case studies of land-lockedness in this volume from many parts of the developing world this view is regretfully being proved correct.

There are significant differences between those land-locked states which emerged from the disintegrations of empires and those which arose from colonial origins. There are also gradations of severity of land-lockedness which need to be considered in any assessment of impact on potential for economic development. It might be suggested that there are solutions available to overcome the problems of land-lockedness – through bilateral agreements with coastal neighbours, through diminishing reliance on external trade whilst emphasising internal commerce and development and, lastly, by creating general regional organisations backed by multinational treaties. In essence land-lockedness in the third world, like other geographical factors, needs to be accepted and accommodated rather than fought against.

NOTES

1. *Bibliography on Land-locked States*, 3rd ed. (Dordrecht: Martinus Nijhoff 1991).
2. I. Brownlee, *African Boundaries* (London: Hurst/RIIA 1979) pp.5–6.

3. This is recognised by movements such as the Kurdish Democratic Party and the Patriotic Union of Kurdistan. Cf. M. O'Shea, 'Between the map and the reality', *Peuples Méditerranéens* 68–69 p.173.

4. The Russian ambassador to Iran, Mr Tretiakov, made clear in a conference address in Tehran on 10 December 1995 (Oil & Gas Prospects in the Caspian Region, Conference, Tehran Institute of Political & International Studies, 11–12 Dec. 1995. ) that no oil or natural gas would be exported from any of its former possession without specific Russian approval.

5. R. Bridges, 'Africa, Africans and the sea' in J.C. Stone (ed.), *Africa and the Sea*, (Aberdeen: Aberdeen University African Studies Group [Proceedings of a Colloquium, March 1984] 1985).

6. Buffer-zone is defined in the Ingalls view 'as...a small political or administrative unit located between and separating two larger opposing powers.' G.L. Ingalls, 'Buffer states: outlining and expanding existing theory', in J. Chay and T.E. Ross (eds) *Buffer States in World Politics* (Boulder, Colorado: Westview 1986) p.233.

7. M.Z. Ispahani, *Roads and Rivals: the Politics of Access in the Borderlands of Asia*, (London: I. B. Tauris 1989) p.2.

8. J.S. Roucek, 'Afghanistan in geopolitics', in *Eastern World* 17/12 (1961) p.4.

9. Germany was an outside contender in the period after 1910 but, although a commercial rival to GR and Russia, never took political risks to sustain its position.

10. The US view of 'dual containment' is encapsulated by T.R. Mattair, 'Horizons for cooperation in the Gulf and the Oman Sea: The view from Washington' in *The Iranian Journal of International Affairs*, (Tehran, Vol.7/3 1995), pp.576–84.

11. K.S. McLachlan, 'Geopolitics of oil and gas in the Caspian Region', in *Oil and Gas Prospects in the Caspian Region*, (Institute for Political and International Studies/Institute for International Energy Studies, Tehran 1996), pp.26–48.

12. Laos was part of French Indochina before this date.

13. E.C. Semple, *Influences of Geographic Environment* (London: Constable & Co. 1911) pp.139–41. Semple made the point that 'A state embedded in the heart of a continent...if weak, its very existence is imperiled because of encroachments on every side'.

14. By Professor Ira Glassner of Southern Connecticut State University who kindly contributed the penultimate paper to this volume.

# The Experience of Land-lockedness in Africa

## IEUAN Ll.GRIFFITHS

In May 1993 Ethiopia became the fifteenth land-locked state in Africa when Eritrea achieved independence. That followed a thirty-year war of secession and a longer delayed self-determination referendum. A former Italian colony, Eritrea had been controversially incorporated into Ethiopia in 1961 largely because it blocked Ethiopian access to the sea. Ethiopia's new status is due to the break up of an empire, a genesis shared with the land-locked states which emerged from colonial empires in Africa and, more recently, from the former empires of the Soviet Union and Yugoslavia. Eritrea's independence could also mark the break down of the political status quo which has prevailed since the end of European imperialism in Africa and more specifically since July 1964 when the Organisation of African Unity (OAU) agreed that member states should respect their colonial boundaries. Interpreting Eritrea's independence as the break up of an existing state (Ethiopia) and as ending the long-standing inhibition on African boundary change, could support the thesis that Africa is about to embark on a period of new political instability. For the first time since the colonial partition would the territorial integrity of states, the basic structure of African political geography, be affected. The threatened disintegration of Liberia and Sierra Leone are in this respect also ominous, as are, in a different way, the rash of African boundary disputes now being referred for solution outside Africa. The multiplicity of land-locked states represents a fundamental flaw in the basic political geography of Africa which, similar to the flawed international boundaries, has a colonial cause and poses a threat to independent development.

Given the large but compact continental landmass of Africa, its lack of great sea inlets, its short coastline in relation to area, and its division into fifty-two independent states, more than any other continent,[1] some land-locked states are to be expected. Add that Africa was partitioned by alien imperial powers who then relinquished direct colonial rule for indirect neo-colonial power, easily asserted over a balkanised continent of small, politically and economically weak states, it is inevitable that there are many African land-locked states. In all there are 15, in three blocks, west, east and south-central, plus Ethiopia in the north-east and the small isolated states of Swaziland and Lesotho in the south.

The western land-locked states are all former French colonies.[2] Mali (French Sudan), Burkina Faso (Upper Volta) and Niger were part of the *Afrique Occidentale Française (AOF)*. Together they cover a vast, sparsely populated area between the coastal states of West Africa and the Sahara. The Central African Republic (CAR) (Obangui Chari) and Chad formerly part of the *Afrique Equatoriale Française (AEF)* are also enormous, extending from the central Sahara to the tropical rainforest of the Congo. French dominance of Mali, Burkina Faso and Niger came from an imperial thrust, from Dakar to the inland Niger and eastwards, aimed at preventing inland expansion by other colonial powers from the Guinea coast. Large tracts of these territories were long into this century not even given the status of colonies but were under military rule. Upper Volta appeared (1919), disappeared (1932) and reappeared (1947) at the changing whim of French colonial administrators. All five sparsely-ruled territories were remote and possessed few natural resources (*seche* rather than *utile)* to attract colonial attention. Economic development was very limited and the French created few opportunities for improvement.

There was little modern transport access from the sea in the colonial period. The French military thrust to the navigable middle Niger (1880s) was backed initially but belatedly by a 310 mile (496km) metre-gauge railway from Kayes on the navigable upper Senegal river to Bamako (1904), with 555 miles (888km) of river transport to St. Louis at the river mouth which was connected to Dakar by a further 164 mile (262km) railway. In 1910 the French completed a second railway 222 miles (355km) to the Niger from Conakry to Kouroussa, 368 miles (589km) upstream of Bamako. This reduced greatly the distance to the sea but both routes were limited by the marked seasonal flows of the Senegal and Niger rivers. Only by 1924 was the Bamako/Kayes railway extended direct to Dakar 769 miles (1230km) via Tambacounda. From Abidjan the French built a railway to Bobo-Dioulasso in 1934, extended to Ouagadougou, 743 miles (1189km), in Upper Volta in 1954 primarily to facilitate labour flow to the coastal region. Niger and Chad, even more remote, were totally unsullied by modern surface transport whilst Obangui-Chari was reached by 718 miles (1149km) of river transport to Bangui from Brazzaville, itself 319 miles (511km) from Pointe Noire on the coast by another metre-gauge railway (1934) which opened up the Congo basin to the French. The five land-locked territories were colonial backwaters, extremities of a far-flung empire, occupied as much to keep other powers out as for their own value.

In east Africa Uganda was a British 'protectorate' where indirect rule and Christian missions flourished. The land-locked protectorate controlling the source of the Nile had few white settlers or mineral resources but possessed rich agriculture. Cotton, coffee, tea and sugar cash crops were encouraged by the colonial administration and to some extent by the strategic metre-gauge Uganda railway built from Mombasa, at first (1901) as far as Port Florence (Kisumu) (572 miles, 915km) on Lake Victoria, but by 1931 extended to Kampala (725 miles, 1160km). Rwanda and Burundi result from the division of the League of Nations trust territory of Ruanda-Urundi which in turn had been carved out of German East Africa (Tanganyika) and given to Belgium as reward for being on the winning side in the First World War. The rationale behind this particular reward was that it was contiguous with the Belgian Congo and, unlike the west coast territory Belgium coveted, had been German and was not strategically important. Similar in some respects to Uganda, Ruanda-Urundi had few white settlers but many Christian missionaries; few mineral resources but rich agricultural land supporting a high density of population. The territory was very remote, over 1720 miles (2750km) from the sea at Matadi, with few development prospects. The Belgians established no modern surface transport access to the sea. Even the river port of Stanleyville (Kisangani) was 413 miles (660km) distant by atrocious dirt tracks.

Ethiopia became land-locked only in 1993, but was land-locked prior to the Italian invasion of 1935 as it had been over centuries of history. The colonial boundary of Eritrea which re-emerged in 1993 was one of the few ever to disappear from the political map of Africa. The 1961 Ethiopian take-over of Eritrea had been pure African imperialism, aided and abetted for strategic cold-war reasons by the United States which elsewhere supported formal decolonisation. Land-locked Ethiopia is served by a 776km metre-gauge railway built by the French from Djibouti to Addis Ababa and opened in 1908.

Nyasaland (Malawi) and Northern Rhodesia (Zambia) with Southern Rhodesia (Zimbabwe), together comprised the short-lived Federation of Rhodesia and Nyasaland (1953–63). The Federation was an attempt by white settlers, mainly in Southern Rhodesia, with active Conservative support at Westminster, to create a system of government between what they saw as the extremes of, as yet untried, black majority rule and white minority rule epitomised by the emergent sterile apartheid state of South Africa. Their 'Partnership' erred towards apartheid offering too little to the majority, particularly in the northern territories. In 1963 the Federation broke up, unable to withstand the wave of African nationalism then sweeping the continent. Malawi and Zambia attained independence separately in 1964, leaving a re-named Rhodesia, replete with a large (250,000) settler population, to follow a troubled, rebellious path to independence with majority rule in 1980 as Zimbabwe.

Nyasaland was a model British African Protectorate: few settlers, many missionaries, high density of population, few minerals but rich in agriculture with tea and tobacco important cash crops. It was remote, first with access by the Zambesi and Shire valleys, via Chinde, the British-leased port at the mouth of the Zambesi, and from 1935 by direct rail link with Beira.[3] Northern Rhodesia, also a British Protectorate, lay athwart the spinal railway from the Cape across the Zambesi (1905) to the Katangan copper mines (1910). It too was an archetypal British Protectorate except in the south and centre. White settlers crept in along the 'line of rail' to alienate land for commercial agriculture and from the late 1920s the Copperbelt was opened up. The copper companies developed mines and mining camps which mushroomed into towns. The modern development of mining was to create problems for a future independent, land-locked Zambia as it generated bulk exports of copper. In colonial times, however, copper exports stimulated the creation of alternative rail routes of access to the sea. The original spinal route was over 3000km from the Copperbelt to the Cape ports. There was a circuitous, 2000km rail route to Beira but that port was unable to cope with the bulk of copper traffic. In 1929 the Belgians opened a new railway to Port Francqui (Ilebo) on the Kasai river over 800km by river from Leopoldville (Kinshasa) itself 374km by rail from the Congo estuary seaport of Matadi. The route was marred by double trans-shipment and great overall length (3395km). The completion of the Benguela railway from the Angolan west coast in 1931, a private venture specifically to tap the copper trade, was a marked improvement but the sea was still 2500km distant. Southern Rhodesia was white-settler country with the more fertile and more accessible half of the land area alienated. Early white hopes of great mineral riches, another Witwatersrand, were never realised and settlers were 'given' land by the British South Africa Company (BSAC) in compensation. Nevertheless Southern Rhodesia developed mining, a rich, settler-based commercial agriculture and, in time, a large manufacturing sector. Rhodes fought to prevent his new empire being blocked from the sea by Portuguese Mozambique, but all his efforts to bluff, bully or buy a corridor of access failed.[4] So Southern Rhodesia remained land-locked, its high level of economic development and settler population, anomalous among Africa's land-locked territories. In early colonial times land-lockedness did not matter as Rhodesia was seen as a potential fifth province of South Africa and as such was similar to the land-locked Transvaal and Orange Free State. But in 1922, before BSAC rule ended, the settlers opted in a referendum for 'responsible self government' rather than union with South Africa.[5] Early rail routes to ensure the survival of the colony were to the Cape ports (1897) and Beira (1900). As the settler-led economy grew a railway was built direct to Lourenco Marques (Maputo) in 1955, avoiding South Africa to maintain independence but giving access to a more efficient port.[6] The Beira corridor was further enhanced by a tarred road and an oil pipeline. During the death throes of the illegal settler government (1965–79), the policy of independence from South Africa was abandoned in the interests of survival. The long-delayed rail link with South Africa via Beit Bridge was opened in 1974 in a futile attempt to prevent the inevitable by establishing an economic lifeline to the apartheid state before access to the sea was denied (March 1976) by the incoming FRELIMO government in newly independent Mozambique.

Bechuanaland (Botswana), Basutoland (Lesotho) and Swaziland also escaped union with South Africa because Britain honoured treaties with African chiefs who did not want it. Later, despite pressure from white South Africa and debate in Britain,[7] the option became increasingly unacceptable, especially as the apartheid state emerged in South Africa. Bechuanaland embraced much of the Kalahari desert and had a very sparse population living mainly near its better-watered eastern border. In the colonial period it was a typical British protectorate: remote, few resources except indigenous agriculture, few settlers and many missionaries. Contiguous with South Africa, it supplied that country with meat and labour. Rhodes' rail 'road to the north' gave access from the south. Swaziland loosely based on the traditional Swazi kingdom became a British Protectorate after the Anglo-Boer war before which it was administered by, but not absorbed into, the South African Republic (Transvaal). Before independence in 1968, unlike other British protectorates, more than half of Swaziland was alienated, largely by white South Africans. In the 1930s asbestos mining was developed but did not open up Swaziland because it was marginally located and exports went via aerial ropeway to the South African railhead at Barberton. Basutoland (Lesotho), another African kingdom which had emerged during the early nineteenth century Mfecane, sought British protection against Boer encroachment in 1868. Lesotho had few natural resources and relied on large-scale labour exports to South Africa. A rail spur from South Africa (1905) extends one mile into Lesotho to facilitate this human traffic. Among African land-locked states Lesotho uniquely is doubly disadvantaged being completely surrounded by a single country, South Africa.

Independence came to European colonies in Africa individually. Most of the land-locked ones became neo-colonial backwaters, no longer part of over-arching empires. Whether decisions to give independence to colonies rather than to colonial federations were deliberate acts of balkanisation to facilitate neo-colonialism is debatable. The effect is evident: emergent land-locked states were seriously disadvantaged.

Land-locked states, by definition, lack direct access to the sea and depend on another state or states for such access. Important considerations are: the absolute distances involved; the quality of the route in respect of modern transport availability and maintenance; alternative modes of transport (rail, paved road, lake and river ships) on individual routes; modal trans-shipments; the number of international borders crossed by individual routes to the sea; and the availability of alternative routes of access. At independence some African land-locked states had no modern transport links with the sea, some had grossly inefficient circuitous colonial links, others found colonial routes of access denied them and had to upgrade alternative routes as a matter of urgency. Because at independence there were few paved roads in Africa, the expense of creating such links with the coast fell on the new land-locked states. Always there is dependency, for access itself, for building and maintaining, operating and prioritising transport links including port facilities.

In Africa sheer distance is often a problem. The capitals of CAR, Chad and Rwanda are more than 1600km from the sea by any overland route. Botswana, Burkina Faso, Burundi, Mali, Niger, Uganda and Zambia are all more than 800km from the sea. In contrast the Swaziland capital Mbabane is only about 220km from Maputo.

Chad, CAR and Uganda still have only one basic route to the sea, although Uganda has both road and rail links with Mombasa. Rwanda and Burundi have more than one access route available but the alternatives are little used because of distance and the need for trans-shipments. Lesotho has two access routes, each served by two different transport modes; but both are to ports in the same seaboard state, South Africa.

The only modern transport access routes available to CAR and Chad require trans-shipment, between river and rail for CAR, road and rail for Chad. The CAR suffers from the worst quality of route because its only means of access is by slow river transport from the Brazzaville or Kinshasa railheads. Rwanda has no modern surface route to the sea that does not cross two other states. Burundi's current main access route crosses three other states, Rwanda, Uganda and Kenya.

At independence Chad, Niger and Rwanda did not have modern transport access to the sea. Burundi and CAR depended on lake or river transport in conjunction with rail which elsewhere was the only modern mode. The exception was Zimbabwe where late independence (1980) ensured paved road and pipeline access as well as rail links to the coast.

Some other land-locked states in Africa suffered from their colonial access routes being longer, and involving more intermodal trans-shipments, than the most direct route to the sea through the former colony of a different European power. This predicament was well illustrated during the First World War when the French faced the Senussi rebellion in Niger.[8] Troops were sent to Agades from Dakar by the 4350km-long, slow, multi-modal (rail, river, rail, river, desert track) all-French colonial route. An advance party was rushed to the scene in arrangement with Britain (then wartime ally rather than colonial rival) by sea to Lagos, less than 2000km by rail to Kano and desert track to Agades.

Throughout the colonial period Chad was normally reached by the all-French route of: rail from Pointe Noire to Brazzaville, thence by river up the Congo to Bangui then via unsurfaced road to Fort Lamy (N'djamena). The route traversed three colonies (now independent states), with two trans-shipments and a total distance of about 2900km. A shorter (1470km) road/rail route through Cameroon to Douala was developed after the German colony became a French-administered League of Nations mandate but was completed only in the 1970s. Marginally the shortest route from Chad to the sea at Port Harcourt is about 1460km with no trans-shipment necessary by road, or one by road/rail at Maiduguri. This route still has 150km of unsurfaced road and crosses two frontiers. The former Belgian Mandates of Rwanda and Burundi were served by a long (3550km) and complex (lake, rail, river, rail, river, rail) all-Belgian route to Matadi on the west coast compared with about 1440km (lake, rail) to Dar es Salaam on the east coast. Despite its greater length and complexity, traffic on the all-Belgian route grew dramatically in the inter-war period.[9] The all-British route from Cape to Copperbelt by rail was about 3440km compared with the post-independence Tanzam route from Dar es Salaam of about 1810km.

Since independence several African land-locked states have found or at least felt it necessary to develop alternative, sometimes shorter, routes to the coast. They include the Tanzam route from Zambia over which pipeline, tarred road and railway were completed between 1968-75, and the new rail link between Malawi and the Nacala line completed in 1970. In addition, roads from Mali to the Abidjan railway, from Burundi to Rwanda and thence to Uganda and Kenya, from Ethiopia to Djibouti and Assab, and from Burkina Faso into northern Ghana have all been surfaced.

It was for the first time, in the post-World War II period in Africa, that the niceties of legal argument about right of access were supplanted by the brutality of *realpolitik*. Some new access routes to the sea were developed by African land-locked states as a matter of necessity following border closures by access states.

Immediately before independence, in 1960, Africa's first modern land-locked state, Mali, had its only rail route to the sea:

> cut by the Senegalese, the tracks torn up near the border, and the rolling stock confiscated.[10]

As the route had carried 80 per cent of all Mali's foreign trade, mainly the export of groundnuts, alternative transport arrangements had to be found. The new route selected was a road link to the Abidjan/Ouagadougou railway which involved the costly construction of a 571km paved road from Bamako and the purchase of a fleet of 400 lorries. In June 1963 the Mali/Senegal frontier was re-opened but the route never fully regained its dominant colonial position in relation to Mali's external trade.

More spectacular was Zambia's quest for alternative routes to the sea. At independence in 1964 Zambia's main external trade route was through Rhodesia, and the country depended on this route for its vital bulk copper exports. In 1965 the Rhodesian settlers illegally and unilaterally declared independence (UDI). Britain, the colonial power, imposed an oil embargo, extended by the United Nations to wider trade sanctions. British frigates in the Mozambique Channel prevented oil shipments via Beira and the oil pipeline to Umtali (Mutare) where Rhodesia's only oil refinery was located. Success was more apparent than real because Rhodesia's oil imports were simply re-routed via Lourenco Marques (Maputo) and the Malvernia (Chicualacuala) railway.[11] Rhodesia's oil imports continued by this route until the FRELIMO government of newly independent Mozambique closed the frontier in March 1976. Zambia was less fortunate because Rhodesia blocked the transit of its oil imports from late 1965. Thus the main effect of the British blockade of Beira was to prevent Zambia, rather than Rhodesia, getting oil via its traditional route. Emergency sources of supply were necessary to keep Zambia's vital copper mining industry going and a secure route was needed for the all-important copper exports. The Zambian government, acutely aware of what it had long feared, that the southern route was politically unreliable, accelerated plans for a re-orientation of trade routes.

The Tanzam route to Dar es Salaam was selected for modernisation. Between 1968 and 1975 an oil pipeline, paved road and railway were completed in that order by the Italians, Americans and Chinese, respectively. The variety of aid sources tells a story. The West was not convinced of the economic viability of a railway and various feasibility studies rejected the project largely because they made wrong assumptions and asked the wrong questions. Only the Chinese grasped the point that the railway was political rather than *economic*.[12] Zambia, in attempting to break away from the hegemony of minority-ruled southern Africa, was making a political decision – not one based on projected financial profitability. The railway, completed on time in 1975, has not been as successful as originally anticipated. The reasons are only partly those predicted by Western aid agencies and the World Bank. The line was constructed cheaply with light rails, tight curves and steep gradients and has a low carrying capacity. Although of Cape gauge [13ft 6ins (1.067m)], it is operated separately from the rest of Zambian railways. Most significant is the low standard of maintenance of permanent way, locomotives and rolling stock. Within eight years of opening, 90 per cent of the railway's locomotives had been cannibalised to keep the other 10 per cent in running order. Dar es Salaam's port is unable to handle the volume of Zambia's bulky copper exports, and little capital is available to improve and extend it. East London is now the main port for Zambian copper, twice as far from the Copperbelt as Dar es Salaam.

Two other rail routes lead from Zambia to ports on the west coast of Africa. The all-Congo (Zaire) route to Matadi is of great length and involves two trans-shipments. It cannot cope with copper exports from Zaire itself, let alone Zambia. Today they are shipped out mainly via the spinal railway and South Africa. The Benguela railway links with the Angolan port of Lobito. It has not operated since 1975, closed by UNITA in Angola's civil war. When that war ends, the line will not be operational for years as it needs complete refurbishment after twenty years of neglect and war damage. Zambia's continued dependence on the southern route reflects not only South Africa's determination in the 1970s and 1980s to keep its hegemony over Zambia, but also the inability of Zambia and its friendly access states to maintain efficient trunk transport routes. Zambia's response has been to press within SADC for even more alternative outlets to the sea, whereas making existing routes viable might be more effective and less expensive.

The creation of alternative routes to the sea may be necessary but even where routes exist, the land-locked state has to see that they are kept open sometimes in the face of military threat. This situation was faced by Zimbabwe during the Mozambique civil war in the 1980s by deploying troops to keep the Beira corridor open.[13] Lesotho is not only land-locked but is an enclave, entirely surrounded by South Africa, with no alternative means of access except through South Africa. In January 1986 the Lesotho government of Chief Jonathan was toppled in a *coup d'état* engineered by the South African government by means of a deliberate and blatant trade blockade. The Lesotho government was targeted because of the South African white minority regime's hostility to the policies of Chief Jonathan who allegedly gave sanctuary to members of the African National Congress (ANC), and introduced North Koreans to train special para-military units.[14] The blockade was enforced by South African military forces who closed the boundary between the two countries to all traffic and therefore between Lesotho and the world.

Lesotho's new military leader, Major-General Justin Lekhanya stated the plight of his country in a telex to the United Nations:

> The situation is deteriorating rapidly to a point where the safety and security and well being of Lesotho as a sovereign state are now in

jeopardy. We are merely seeking your assistance to address what has become an emergency and a difficult situation unique in the history of our small, land-locked state.

The United Nations' response was limited to 'grave warnings.'

These are only some of the problems faced by African land-locked states. In 1985 Nigeria refused passage of food shipments for Chad because of alleged congestion in the Nigerian transport system though the decision was more probably related to a contretemps between the two governments over the border area. The goods were diverted via Cameroon. The Chad government was not threatened but the hostile action illustrates the vulnerability of land-locked states. In east Africa in 1979, imports of military supplies and petroleum to Uganda were stopped by the Kenyan government. This facilitated the toppling of Amin in Uganda. Few cared about the blockade at the time, indeed many welcomed it and Amin's overthrow, but again the vulnerability of land-locked states was demonstrated. The decision to close the border, however praiseworthy, was by Kenya not Uganda. In 1987 Kenya again closed the Ugandan border. As Uganda's only feasible route to the sea is via Kenya any closure is of serious concern to Uganda. The decision by a seaboard state to close its borders may have nothing to do with the land-locked state using its route for access to the sea. When in 1984 Nigeria sealed its borders following a military *coup d'etat* essentially internal to Nigeria, Chad and Niger had no option but to depend entirely on alternative routes to the sea.

African land-locked states, with few exceptions, are small (not always in area), remote, economically and politically weak, underdeveloped and dependent. Eleven African land-locked states are among the world's poorest states with GNP per capita of less than US$500 per annum. By this measure Botswana is the only land-locked state among the ten richest African states. Of the African land-locked states, Zimbabwe and Ethiopia alone have a total GNP in excess of US$6 billion. Ethiopia and Uganda alone have populations over 15 million.

African land-locked states also lack political influence. Ethiopia apart, on average land-locked states have less than half the number of resident diplomatic missions from other African states than do African seaboard states, despite having more direct neighbours or a higher contiguity factor. Ten land-locked states ranked below 30 out of 52 African states in the Human Development Index (HDI). By most measures of size, wealth, influence and general well-being land-locked states are clearly among the weaker states of Africa. The western, ex-French, mainly Sahelian land-locked states of Mali, Burkina Faso, Niger, Chad and CAR have a GNP per capita in the range of US$200–390 accompanied by low levels of life expectancy and literacy. The east African land-locked states of Uganda, Rwanda, Burundi, Ethiopia and Malawi are even poorer with a GNP per capita range of US$100–220 but higher HDI scores. The land-locked states of southern Africa, Zambia, Zimbabwe, Botswana, Swaziland and Lesotho, are the richest in all respects but compare unfavourably with most seaboard states.

The absolute poverty of so many African land-locked states makes the condition of land-lockedness much more serious in Africa than in, for example, Europe. Land-locked African states cannot easily meet the costs of maintaining modern transport links with the sea let alone establishing alternative routes. The wider African context of poverty also has an impact. In many African states infrastructural development is limited, so that a land-locked state cannot assume that its thrust to the sea will be welcomed with appropriate investment by its seaboard neighbour, nor assume an adequate level of pre-existing transport development there.

In addition to being poor and dependent on other states for access to the sea, land-locked states are usually weaker than their seaboard neighbours. They are therefore less able to influence those neighbours and more vulnerable to pressure from them. The contrast between Lesotho and South Africa is an obvious extreme but other ill-balanced relationships between land-locked states and seaboard ones are found throughout Africa. For example, between Botswana and South Africa, Uganda and Kenya, Chad and Cameroon or Nigeria, Burkina Faso and Ivory Coast, and Mali and Senegal or Ivory Coast.

Even with the development of road transport, only eight of the 15 land-locked states have modern transport routes through more than one seaboard country. They are vulnerable not only to hostility from their seaboard neighbours but also to unrelated political unrest in those states, for example, the impact of civil war in Angola and Mozambique on Zambia, Malawi and Zimbabwe. Land-locked states might plead for special aid, but a case for an additional route to the sea, if possible, is unlikely to be persuasive because of the difficulty of making an essentially political or strategic aim meet the economic criteria normally set by funding agencies.

Accessibility is more than the simple existence of a route even where that route is through the territory of a constantly friendly neighbour. Bottlenecks arise at sea-ports, river-ports and river-ferry crossings beyond the control of the land-locked country. Unintentional delays are caused at customs and immigration posts by the welter of bureaucratic paper-work in which such places delight. Customs duties, freight rates, road transport licensing and insurance are essential details to be sorted out. Railway locomotive and rolling stock deployment and operating schedules are subject to bi-lateral agreement and implementation. Maintenance of vehicles, locomotives, rolling stock signalling and on the route itself needs to be carried out systematically. All these operational matters call for the closest international co-operation and co-ordination. This is rarely achieved, sometimes just because of inefficiency, but also because access states inevitably and all too frequently have different priorities from their land-locked neighbours in the allocation of scarce resources. In matters of route development and capital investment land-locked states are also disadvantaged especially when it is realised that on average two-thirds of the length of all paved access roads to land-locked states in Africa built in the post-independence period are in fact in the seaboard states. Infrastructural development to the borders of land-locked states is not always complemented, matched or met within the seaboard access state. Thus the 805km paved road south from Addis Ababa to Moyale on the Kenyan border is met by 527km of rough murram road from the border to Isiolo 285km north of Nairobi:

> The smooth tarred Ethiopian road north of Moyale becomes dirt track to the south…Every now and then we hit a run of shallow ruts and for 15 seconds it's like   being in cocktail shaker.[15]

A variation on this theme is found in northern Cameroon where 780km paved road access is provided from Chad to the Cameroon railhead of Ngaoundere but not from Chad across the northern tip of Cameroon to link with the paved road at the Nigerian border which is continuous to the Nigerian ports. By leaving the 157km dirt road between Maltham and Fotokol unsurfaced the Cameroon government protects its position as the main access route to Chad. This further illustrates the dependency of land-locked states. Taken altogether these are potential sources of international friction as well as serious impediments to the smooth flow of trade. Because it is their vital external trade arteries which are threatened, the impediments and the friction are most seriously felt by the land-locked states.

## NOTES

1. Roy Bridges, 'Africa, Africans and the sea', in Jeffrey C. Stone (ed.) *Africa and the Sea*, (Aberdeen: Aberdeen University African Studies Group, Proceedings of a Colloquium at the University of Aberdeen March 1984) pp.14–26.
2. Joel Vernet (ed.) *Pays du Sahel: du Tchad au Senegal, du Mali au Niger* (Paris: Autrement 1994).
3. Ieuan Ll. Griffiths, 'Changing port location in southern Africa', *African Urban Quarterly*, 9/1 (1994) pp.133–46.
4. Ieuan Ll. Griffiths, 'The quest for independent access to the sea in southern Africa', *The Geographical Journal*, 155/3 (1989) pp.378–91.
5. Robert Blake, *A History of Rhodesia*, (London: Metheun 1976).

6. Anthony Croxton, *The Railways of Zimbabwe*, (Newton Abbot: David and Charles 1982).
7. Margery Perham and Lionel Curtis, *The Protectorates of South Africa: the Question of their Transfer to the Union* (London: OUP 1935).
8. UK, Naval Intelligence Division, *French West Africa: the Colonies, Vol.II* (London: HMSO, Geographical Handbook Series 1944) p.377.
9. UK, Naval Intelligence Division, *The Belgian Congo*, (London: HMSO, Geographical Handbook Series 1944) pp.362–3.
10. Alexandre, in Z. Cervenka (ed.) *Land-locked Countries of Africa* (Uppsala: Scandinavian Institute of African Studies 1973) p.140.
11. Thomas Bingham and Gray, 1976.
12. Richard Hall and Hugh Peyman, *The Great Uhuru Railway: China's Showpiece in Africa*, (London: Gollancz 1976).
13. Jose Smith, 'The Beira corridor', *Geography*, 73/3 (1988) pp.258–61.
14. Robert Edgar, 'The Lesotho coup of 1986' in Glenn Moss and Ingrid Obery (eds.), *The Geographical Journal*, 155/3 (Johannesburg: Ravan 1987).
15. Michael Palin, *Pole to Pole* (London: BBC Books 1992) p.196.

# Chad:
# Power Vacuum or Geopolitical Focus

GEORGE JOFFÉ

Land-locked states differ from other states in one vital respect. Their physical contiguity with neighbouring states means that they are dependent on such states for access to the outside world. They do not have, in short, the type of unlimited and unconstrained access to freedom of movement on the high seas, an innate right of the majority of states, which provides them with unfettered control over commercial activity and lines of communication. The result is that such states have, as a major, if not the major, goal of their foreign policy the requirement of negotiating and maintaining transit regimes with their neighbours, usually from a position of normative diplomatic weakness. Conversely, surrounding states have the potential to seriously affect both the foreign and domestic policies of their land-locked neighbours by the way in which they respect such transit regimes, whatever the status of the legal instruments guaranteeing them in international law. Unlike the situation where a state's maritime access to the high seas through a channel is controlled by a transit regime based on the universal right of 'innocent passage' under international law[1] or where airspace over a particular state is governed by a similar concept,[2] land-locked states have no general international legal principle to help them in their diplomatic and commercial relations with their neighbours.

One of the reasons for this is that, unlike states where there is a coastline, the definition of the borders of land-locked states does not necessarily have any innate, inherent or internal rationale. Indeed, even though these borders may appear, at first sight, to enjoy such characteristics, this appearance is usually coincidental and does not reflect the original justification for defining, delimiting and demarcating the border in the precise way in which it appears today. In fact, such boundaries often reflect the innate power-relationships between neighbouring states more than any other factor.[3] Thus, although in general terms, borders are no longer necessarily defined in terms of ethnic, geographic, topographic, ecological, environmental, historical or functional divides,[4] such factors usually have some instrumental part in boundary definition and delimitation or demarcation. In the case of land-locked states, however, such a role, if it does exist, is not perforce instrumental. Of course, statements of principle

MAP 1

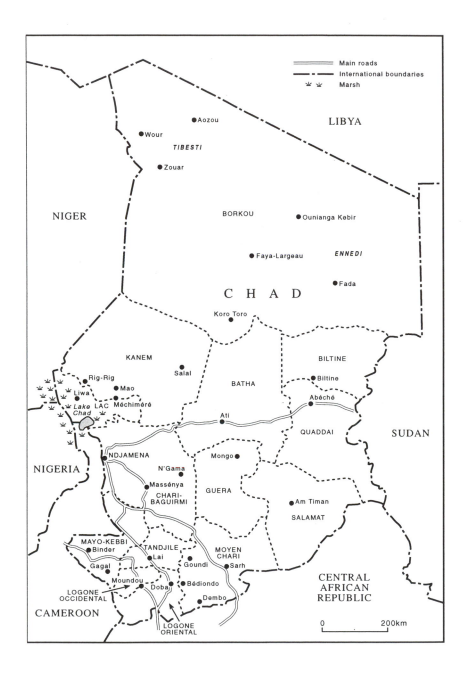

such as these can always be countered by specific examples. Nonetheless, the factor of terrestrial contiguity between neighbouring states when one is land-locked does mean that this somewhat artificial distinction has practical value in enabling us to distinguish the characteristics of land-locked states as opposed to other states in terms of border definition and the consequent nature of the state itself.

This type of distinction is particularly useful in Africa where so many states are completely artificial post-colonial constructs, preserved in terms of their border definition by the artifice of the Organisation of African Unity's 1964 Cairo Declaration which affirmed the intangibility of colonial boundaries.[5] The result of this process has been that, even though the Cairo Declaration might have limited inter-state conflict over boundary disputes – and there is plenty of evidence that this prohibition has been honoured more in the breach than in the observance, as in the Western Sahara issue, the Ogaden conflict and the Libya–Chad dispute over the Aozou Strip, to name but a few examples, make clear – African states have been hampered in achieving genuine internal political and economic coherence. Ethnic groups have been divided by colonial boundaries which often defy geographic logic as well as ethnic coherence.[6] Traditional patterns of economic interaction have been disrupted and entities that negate coherent economic principles have been created. The infrastructural dependence of the SADDC states or of Botswana and Swaziland on South Africa is a good example of the economic consequences of the Cairo Declaration, whilst its political consequences can be seen in the Western Sahara issue or the Libya–Chad dispute.

In short, African states have suffered dramatically in terms of their ability to construct viable nations by which to legitimise their political structures, in part because of the historical origins of their boundaries. Of course, this is not the whole story and many other factors have significantly contributed to the crisis of identity and legitimacy that many of them face. Nonetheless, the role of boundary definition in this process, especially in the case of land-locked states, should not be under-estimated. Chad is a particularly acute example of the consequences of this essentially historical process. The civil war that has raged virtually permanently since independence in 1960 is the political symptom of some of the most adverse potential consequences of 'land-lockedness'. Of course, such an outcome is not an inevitable consequence of 'land-lockedness'. Nevertheless, the propensity of a new state for domestic instability, particularly in circumstances where there is no indigenous and homogeneous population to provide government with legitimacy,[7] is significantly intensified by the historical, diplomatic, ethnic and social problems created by 'land-lockedness', as an investigation of the history of modern Chad makes clear.

**The Pre-colonial Reality**

Before the French occupied what has now become modern Chad – which during the colonial period formed part of French Equatorial Africa – there was no political entity which approximated to the modern state. Instead, there were three zones of population settlement in which different types of political structures existed. Furthermore, these structures often extended beyond the boundaries of the modern state, thereby providing a demographic, ethnic and sociological continuity with its modern geographic environment.

In the north of Chad – the semi-arid and arid zone shading northwards into the Sahara desert and including the two great mountain massifs of Tibesti and Ennedi – there was a scattered nomadic and transhumant tribal population equivalent, probably to around 5 per cent of the total population of the modern state. It was divided between two major tribal groups. The first was the Tubu[8] around the Tibesti massif but also in Borkou and reaching across the modern border westward, towards the Bilma and Kawwar oasis chains and divided between the Tedaga and Dazaga. Some of the Tubu, particularly those in the Tibesti massif, also migrated northwards as part of their nomadic cycle and traded with Murzuq and Kufrah in southern Libya. The second group was comprised of the Bideyat and the Zaghawa, both different branches of the Beri, who were located around the Ennedi massif and extended into Darfur.[9] Both groups were the remnants of one of the three great Saharan tribal groups – the Moors, the Touareg and the Tubu – and had formed part of one of the early imperial systems of the southern Saharan fringe, the Zaghawa empire of the eleventh century.[10]

Intermixed with these groups were two others; the sedentary Kanouri and Kamadja, found in Borkou and in Bilma or Kawwar, and various Arab tribal communities.[11] One Arab group was derived from the Awlad Sulayman of the northern Fezzan who moved southwards into the northern part of the Kanem region after being displaced from Libya in 1842 by the Ottomans after the second Ottoman occupation of Libya in 1835. Another group which, like the first, came from Libya but, unlike it, was sedentary, was made up of traders located in the major oasis complexes of Borkou. It replicated many of the major tribes of Libya itself, such as the Qadhadhfa and the Zuwaya. The third group was composed of factions of eastern Arab tribes, such as the Djellaba, the Toundjour, the Djcheina and the Hassaouna, who had migrated westwards into the region over the previous millennium. The Djcheina and the Hassaouna fused in the fifteenth century into the Mahamid and became the major slavers of central Chad, thereby sustaining the trade routes across the Sahara which were controlled by the Tubu and Touareg.

The Arab tribes from Egypt and Sudan also created a series of small Muslim sultanates in central Chad – Kanem, Baguirmi (both remnants of the tenth century Bornou empire) and Ouaddai. Their populations – probably around 15 per cent of the total population of what is today Chad – were largely pastoralist, although there were also sedentary groups, such as the Hadjeray in what is today the Guera Prefecture. The sultanates acted as a barrier between the acephalous non-Arab populations of the Saharan fringe – largely animist in culture and linked into the far flung subsistence economy of the Sahara with migratory and trading links into the Fezzan and Kufrah – and the sedentary agriculturalist populations of the extreme south of Chad. By the nineteenth century, the Sultanate of Ouaddai had also enforced its control over the Beri and had begun to Islamise them.

These southern populations – mainly acephalous decentralised animist communities based on lineage affiliation – were dominated by the Sara who also extended into modern Cameroon and Central Africa. The Sara formed a complex and hierarchical village-based society, dominated by a system of chiefs. The other major southern group were the Moundang, who were derived from the Fulbe populations of West Africa.[12] Unlike the situation further north, there was no centralised authority and the southern part of Chad was constantly ravaged by slavers, particularly towards the end of the nineteenth century. Indeed, the first French advance into Chad was directed against the major Sudanese slaver, Rabih, who had conquered the sultanates of Kanem and Baguirmi and was preparing to turn against Ouaddai but whose defeat at French hands occurred close to the site of the capital of modern Chad, N'Jamena.[13]

Islam also came to the Tubu, largely as a result of the expansion of the Sanusi Order southwards from Jarabub and Kufrah at the end of the nineteenth century.[14] The Sanusi Order, founded in the early nineteenth century and originally based along the eastern Libyan Mediterranean littoral at al-Bayda, was a powerful agent of Islamisation amongst the Saᶜadi tribes of Cyrenaica and also came to control trade routes and to administer tribal life from its *zawiya-s* which were dotted throughout Cyrenaica and extended into the Fezzan, Tripolitania and even Egypt. It maintained an uneasy *modus vivendi* with the Ottoman administration of the Mediterranean coast of Libya, whereby the Ottomans tacitly ceded administrative authority for the interior to the Sanusi Order. The Order also became a powerful agent for resisting colonial penetration, particularly through its migration southwards into Chad where, in addition to penetrating the Tubu and Beri regions, it also established a presence in Ouaddai. By the end of the nineteenth century, it had begun to prepare resistance to French penetration eastwards and northwards.[15]

## The Colonial Period and Chad's Boundaries

The French occupation of modern Chad slowly developed over the first two decades of the present century. In part it was a response to the need to protect French colonial acquisitions in West Africa and was carried out with very small logistical and military resources. The conquest actually took 15 years to complete between 1900 and 1915 and, after a hiatus during the First World War, a further forty years were spent organising the administration of the new colony. As one authority puts it:

> C'est ainsi que le Tchad 'est né de quelques actes de bravoure accomplis par les soldats persuadés de servir un grand dessein national, et de nombreux traités signés, puis modifiés et rectifiés dans les chancelleries européennes.' [16]

In part the conquest corresponded to the grander design of linking together the two components of the new French colonial empire created during the nineteenth century, French West Africa and French North Africa. The extent of the French advance into Chad was governed by the 1898 Anglo-French Spheres of Influence Agreement which, according to the subsequent 1899 Declaration, divided Central Africa between the two countries along a line, '…which shall start from the point of intersection of the Tropic of Cancer with the 16th degree of longitude east of Greenwich…shall run thence south-east until it meets the 24th degree of longitude east of Greenwich.' [17] It was only after the First World War that a very limited French presence was permanently established in the extreme north of what was to become known as the BET (Borkou–Ennedi–Tibesti) Region.

The French presence created several new facts about Chad. Firstly, it defined a territorial extent and administrative boundaries to the new political entity. Many of the territorial limits to the new colony resulted from internal French colonial administrative decisions. The Central African Republic–Chadian border, for instance, developed from an administrative delimitation which was only finalised in 1941–42 and, even today, is not subject to formal treaty definition. [18] The same is true of the Chad–Niger boundary, which was established by a whole series of administrative decisions between 1912 (just two years after French Equatorial Africa was formed and Chad and Niger ceased to be French military territories) and 1958 (when Chad became a member of the French Community, just two years before it was granted independence). The most important instrument in this respect was a French administrative memorandum in 1931 which defined the border south of the tripoint with Libya to the dogleg at Siltou, while the final line of the border section from Siltou to Molo on Lake Chad was only established by agreement between the governors of Niger and Chad in 1957. [19]

The Chad–Cameroon border, strangely enough, was the result of an international agreement, although Cameroon itself formed part of the French African empire. The reason for this was the fact that Cameroon, before the First World War, had been a German possession. As a result, its boundaries were defined by a series of instruments; the Franco-German protocols of 1885 and 1894 and two Franco-German Conventions signed in 1908 and 1911 respectively.[20]

The remaining three borders of Chad were the subjects of international instruments for they all involved Chad's abutment against the colonial possessions of other European powers – Britain in Nigeria and Sudan and Italy in Libya. The Chadian boundary with Nigeria is simply a maritime delimitation, for it runs through Lake Chad and results from the delimitation of two tripoints. The tripoint with Cameroon was eventually established by the Anglo-French Exchange of Notes in 1931, which clarified an earlier Anglo-French convention and the 1908 Franco-German convention over Chad's border with Cameroon. The tripoint with Niger was established by an Anglo-French convention in 1910.[21] The boundary of Chad with Sudan derives in part from the 1898 and 1899 Anglo-French Spheres of Influence Agreement and Declaration, but the actual alignment of the frontier was settled in 1924 by a protocol and a subsequent exchange of notes.[22]

Interestingly enough, although imprecisions still exist in most of these boundary definitions, they have not been the source of significant dispute between the modern independent states of this part of Africa. The same cannot be said to be true of Chad's final boundary, that with Libya. Although this was originally defined in the 1898 and 1899 agreements between Britain and France, the section between the 16th and 24th degree of longitude east of Greenwich was essentially redefined by a 1919 Franco-Italian Exchange of Notes, after Italy had ousted the Ottoman empire from Libya in 1911 but before the subsequent Italo-Sanusi wars had been ended. The redefinition occurred because the original 1898 agreement was not accompanied by a map and France was able unilaterally to redefine the boundary in favour of its new colony by insisting that the two lines of longitude involved were linked by a line running east-south-east, rather than south-east. This had first been suggested in a secret Franco-Italian agreement drawn up in 1902 which actually referred to the non-existent 1898 map as its spurious justification. The section to the west, from the Tummo oasis to the 16th line of longitude east of Greenwich, was established by the 1919 protocol.[23]

This arrangement was modified on two subsequent occasions: in 1934, Italy and Britain reached an agreement on the so-called 'Sarra Triangle Dispute', which involved the portion of land to the north of the 1919 line and between the 22nd and 24th lines of longitude east of Greenwich. The following year, Italy and France negotiated and ratified an agreement – the Mussolini–Laval Agreement – which ceded a strip of territory 100 km deep south of the 1919 line to Italy. This strip of territory has since become known as the 'Aozou Strip'. The justification for this seems to have been a French desire to settle Italian claims to rights for its citizens in Tunisia – a French colony but in which the Italian community was the largest European element – as well as removing irredentist Italian claims to Nice and as a means of diverting Fascist Italy away from close treaty links with Nazi Germany. In the latter respect, French policy failed, for two years later Italy signed the Pact of Steel with Germany and the instruments of ratification of the Mussolini–Laval Treaty were never exchanged.

Nonetheless, until 1955, the Franco-Italian border in Central Africa was conventionally assumed to be the new line established by the Mussolini–Laval Treaty. It was only after the independence of Libya in 1951 and the signing of a Franco-Libyan Friendship Treaty in 1955 that the issue of the 1935 treaty re-emerged. This required Libya to recognise existing boundary agreements. At French insistence in a subsequent exchange of notes in 1956, the various treaties considered to define the boundary were listed but no specific boundary definition was provided. The result of this has been that Libya did not accept the 1919 line as its boundary with Chad, arguing instead that no boundary had ever been properly delimited and that the closest approach to such a delimitation was the 1935 Mussolini–Laval Treaty.

One reason for this view has been that Italy never defined the southern limits of its Libyan colony in its Treaty of Peace with the Ottoman empire at the end of its initial occupation of Libya in 1912. Libya considered that both the penetration of the Sanusi Order into northern Chad – where it established a significant administrative role between 1890 and 1913 – and a belated Ottoman presence there between 1908 and 1912 provide it with a claim based on *uti possidetis juris* to a large area of Northern Chad. Libya also argued that the French occupation of Northern Chad – of the BET region – was never 'effective' in the sense that a permanent and effective administrative presence was never established. Its more limited claim to the Aozou Strip was, therefore, a concession. Chad, of course, basing its case on the 1955 Franco-Libyan Treaty and its rights as a successor state to France, did not agree.[24] The issue was eventually debated before the International Court of Justice at The Hague and, in early February 1994, the Court decided to accept the 1955 Franco-Libyan treaty as legitimising the international boundary as then accepted. Libya's claim to the Aozou Strip was thus rejected.

## The Colonial Period and Internal Change

Even though the French presence in the BET region was always minimal and was mainly concerned with attempting to preserve a fragile peace while leaving local society relatively untouched, the same was not true of central and southern Chad. Indeed, even in northern Chad, sporadic attempts were made by the authorities to interfere with the traditional migratory links between the Tubu and southern Libya and to prevent Beri movement in and out of Darfur in Sudan. The French military and administrative presence was, however, far too weak for this to be done by direct control and French administrators had to depend on local power structures, such as the Derde of Tibesti, for this purpose. The result was that control of the northern borders was ineffectual and traditional migratory patterns persisted. Furthermore, French military control of the BET region only ended in 1964, four years *after* Chad had become independent.

In the old Muslim sultanates, the existing order was preserved and France ruled through a system of indirect administration. French officials introduced new taxation systems, for the colony had to be as financially viable as possible, and ended the tradition of the *ghazaw* southwards. Apart from these modifications, however, the old Muslim heartland of Chad was left relatively untouched, as was the traditional pastoralist economy based on transhumance. Indeed, the relative calm brought by French administration opened up the possibilities of livestock trade southwards as well as eastwards into the Sudan.

In the south, however, particularly in the Sara heartland, the colonial experience brought dramatic change. The old village chieftain system was uprooted, as chiefs were replaced by personalities loyal to the new administration. In 1921, cotton cultivation was introduced into southern Chad, a development which had profound social and economic implications. Firstly, the administrative system based on the new, compliant chiefs, was redirected towards the creation of an economy based on cotton mono-culture. Secondly, all French developmental interest in Chad was now directed towards the south. Thirdly, a monopoly private company, COTONFRAN (later known as COTONTCHAD) came to dominate the national economy. This was accompanied by an administrative decision to favour the south in terms of educational facilities, in order to create a native administration based on the Sara, while the Muslim regions of the country were left to stagnate through social and administrative neglect. Southern Chad had now become the 'Tchad Utile' for France.

This development had two further consequences. Firstly, it upset the pre-colonial social and political balance, in which the sultanates of central Chad had been the dominant element. Secondly, it increasingly integrated

Chad into the political development of West Africa through Cameroon. After the creation of the French Union in 1946, political parties began to develop in West Africa. Political agitation for independence was first voiced through the *Rassemblement Démocratique Africaine*, founded by Félix Houphouet-Boigny in 1951 and Chad was represented at its founding conference. A year later, the *Parti Progressiste Tchadien* was founded in N'Jamena by Gabriel Lisette, an administrative official from Guadeloupe. This became the dominant political formation in Chad and was dominated by Chad's southern Sara populations, although it was originally also open to persons from northern Chad, such as Abba Siddick. Most northerners, however, were gathered into a new party, dominated by the Muslim elite of the old sultanates, the *Mouvement Socialiste Africaine*, until they left it in 1958 to create the *Union Nationale Tchadienne* which was dominated by young activists and from which was to emerge the eventual national independence movement, *FROLINAT*.[25]

## Independence

The striking feature of Chad at the eve of independence was the fact that the pre-colonial disposition of power inside the new state had been inverted. Whereas power had originally been based in the central Muslim sultanates, with the north of the country isolated by its links into the Sahara and southern Libya and the south dependent and subjected to central domination, now it was the Sara-dominated south of Chad that controlled the political process and sought to control power once independence was granted. Furthermore, the old links outside the territory of the new state, which had defined political structures in pre-colonial times, had been disrupted by the administrative functions located within the new boundaries. The northern populations found their ability to maintain close links with southern Libya circumscribed, as did the populations of the eastern BET region with Sudan or those of the central part of the country with areas across the borders to the east and the south. Chad had become, as a result of the colonial experience, an embryonic unitary state, although it was far from being a nation as well. Its three-to-four million-strong population was dispersed between around 100 different ethnic and linguistic groups. There were also at least three distinct religious identities and old political loyalties reinforced the ethnic and religious divides.

Not surprisingly, independence produced a southern Sara-dominated government under François Tombalbaye and, within five years, the precarious unity of the state collapsed as a Sara-dominated administrative structure alienated the large non-Sara minorities in the centre and the north of the country. The simple fact was that the administrative structure of Chad failed to coincide with any other political or cultural reality so that, once the Sara-dominated government faltered, its whole basis of legitimacy collapsed. The first sign of the troubles to come appeared in Mangalme in October 1965, with a tax rebellion amongst Moubi transhumants. Soon, in the wake of the withdrawal of French administrators from the BET region, tensions between the government administration and local political structures there generated a new dimension for the rebellion. Within one year, activists of the northern-dominated *Union Nationale Tchadienne* had moved into active rebellion against the Tombalbaye government and, under the leadership of a Nigerian who had moved to Chad, Ibrahim Abacha, had formed a guerrilla movement, *FROLINAT.*

The outbreak of Chad's first civil war was, in essence, an attempt to redress the geopolitical balance inside the country.[26] The Sara-dominated government – in which President Tombalbaye was replaced by Felix Malloum in 1974 – now confronted an increasingly powerful armed opposition which, although it claimed to represent all Chadians, was actually dominated by the once marginalised Tubu. Furthermore, the leadership of *FROLINAT* itself split along ethnic lines, between the Teda of Tibesti and the Daza of Faya Largeau in Borkou, represented by the son of the old Tibesti *Derde*, Goukouni Oueddei, and a French-educated Daza lawyer from Faya who had returned to Chad as a member of the administration and then defected to *FROLINAT* in 1971, Hissan Habré. This internal split had been powerfully aided by the former colonial power, France, which, in 1969, in response to a desperate plea from the beleaguered Tombalbaye government, had sent in troops to isolate *FROLINAT* within the BET. This, in turn, led *FROLINAT* to turn to Libya for aid. By the start of the 1970s, therefore, Chad had not only collapsed in civil war, it had also become the arena for a surrogate conflict between outside powers.[27]

In late 1972, Libya unilaterally annexed the Aozou Strip, claiming that François Tombalbaye, while president, had recognised the validity of Libya's claim to the 1935 boundary line. This action was the direct cause of the 1974 split inside *FROLINAT* between supporters of Goukouni Oueddei who was prepared to tolerate the Libyan action for the sake of Libyan support and Hissan Habré who was not. Eventually Habré allied with the Malloum government but, in 1979, the combination of tensions inside N'Jamena and a *FROLINAT Forces Armées du Nord* (FAN) offensive under Goukouni Oueddei ended the southern-dominated Malloum regime. As a result of sustained prodding by Nigeria, the Organisation of African Unity eventually imposed a peace plan, the Lagos Accords, which provided for a transitional government, the GUNT, which was supposed to hold elections eighteen months later.

By March 1980, however, tensions between the two reunited wings of

*FROLINAT* had broken out into renewed fighting which ushered in the second civil war. Libyan intervention in June ensured victory for the Goukouni Oueddei faction, but, within a year, Hissan Habré had amassed Sudanese and Egyptian support, because of the threat Libya was seen to pose through its presence in Chad. By 1982, Libyan forces in central Chad had withdrawn and the Oueddei government fell, to be replaced by a Habré administration dominated by the Daza Tubu. Twelve months later, a Libyan-backed rebellion led by Goukouni Oueddei had occupied all of Chad down to the 16th parallel and the Habré government had had to call on France once again. The USA, given its ferocious hostility towards the Qadhafi regime in Libya, had by now entered into the picture, competing with France to arm the Habré regime and bolstering Egyptian and Sudanese support for it too.

In the early months of 1987, Libya suffered a staggering defeat at the hands of the *Forces Armées Tchadiennes* (FAT), led and trained by Habré's Zaghawa supporters, Hassan Djamous and Ibrahim Deby. Libya was left with a toehold on Chadian territory at Aozou and was eventually persuaded by Algeria and Morocco to place its claim before the International Court of Justice at The Hague. Habré, as victor in the conflict – Goukouni Oueddei had been eclipsed and many of his supporters had in any case defected to the Habré government in N'Jamena – was fêted in Paris and Washington.

The Habré regime was, however, in trouble. Ethnic tensions within Hissan Habré's own UNIR movement, between his own Daza faction and erstwhile Hadjeray and Zaghawa allies, led, first, to a rebellion in Guera, the heart of Hadjeray country, and a year later, to a mysterious coup attempt in N'Jamena which left Djamous dead and Deby in exile. At the same time, tensions erupted over proposed political changes which seemed to threaten southern Chadian interests. Deby sought and obtained Libyan support and, operating through the Sudanese border at Darfur, amongst his own ethnic Zaghawa group, soon ousted Habré. The Deby government is still in power, despite at least one coup attempt and hostile US and French pressure. At the same time, it is attempting to resist too close a Libyan embrace. Chad itself is bankrupt and prostrate after 27 years of continuous warfare.[28]

## The Reasons

There is little doubt that the major cause of this chronic state of tension and warfare has been the administrative dispensation bequeathed to Chad by the French colonial experience. The definition – or, rather, the lack of adequate definition – of Chad's borders, particularly that with Libya, provided an inevitable opportunity for inter-state conflict. Chad's location in the centre of Africa made it impossible for surrounding states to ignore such a conflict.

Nor, indeed, does the February 1994 International Court of Justice's rejection of Libya's claim to the Aozou Strip necessarily clarify the issue, for Libya cannot be forced to accept the Court's judgement[29] and Libyan public opinion was certainly very hostile to it. The unhappy accident of US hostility towards the Qadhafi regime in Libya forced Chad into becoming the arena for a surrogate struggle designed to undermine the Libyan government, in which France was goaded and coerced by the USA to act more decisively than it otherwise might have done.

These external tensions were intensified by the complete failure of national integration or of the creation of a cohesive political culture inside Chad after independence. This, in turn, was due to the way in which France had chosen to manipulate Chadian society during the colonial period which had reversed the original balance of power inside the country in ways that were intrinsically unstable. Additional tensions, caused by the chronic predominance of tribal factors inside political movements in Chad had ensured further fragmentation of the domestic political scene, thereby dragging in intensified external power attention. The political vacuum created by the failure of domestic governmental competence and by foreign intervention in independent Chad had, in short, turned it into a geopolitical focus. It is not yet clear whether Chad can escape this political legacy.

Nor is the fact that Chad is such a profoundly land-locked state completely alien to the problems it has faced in terms of national cohesion. This factor has meant that groups within the Chadian population have been able to preserve their ethnic distinctiveness and political isolation from central government control by calling on external patrons or supporters. In effect the linkages of distinct population groups north into Southern Libya, east into Darfur and south into the Central African Republic has reinforced their distinctiveness whilst the links westwards into Nigeria and Cameroon provided economic choke points that the Nigerian government used very effectively to force warring factions to accept the Lagos Accords in 1979. At the same time the intrinsic weakness of Chad as an integrated state caused by these exogenous linkages has encouraged surrounding states to intervene inside Chadian affairs, as occurred in 1980 with Libya's intervention in the civil war which lasted until 1983. Even the current apparent calm in Chad's political affairs is a consequence of externational interaction, for it was Libya that supported the Deby regime in its successful attempt to wrest control of the state from Hissan Hibre – himself backed by Egypt and Sudan in December 1992.

The transformation of FROLINAT from a movement for national revolution into a Tubu-dominated and Libyan-supported movement, more concerned with tribal control than with national revival, is a good case in point. Similarly, the success of the current Zaghawa-dominated government of Idris Debay was due in no small part to its ability to recruit amongst its kinsmen in Darfur, in neighbouring Sudan, quite apart from the patronage it enjoyed from Libya and, to a far lesser extent, from Sudan. Similar factors were evident in the Sara-dominated South, during periods of unrest against the Habré government. In economic terms, too, Chad has survived the civil war as a series of separate regions largely because each region was able to develop economic and commercial links with neighbouring regions of other states, rather than as part of an integrated national economy. It is quite clear that neither of these aspects of the instability of the Chadian state would have developed so easily or with such success had Chad not been a land-locked state. It is not yet clear, in short, whether Chad's future will be determined by its political, rather than by its geographic legacy, for it may well be the land-locked nature of the state that determines its ability to survive as an integrated national or federal state.

## NOTES

1. R.M.M. Wallace, *International Law*, (London: Sweet and Maxwell 1986) pp.129–30.
2. J.R.V. Prescott, *Political Frontiers and Boundaries*, (London: Allen and Unwin 1987) p. 27.
3. P.J. Taylor, *Political Geography: World-economy, Nation-state and Locality* (Harlow: Longman 1989) pp.144–6.
4. Prescott, pp.98–9.
5. L. Brownlie, *African boundaries, a Legal and Diplomatic Encyclopedia* (London: Hurst/RIIA 1979) p.11.
6. viz P.O. Adeniyi and A.I. Asiwaju (eds), *Borderlands in Africa: a Multidisciplinary and Comparative Focus on Nigeria and West Africa* (Lagos, Nigeria: University of Lagos Press 1989) pp.25–85.
7. E.G.H. Joffé, "The International Court of Justice and the Western Sahara dispute" in R. Lawless and L. Monahan (eds) *War and Refugees: the Western Sahara Dispute* (London: Pinter 1987) p.21.
8. J. Chapelle, *Nomades noirs du Sahara* (Paris: L'Harmattan 1982) pp.66–165.
9. J. Tubiana and M.J. Tubiana, *The Zaghawa from an Ecological Perspective* (Rotterdam: Balkema 1977) pp.1–11.
10. J. Wright, *Libya, Chad and the Central Sahara* (London: Hurst 1990) pp.32–3.
11. A. Le Rouvreur, *Saheliens et Sahariens du Tchad* (Paris: L'Harmattan 1989) pp.13–43.
12. G. Gali NGothe, *Tchad: Guerre Civile et Désagrégation de L'Etat*, (Paris & Dakar: Présence Africaine 1985) pp.21–5.
13. J-C. Zeltner, *Les Pays du Tchad dans la Tourmente 1880-1903* (Paris: L'Harmattan 1988) pp.152–70.
14. J-L. Triaud, *Tchad 1900-1902: Une Guerre Franco-Libyenne Oubliée?* (Paris: L'Harmattan 1987) pp.13–76.
15. G. Ciammaichella, *Libyens et Français au Tchad (1897-1914)* (Paris: CNRS 1987) pp.73–80.
16. Gali NGothe, p.31.
17. Brownlie, p.123.
18. Ibid., pp.589–91.
19. Ibid., pp.609–11.
20. Ibid., pp.533–9.
21. Ibid., pp.613–16.

22. Ibid., pp.617–39.
23. Ibid., pp.121–5.
24. viz B. Lanne, *Tchad-Libye: La Quérelle des Frontières* (Paris: Karthala 1982) p.184.
25. Gali NGothe, pp.173–8.
26. M. N'Gangbet, *Peut-on Encore Sauver le Tchad?* (Paris: Karthala 1984) pp.9–10.
27. R. Buijtenhuijs, *Le Frolinat et Les Révoltes Populaires du Tchad, 1965–1976*, (The Hague: Mouton 1978) pp.456–61.
28. E.G.H. Joffé, 'Turmoil in Chad' in *Current History* (April 1990) pp.176–7.
29. In fact, in mid-1994, the Libyan regime decided to accept the Court's ruling and signed an agreement with Chad to that effect. It is not certain, however, that the issue will not be re-opened at some later date or by a subsequent regime.

# Land-locked Niger and its Alternative Seaport Accesses

## ALI DJIMBA

Strictly speaking, the term 'land-lockedness' refers to countries having no physical access to a sea coast. From the geographical viewpoint, these states are located inland and used to be called 'hinterland'. Up to 1990, 44 countries have been identified around the world as being land-locked of which 15 are located in Africa. The Republic of Niger is one them and one of the poorest as well.

Basically, apart from the known problems faced by developing countries, the land-locked countries of Africa particularly suffer from :

- their total isolation from sea interfaces
- their dependency on the surrounding transit states
- the general deficiency of their transport infrastructures
- the permanent disequilibrium of their balance of trade in favour of importations
- their dependence on a very small number of commodities both in the import and export markets.

This paper does not aim to cover all these issues, but just briefly to present the Republic of Niger in its daily fight against distance. Hence, the author will focus on the following aspects:

- a quick overview of Niger, a West African land-locked country (history and economy)
- the major land corridors used to gain access to the sea
- suggestion of some approaches which could help to overcome the handicap of land-lockedness in Niger, focusing on the vital necessity of looking at the Nigerian corridor as a potential outlet to the sea coast.

## Brief Historical Background

In many cases, land-lockedness is just an accident of history. A look at Niger's past would help a better understanding of the history of the largest land-locked state of Africa. As Uka Ezenwe stated, history is retrospective

MAP 1

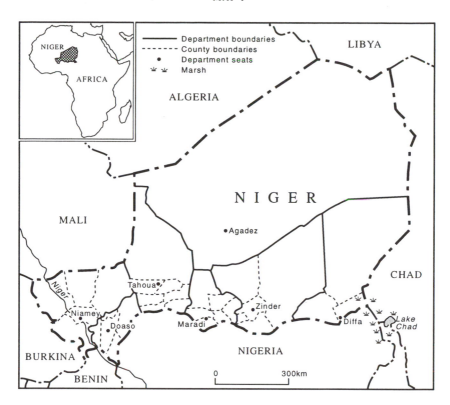

whereas economy is prospective, 'They speak the same language and they nourish each other.'[1]

*The Pre-colonial Period*

Prior to the European invasion, trade between the people in the region flourished, despite the lack of paved roads. Long-distance transport was assured by camel caravans from north to south and from east to west. Touaregs, in the northern arid area, were nomadic pastoralists. Their mobility allowed them to move through hundreds of kilometres in search of grazing lands and water for their herds. In so doing, they developed a flourishing trans-Sahara trade in West Africa. Milk, salt and butter were exchanged against food crops, millet and sorghum in the South where the Zerma-Songhai, Hausa-Fulani and Kanuri, thanks to their sedentary ways, had established a more stable society. Undoubtedly, a well-organised intra-African trade 'with an elaborate network of routes over land'[2] existed.

*The Colonial Period*

From the fourteenth to the nineteenth centuries, Africa had been suffering from slavery. But the years 1830–85 saw a complete and important change in the system, characterised by a change in the trade pattern: the slave trade was replaced by the exportation of raw materials from Africa to Europe. The profitability of such international exploitation was so exciting that conflicts arose among the colonial powers (Britain, France, Germany and Belgium) over African properties. A compromise was reached at the Berlin Conference of 1884-85: the continent was cut up into economically weak coastal and land-locked states. Since the objective was concentrated on the exploitation of raw materials, emphasis was put on roads, railways and waterways according to the interests involved. As a matter of fact, there was not any real interest in building infrastructure where there were no raw materials! Inland areas were systematically neglected. The incredible thing was that neighbouring peoples with identical ancestral traditions found themselves suddenly subjected to different languages and different practices in schools and administrations.

The 'ideal-typical sequences' model of Taafe, Morill and Gould (1963)[3] may help to understand the colonial strategy concerning transport policy. The model identifies three consecutive phases:

* *Early phase*: This step corresponds to the earlier colonial period when interests were essentially focused on ports infrastructure and just a very few inland connections were built.

* *Middle phase*: More important sea interfaces with more inland opportunities in terms of raw materials and cash crops were set up.

* *Late phase*: This last phase corresponds to the present period when more efficient ports and inland connections relying on economic and strategic centres were established.

In short, the 'ideal-typical sequences' of Taafe, Morill and Gould, shows that the construction of road networks were determined by the priority given to transport links between primary producing centres and seaports with Europe at the expense of regions presenting no immediate interest. The colonial settlers' main purpose in constructing railways in Dahomey (present day Benin), was to transport raw materials from the northern regions to ports where ships bound for Europe were loaded.

*Independence*

By 1960, many African countries had become independent. The main characteristic of these independent countries was their structural

FIGURE 1

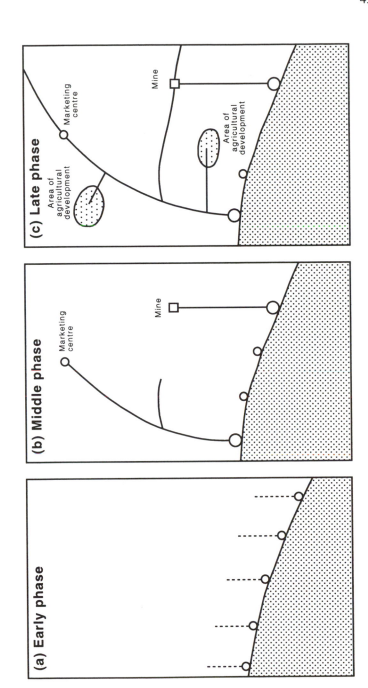

(a) Early phase

(b) Middle phase

(c) Late phase

Marketing centre

Mine

Area of agricultural development

Area of agricultural development

dependence on the colonial settlers. For instance, each French-speaking land-locked country would use primarily French-speaking coastal countries' ports. Louis Sabourin referred to this as a 'dependency syndrome'.[4] As a result of this structural dependence, about 95 per cent of all imports and exports in Niger pass through the ports of Lome in Togo and Cotonou in Benin. With some improvements the Nigerian ports could be a better alternative for the eastern regions (Maradi and Zinder) which culturally and geographically are closer to Nigeria.

## The Geographical Handicaps

As the distances inside and outside the borders of a land-locked country increase, so do the costs of imports while there is less return on exports. The Republic of Niger is the widest country in West Africa, and its inland location adds another dimension to the effects of its size. Focus in this descriptive section will be on the transportation problems encountered by such a geographically disadvantaged country.

### The Area of the Territory

The Republic of Niger is often qualified as 'a geographical monster'. Of the 19,000,000 km$^2$ for the whole of Africa, Niger alone covers a wide area of 1,267,000 km$^2$. Unfortunately, due to the adversity of its topography, only one third is really useful in terms of agricultural production.

Another source of logistical problems is the spread of the economic centres and villages, which are situated far from each other. Certainly, some efficient paved roads exist between the main cities, but when it comes to hauling cargoes to the villages (where about 85 per cent of the population lives) then transport becomes a matter of concern.

### The Location of the Territory

Niger is surrounded by developing countries upon which it heavily depends. Eight countries share a border of about 5,000 km with Niger. Three of them are land-locked (Chad to the east, Burkina Faso and Mali to the west) and four are coastal (Benin and Nigeria to the south and to the north, Algeria and Libya). At present, the most used but not necessarily closest port, is Cotonou in Benin, through which about 90 per cent of the total sea-borne trade of Niger is shipped.

Despite the bilateral agreements between Niger and its coastal neighbours, the country does not have effective control of the movement of its goods over the national frontiers as far as the following are concerned:

• port policy in which pricing is of paramount importance

- political troubles which often arise

- customs and administrative procedures in use and

- communication networks.

*The Geographic Distribution of the Population*

Niger is divided into seven administrative departments, namely: Niamey (the capital city), Dosso, Maradi, Zinder, Tahoua, Agadez, and Diffa. According to 1994 estimates, the population of Niger is 8,871,605. For the purpose of this study, they can be grouped into three main distribution centres in considering the density of population and economic interests:

- *The north-centre*: This area is occupied by the nomadic Touaregs whose population is difficult to determine due to their constant mobility. But the most important thing is the presence of uranium and coal mining activities in this area. Uranium is the main export product of the country: it contributed 24.3 per cent to the GDP in 1980.[5] Today, it contributes less than 18 per cent.

- *The south-east*: With a population of 1,389,433 inhabitants in the Maradi Department, 1,411,061 in Zinder and 1,308,598 in the Tahoua Department, the Hausa represent about 50 per cent of the national population. This ethnic group is one of the largest and most influential in West Africa (more than 100 million people communicate in Hausa). The Hausa of Niger draw great advantages from their proximity to Nigeria, with which an extensive trade network has been organised. Unfortunately these trading activities are difficult for the central government to control. In the extreme south-east, around Diffa, the Kanouri and the Boudouma represent 5 per cent of the total population.

- *The south-west*: This region is occupied by the Songhai-Zarma-Dendi who represent about 24 per cent of the population. The main cities of Niamey and Dosso are closer to Cotonou. The Pular are spread out throughout the country.

**The Economy of Niger**

According to the United Nations criteria, the Republic of Niger has been classified among the very poorest of the developing countries. The Gross National Product per capita (GNP) is estimated at about US$300 in 1990, whereas in Switzerland and Austria (land-locked countries of Europe) the GNP per capita were respectively US$15,710 and 27,693. Economic activity in Niger may be classified into two co-existing sectors.

*The rural sector* (agriculture and livestock) which employs 90 per cent of the active population, contributed only 39.1 per cent to the GDP (Gross Domestic Product) between 1980 and 1989. Many factors explain this low contribution:

• the adversity of climatic conditions

• the invasion of grasshoppers

• the consequent problems of diversification

• the scarcity of arable land and poor soils

• a demographic growth rate higher than that of the economy (3.2 per cent against 1.7 per cent)

• the remoteness from distribution centres and lack of rural infrastructure.

As a result of these factors, the country is bargaining for international food aid and purchasing additional quantities of cereals from international markets.

*The modern sector* is dominated by the mining sector. Actually, Niger's uranium reserves have been estimated by the United Nations at 360,000 tons, which represents 100 years of reserves assuming an extraction rate of 3,600 tons per year. Today, Niger is among the five major producers of this mineral in the world. In 1978, uranium contributed 14.5 per cent to the GDP and 81 per cent to the exports of goods. Before the crash in international uranium prices, this product was the driving force of the national economy. However, since 1989, uranium's share in GDP fell from 14.5 per cent to 5.7 per cent.[6] In 1991, the production costs at the mines were put at 22,000 FCFA/kg while the market selling price was 12,000 FCFA/kg. But worst of all was that the average world 'spot-market' price for uranium was about 9,000 FCFA/kg.

**The Alternative Sea Port Accesses**

The conditions of the use of transit ports are embodied in a number of international and bilateral agreements:

• Treaty of Versailles (28 June 1919)

• Genoa Convention (1923)

• Barcelona Declaration (20 April 1920)

• New-York Convention (8 July 1965)

• UNCTAD Code of Conduite ( 6 April 1974)

- Montego Bay Convention (10 December 1982)

- PAC-EEC Convention of Lomé

- TRIE Convention (Transport Routier inter-Etat)

- Benin-Niger agreement signed in January 1975

- Togolese Presidential Order No. 77-24/CAB/PC/MTP published on 28 February 1977 by which Niger was allocated in the Port of Lomé an indefinitely leased area of 24,000 m at a symbolic sum where a warehouse for Niger has been built.

All of these agreements aim to facilitate the use of sea facilities for land-locked countries. Although their application is very often jeopardized by local political or social conflict, they remain the only legal instrument used by inland countries for access to the sea coast.

Five alternative accesses to an international seaport are available to Niger: Abidjan (in Côte d'Ivoire), Tema (in Ghana), Cotonou (in Benin), Lome (in Togo) and Lagos (in Nigeria). The most used are the last three corridors as illustrated by schemes 1a, 1b and 1c.

*The Benin–Niger Corridor*

This section presents each land corridor, highlighting the advantages and disadvantages for Niger.

As scheme 1a shows, this corridor includes 438 km of railways in Benin and 618 km of paved road, of which 324 km are located in Benin. This route is of prime importance, as about 80 per cent of cargo (imports and exports) are carried on it. There are a number of advantages to this route:

- the distance (1056 km from Cotonou to Niamey) is shorter than it is to the other ports.

- the geographical situation: from Cotonou to Niamey, there is no other transit country, such as Burkina Faso when transiting via Lomé or Abidjan.

- the same official language (French) is spoken in both countries due to their common colonial background.

Based on these advantages, a number of arrangements have been established in order to improve the use of this route:

- OCBN (Organisation Commune Benin Niger des Chemins de Fer), jointly owned by the two governments and established in 1959. This railway company has a monopoly on Niger's transit traffic although the rail is extended only 438 km in Benin territory. Although a brand new

SCHEMES 1a, 1b and 1c

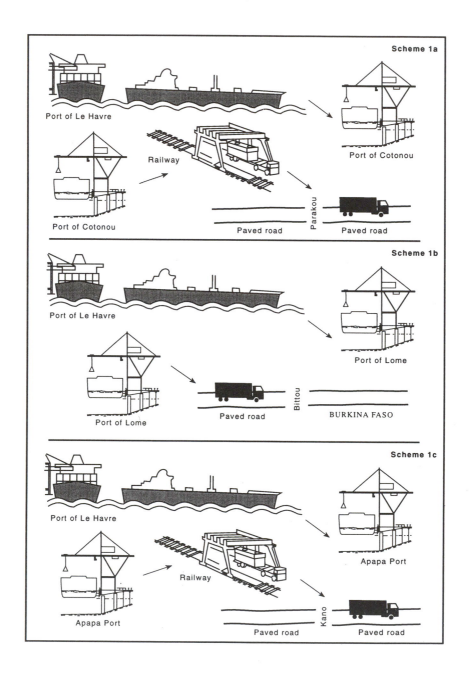

Scheme 1a

Port of Le Havre

Port of Cotonou

Railway

Port of Cotonou

Parakou

Paved road          Paved road

Scheme 1b

Port of Le Havre

Port of Lome

Port of Lome

Bittou

Paved road          BURKINA FASO

Scheme 1c

Port of Le Havre

Apapa Port

Railway

Apapa Port

Kano

Paved road          Paved road

highway financed by the World Bank can today join Cotonou to all of the cities of Niger, land transport is still forbidden to carriers.

• the agreement signed in Niamey in January 1975 provides Niger with some facilities to gain access to the Port of Cotonou.

The major disadvantages of this route are:

• the trans-shipment at Parakou. After goods are transported 438 km by rail from Cotonou to Parakou, cargo has to be trans-shipped onto trucks to Niger.

• the distance from the port of Cotonou to the eastern regions of Niger (Maradi and Zinder, where 55 per cent of the national population lives) is longer than from Lagos.

*The Togo–Niger Corridor*

This corridor is another alternative for Niger to gain access to the Atlantic Ocean. It is illustrated by scheme 1b. By choosing the Togolese port, one has to transit neighbouring Burkina Faso, also a land-locked country. That is one of the disadvantages of using Togo's port. Also the distance to the capital is longer (1250 km to Niamey). However, the fact that hauliers can directly collect their goods at the port represents an advantage for Nigerian importers who own both goods and trucks.

One of the major difficulties of this corridor used to be the irregular stops and expenditures en route. But thanks to the recommendations of the 'cellule de concertation' between Burkina Faso, Niger and Togo, the Togolese authorities decided to organise transport from the port to the border in convoys accompanied by an official escort. Although the system is highly appreciated in terms of cost saving, importers are now complaining about the delays. Actually, to get a sufficient number of trucks to form a convoy could take four days. The system therefore needs to be improved.

*The Nigerian Corridor*

This corridor to the Atlantic Ocean, illustrated by scheme 1c, is most often used by wealthy traders from the south-eastern part of Niger (Maradi and Zinder) who take advantage of the Nigerian central government's total lack of interest in this corridor. The complexity of the transport system is due to many factors, such as the disparity of currency, making this corridor difficult to control. In fact, despite the bilateral agreement signed in 1977 between Nigeria and Niger regarding the use of Nigerian ports, no practical action seems to have been taken to implement the decision. Nevertheless, three main reasons could justify the use of this corridor:

- Historically, there exists a trade tradition linking the eastern region of Niger to the western part of Nigeria.

- Geographically, Nigerian ports are closer to Maradi and Zinder than those of Lomé and Cotonou.

- Financially, despite the devaluation of the CFA (currency in use in Niger), its holders generally benefit from the instability of the Naïra (Nigerian currency).

The major handicap to Nigerian routes is the permanent lack of security. Importers and hauliers fear attacks by gangs on Nigerian highways.

## The Distances from the Alternative Ports to Niger

In observing Table 1 below, it appears that Cotonou and Lagos present the best alternative to the sea for Niger in terms of distance compared with the other ports. Also, considering the two ports, Lagos is closer to all the main cities than Cotonou.

TABLE 1

THE DISTANCES TABLES FROM ALTERNATIVE PORTS TO THE
MAIN CITIES IN NIGER (IN KM)

| Ports to... | NIAMY | MARDI | ZINDER | AGADES | ARLIT | DIFA | NGUIGMI |
|---|---|---|---|---|---|---|---|
| COTONOU* | 1056 | 1454 | 1694 | 1723 | 2137 | 1961 | 2267 |
| LOME | 1241 | 1905 | 2136 | 2182 | 2420 | 2596 | 2726 |
| LAGOS* | 1525 | 1421 | 1391 | 1628 | 1866 | 1851 | 1981 |
| ABIDJA | 1660 | 2324 | 2555 | 2601 | 2839 | 3015 | 3145 |
| ALGIERS | 3710 | 3536 | 3767 | 2769 | 2531 | 4227 | 4357 |

*Source:* Nitra Cotonou and various documents and maps.
* Rail - road network + straight paved road.

## Transport Costs from the Alternative Ports to Niger

The land transport varies between 20 and 42 per cent of the total cost according to:

- the corridor considered

- the distance

- the type of commodity

- the means of transport

Taking as an example the transport of rice, information recently collected shows the followings costs:

- Cotonou–Niamey      fcfa 24,830/ton
- Cotonou–Maradi      fcfa 33,885/ton
- Lagos–Niamey        fcfa 31,250/ton
- Lagos–Maradi        fcfa 24,671/ton
- Lomé– Niamey        fcfa 29,375/ton
- Lomé–Maradi         fcfa 50,859/ton

This cost comparison shows a preference for Lagos for the eastern part of Niger (Maradi and Zinder) and Cotonou for the western regions, all other factors (transit conditions, security and speed) being equal.

**The 'Strengths, Weaknesses, Opportunities, and Threats' (SWOT) of each Alternative Transit Route to Niger**

A final SWOT overview is appropriate for summarising the whole chapter. In this section the competitiveness of each corridor to Niger will be assessed.

*The Strengths*

*Cotonou–Niger*
- Geographic location near the western regions
- Railway joint venture
- Port usage agreement
- Same official language for ease of communication
- Same monetary system
- Better information network
- Low transit costs

*Lomé –Niger*
- Port usage agreement
- Same official language for ease of communication
- Same monetary system
- No trans-shipment by road
- Speed and security in port operations

*Lagos–Niger*
- Geographic location near the eastern regions
- Low cost of port operations as far as cargoes are concerned
- Efficient port infrastructures

- Efficient equipment
- Direct delivery on trucks or railways to hinterland
- Railway network until Kano
- Dry ports at Kano and Kaduna respectively located 300 km and 265 km from Maradi.

## The Weaknesses

### Cotonou–Niger

- Time in port and on road
- Pilferage and loss in port
- Trans-shipment at Parakou
- OCBN monopoly on land transport
- Obsolescence of the rails and wagons

### Lomé– Niger

- Geographic location
- Deficiency of road infrastructure in Burkina Faso
- High transit costs
- Cumbersome formalities in Burkina Faso and time consumption
- Deficiency of communications network

### Lagos–Niger

- Different language of communication and consequent delays in documentation procedures
- Current increases in dues and rates on ships
- Uncertainty and insecurity in the whole transport system
- Deficiency of the Lagos-Kano railway line
- Different monetary system and instability of the Naira
- Deficiency of both internal and external communications systems
- Lack of respect for various bilateral agreements on the Nigerian side

## The Opportunities

### Cotonou–Niger

- New international highway
- Liberalisation of transport system
- Computerisation of port and customs procedures

### Lomé–Niger

- Industrial free zone in the port

### Lagos–Niger

- Improvement of security by military escort

- Implementation of decisions
- Marketing towards Niger particularly the Western region
- Implementation of ECOWAS principles

*The Threats*

*Cotonou–Niger*
- Nigerian ports capacity to attract more trans-shipment cargo
- Improvement of security in Nigerian transport system
- Improvement in transit facilities via Togo

*Lomé– Niger*
- Political troubles and traffic in the Port of Cotonou
- Computerisation of operations in the port of Cotonou and expected future improvements in documentation speed

*Lagos–Niger*
- Instability of the Naira and constant political instabilities

**Some Suggestions**

*The Development of Alternative Routes to the Sea*
Two principal motives justify the search for alternative routes of access to the sea:

- reduction of the dependence on traditional routes

- increasing bargaining power by taking advantage of the fact that Niger could eventually use four route options. One may keep in mind that 'given two ports of similar nautical capacity, equidistant and with comparable land liaisons…it is the more efficient of the two ports which will be chosen'.[7] However, a full analysis of costs and benefits should be the pre-condition for such a choice. The profitability of all aspects may be the decisive factor in the final choice.

Today, Cotonou and Lomé are regularly used. But Lagos, despite the advantages it offers for the eastern regions of Niger, is very little used. In view of the fact that Maradi and Zinder constitute two of the major distribution centres of Niger, the author believes that the Lagos-Niger route should be investigated. Three essential problems must be resolved: currencies, security and communications. From this perspective, the following may be considered as measures:

- *Bilateral agreements*: As with Benin and Togo, Niger could obtain from

Nigeria some facilitation on the matter of tariffs. An instrument of co-operation already exists between the two countries. It is now a question of implementation, including port and transport arrangements.

• *Security problems*: Thieves and pilferage in port and eventual attacks on roads could be overcome if the two countries decided to put their efforts together. In this respect, expeditions from Lagos towards Niger via Kano could be grouped and escorted by army forces until the border. Insurance companies could also participate in these efforts by guaranteeing a sufficient coverage of risks. In a paper presented on 7 March 1991, Suzanne Lamido-Dorayi, the ICNL Managing Director at that time, noted that the principle of armed escorts has been adopted since the break down of the railway system. This is proof that the Dry Ports authorities are conscious of the security problems on Nigerian roads.

• *Documentation procedure:* Apart from its present complexity, the real problem with Nigeria is the administrative language of communication. Shipping documents are in English, while in Niger, customs and administrative clearances are carried out in French. At the bilateral level, the solution is what already has been implemented with success in Switzerland, a European land-locked country. Documents are established in three different languages: French, German and Italian. The same policy could be implemented by Nigeria and Niger and even at the regional level.

• *Monetary system*: This is one of the most complex issues due to the variety of local currencies in use in each country in West Africa. The convertibility of the FCFA and the Naira is a technical problem and the mechanism for solving it could be devised by the monetary specialists of the two countries or at the regional level.

### Conclusion and Recommendations

In this study, emphasis has been placed mainly on surface transport. The reason is that 90 per cent of Niger's foreign trade is organised by ocean transport. In assessing the different alternative options for access to the regional maritime ports, the paper has identified the major transport issues for the Republic of Niger. It appears that transport and related services represent the key cost components of the whole transport chain.

The effects of Niger's geographic isolation from seaports are enhanced by its underdeveloped economic conditions in which transport issues appear just as a facet. As indicated by Thomas Szentes:

The roots of the problem are of a structural character and related to the international division of labour and its impact on the local economies and environment.[8]

In searching for strategies for overcoming these issues, consideration of these internal and external structural factors may be a pre-condition.

## NOTES

1. Uka Ezenwe, *ECOWAS and the Economic Integration of West Africa* (London: C. Hurst & Company Publishers 1983).
2. J.P. Dickenson, A Geography of the Third World HC 59.7.
3. J.P. Dickenson, J.G. Clarke, W.T.S. Gould, R.M. Prothero, A.G. Hodgkiss, D.J. Siddle, C.T. Smith and E.M. Thomas-Hope, *A Geography of the Third World* (London: Methuen 1983) p.210.
4. Zdenek Cervenka (ed.), *Land-locked Countries of Africa* (Upsala: The Scandinavian Institute of African Studies 1973) p.147.
5. United Nations, *Country Presentation: Niger 1990* (Second UN Conference on the Least Developed Countries 1990).
6. Ibid., p.7.
7. Tim Reynolds, 'Port Documentation And Customs Procedures', paper presented at Le Havre (7 Sep.–9 Oct. 1992).
8. Thomas Szentes, in Zdenek Cervenka (ed.) *Land-locked Countries of Africa* (Upsala: The Scandinavian Institute of African Studies 1973) p.273.

# Land-lockedness and Dependency on Coastal Countries: The Case of Ethiopia

## WUHIB MULUNEH

Geopolitics is avowedly state-centric in its premises...the way in which governments conceptualise the distribution of political power beyond their boundaries as a precondition for conducting foreign policy in that special national interest. This is the way state elites make sense of the world in order to respond to or create events to their state's advantage. Through studying such statecraft we can identify codes that are the building blocks of geopolitical world order.[1]

Land-locked Ethiopia depends on the coastal countries of Eritrea and Djibouti for her import and export activities. This raises fundamental questions. How can Ethiopia cope with a more and more interdependent economy? How could Ethiopia handle the import and export economic interactions? Would the spirit of good neighbourliness play a positive economical role? These are some of the questions that this paper examines within the geopolitical *status quo ante* of the Horn of Africa. In order to answer the aforementioned questions the following topics require careful consideration: 1. brief historical, geographical, political and economic appraisal; 2. Ethiopia's dependence on the ports of coastal states; the dependency syndrome; 3. conclusions and recommendations.

### A Brief Historical, Geographical, Political and Economic Appraisal

#### A Brief History

The British historian Arnold J. Toynbee wrote the following in his book entitled, *A Study of History*, 'The wave of Islam and the mightier wave of our modern Western Civilisation have washed around the foot of the escarpment (Ethiopia) without submerging the summit. The oceans on which these later waves have swept upon the highlands have been few and brief; and they are the exception which prove the prevailing rule of Abyssinian (Ethiopian) immunity.'[2] The aforementioned historical observation by Toynbee summarises Ethiopia's History. The Red Sea area, as a strategic region (see map 1) experienced the rise and fall of the major historical powers: the Egyptians, the Turks during the Ottoman Empire and

MAP 1

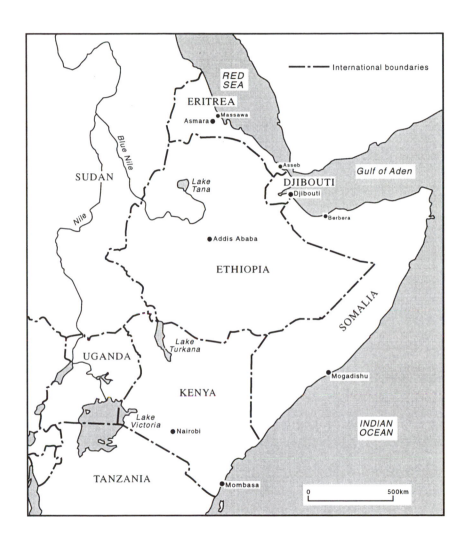

the British, French and Italians during the scramble for Africa. However, the Ethiopian Empire remained independent by keeping at bay all the foreign powers.

The Ethiopian polity, especially in 1800 was not a politically consolidated state. As Seven Rubinson put it in his book, *The Survival of Ethiopian Independence,* Ethiopia of 1800 was a weak state with serious internal problems and little visible cohesion. It was not, however, like many other areas of Africa, the home of a mere conglomerate of more or less closely affiliated tribes. The many centuries of settled agricultural life in Ethiopian highlands, the long history of the Ethiopian monarchy and the Christian Church in the area, had weakened tribal structures in favour of a mere regionally organised society. The politically and culturally dominating element in the region for a while was the Christian and Semitic-speaking highland population who cultivated much of the plateau from the hinterland of Massawa roughly to the big bends of the Abbay (Blue Nile) and the Awash.[3]

The Blue Nile and the Awash River basin, the north-west and south-east escarpments dissected by the famous Rift valley, were and are the most populated sections of the Ethiopian land mass. It is these people who dominated the political history of Ethiopia; Emperor Thewdros (1848–60), Emperor Johanis (1872–89), Emperor Menelik (1889–1913) and Emperor Haile Sellasee I (1930–74).

The coming to power of the Dergie (1974–90), the military dictatorship lead by Col. Mengistu Hallemarion tried to keep the country together by force and imposed a Marxist/Leninist political will upon the Ethiopian people. Since the demise of the former Soviet Union and Eastern European Communist countries, the rise of nationalism , as we have witnessed in the former Yugoslavia, surfaced in Africa in general and Ethiopia in particular. Through political awareness and the armed resistance of the Eritrean people (which lasted for nearly 30 years), the Republic of Eritrea was born. This political reality leaves Ethiopia a new land-locked country in Africa.

*Geographical Location*

Ethiopia is a mountainous country. It is often dubbed as the Switzerland of Africa. When Eritrea was part of Ethiopia, the land mass of Ethiopia stretched approximately between 3 and 18 north latitudes and between about 33 and 48 east longitudes. However, now the maximum northern latitude is about 14 and 30.

Ethiopia is bordered by the Sudan on the west for about 2200 km, Kenya in the south for about 860 km, Somalia on the east and Republic of Somalia on the north west for 1400 km, Djibouti for about 450 km, and Eritrea for about 700 km.

The climate of Ethiopia is influenced by the country's unique terrain. These geographical elements of low land, high land classifications and longitude influence the activities of all human beings. According to Mesfin Wolde Mariam, 'The influences of climate are almost inescapable...the sharp contrast of season in the temperate region of the world impose totally different needs. It is not unreasonable therefore to deduce from these forces that people in such environments must of necessity foresee the cold winter during the hot summer and vice versa.' He further asserts that, '...we can relate the backwardness of the tropical peoples and the progressives of peoples in the temperate regions to climate.'[4]

Geopolitical determinism globally has actually resulted in the north-south divide. Ethiopians, however, influenced by the tropical climate factors, pursued their agricultural life which is seasonally determined.

The area south-west of the Rift Valley experiences an annual rainfall of approximately 1400 mm. In certain areas, over 2000 mm. June, July and August are the three rainy months of the year, with 45 per cent of the total yearly rainfall.

The Central Plateau and the South Eastern Highlands receive their rainfall in June, July and August as well. 'Addis Ababa gets 55 per cent, Debre Margos 57 per cent, Gonder more than 75 per cent of the total rainfall in the three summer months.' Mariam further states that, '...the fluctuation of the rainfall in amount and periodicity from year to year reduces it's reliability...the percentage deviation is 30 per cent for Addis Ababa and 45 per cent for Leqemt.'[5] As a result, Ethiopia's agriculture is affected by the unreliable precipitation.

## Political

The Federal Democratic Republic of Ethiopia appears politically stable. All opposition groups have become spent forces and simply advance psychological and propaganda warfare. For the time being the political landscape is kept in place by the Ethiopian Peoples Revolutionary Democratic Front (EPRDF). The ruling party enjoys external support, especially from the US. The 548 member council of Peoples Representatives is the federal assembly. The elections of June 1994 for the constituent assembly and of May 1995 for federal and regional councils have given the EPRDF the legitimate grounds to govern for five years. The opposition boycotted the election and some are banned; the OROMO Liberation Front (OLF) and the all-Amhara Peoples Organisation (AAPO).

However, the political scene in Addis Ababa appears tense, especially after an explosion at the Ghion Hotel of 18th of January and at the Ras Hotel in Diredawa on 2 February 1996. No opposition party claimed responsibility. Since then the government has reinforced it's security network in order more effectively to maintain law and order as there are some sporadic banditry activities.

On the other hand there is tension along the Ethiopia-Sudan border. The Bashir Government of the Sudan guided by Islamic fundamentalist ideology has become a threat to both Ethiopia and Eritrea. There are accusations and counter-accusations by the governments of both the Sudan and Ethiopia. According to the Economist Intelligence Unit (EIU) in 1996, 'Diplomatic attrition has been accompanied by a flurry of accusations and counter-accusations of military action along the border and reprisals against Ethiopian refugees in the Sudan.'[6] It seems that both countries give refuge to opposition elements. However, internationally isolated Sudan could hardly venture military confrontation with either Ethiopia or Eritrea.

*Economic Appraisals*

Ethiopia is an agricultural country. Over 90 per cent of the people depend on the land. Farming and animal husbandry are the dominant occupations. It is largely a subsistence economy. However, coffee, pulses and oil seeds are grown for export.

Coffee is the major export-orientated cash crop of Ethiopia. Coffee is mainly grown in the south-western and eastern region of Ethiopia, which is closer to Assab and the Djibouti port. According to Ethiopa's Ministry of Industry 1994/95 estimates, total merchandise exports ran at 3 billion Birr (US$505 m). Out of the total merchandise, export coffee is number one. According to the EIU report, 'Coffee earned Birr 1.9 bn, hides and skins Birr 403 m, and gold Birr 136 m (US$1 = 9.5Birr). This compares favourably with 1993/94 when, according to central bank data, coffee earned Birr 920 m. Hides and skins Birr 204 m, and gold Birr 180 m.'[7] However, Ethiopia remains a league member of the least developed countries in Africa.

An average per capita income of $120 (some sources indicate $100) persists to date. According to the African Development Report (1995) the population growth rate is 3.0 per cent which is 0.8 per cent less than, for example, Kenya, which is 3.8 per cent and 1 per cent more than Djibouti, which is 2 per cent. A study made by the UN African Recovery Programme, (UN.5 No2-3 1991), as quoted in *Eritrea and Ethiopia – From Conflict to Co-operation*, gives a clear picture of socio-economic underdevelopment in its negative statistical picture of population income and debt in Djibouti, Eritrea, Ethiopia and Somalia. The following table shows the trend:

TABLE 1
KEY ECONOMIC DATA

| | Djibouti | Eritrea | Ethiopia | Somalia |
|---|---|---|---|---|
| Population (m 1990) | 0.40 | 3.5 | 45.24 | 7.49 |
| Average growth rate % ('85–'90) | 3.05 | N.A. | 2.7 | 2.4 |
| GNP per capita US$ ('89) | N.A. | 150 | 120 | 170 |
| Total debt (US$ m) | 180 | N.A. | 3.88 | 1.18 |
| Debt services as % of export '89 | N.A. | N.A. | 39 | 34 |
| Actual food prod. per capita '86–'89 ('79–81 = 100) | N.A. | N.A. | 90 | 97 |
| Infant mortality '85–'90 (per 1000 live births) | 122 | 137 | 137 | 132 |
| Life expectancy yrs. '85–'90 | 47 | 48 | 44 | 45 |

*Source*: Tekle Amare, *Eritrea and Ethiopia from Conflict to Co-operation* (1994)

The overall GNP of $120 for Ethiopia, $150 for Eritrea and $170 for Somalia indicate that Ethiopia is at the bottom of the league within the Horn of Africa. However the current Ethiopian economic growth shows a positive and optimistic trend in the wake of a good food harvest in 1995. Still, Ethiopia depends on a cash economy, for example, coffee for hard currency for importing oil and chemicals. The export and import deficit underlines the need for a more export-oriented economy.

TABLE 2
ETHIOPIA – FOREIGN TRADE

| Principal Exports 1994 (US$ m) | | Principal Imports 1993 (US$ m) | |
|---|---|---|---|
| Coffee | 320 | Food & live animals | 111 |
| Hides & skins | 68 | Crude petroleum | 79 |
| Gold | 23 | Petroleum products | 64 |
| | | Chemicals | 44 |

*Source*: EIU Country Report, Ethiopia, Eritrea, Somalia & Djibouti (1996)

The $320 m coffee export value, out-balances the total import value which is $298 m. On the other hand, Ethiopia's requirements for chemicals such as fertilisers tend to increase in the long run in order to maximise food production. Estimates from the Ministry of Agriculture of an unprecedentedly large cereal harvest of 9.6 m tons for 1996 was attributed to good climatic conditions. At the same time, it appears that fertilisers played a prominent role as well. Therefore dependence on fertilisers and technology will show an upward trend in the future. Hence, export orientated activities will be necessary to pay for imports. Ethiopia's destination for exports is mainly Germany in Western Europe and Japan in the Pacific economic realm. On the other hand, imports originate from Italy, Germany and the US. Crude petroleum and petroleum products come from Saudi Arabia. According to the EIU the table below shows the percentage of export destinations and origins of imports for Ethiopia.

TABLE 3
ETHIOPIA – SOURCE OF IMPORTS/DIRECTION OF EXPORTS

| Destination of Ethiopia Exports 1993 (% of total) | | Origin of Imports 1993 (% of total) | |
|---|---|---|---|
| Germany | 18.0 | Saudi Arabia | 13.3 |
| Japan | 13.0 | Italy | 11.6 |
| Djibouti | 10.0 | USA | 10.2 |
| Saudi Arabia | 7.7 | Germany | 9.1 |

*Source: EIU Country Report, Ethiopia, Eritrea, Somalia & Djibouti (1996) p.12*

In *Emergent Eritrea*, Gerbre Hiwet Tesfa Giorgis underlined that, 'Assab largely handles Ethiopia's sea-borne trade and requires a different organisational set up to reflect its difference from Massawa, especially now that it has been declared a free port as it relates to Ethiopia.'[8] In 1992 Ethiopia and Eritrea signed an agreement reinforcing the 1991 protocol of understanding for Ethiopia to use Assab as a 'free transit' port. However, the contractual agreement does not reflect what land-locked countries claim as 'access to sea', and therefore the agreement could be 'revocable' anytime.

## Ethiopia's Dependence on the Ports of Coastal States

### The Assab Outlet

Since Eritrea's independence (24 May 1991) there is a protocol of understanding between Addis Ababa and Asmara for Ethiopia's 'free' use of the port of Assab – Ethiopia's concern at being land-locked is thus eased, but the assurances reached in order to maintain Ethiopia's outlet to the sea will depend on the political whims of the government of the day in Asmara. Therefore the Addis Ababa–Asmara axis play a pivotal political role. Ethiopia uses the port of Assab for export and import, therefore Assab plays a vital role in Ethiopia's economic life. The Massawa port, during Emperor Haile Selassie and Col. Mengistu's regime was used as a naval port for military purposes.

Assab's geographical location places the port in an ideal position for exporting coffee, as the road between Addis Ababa and Assab is of a very high standard, and regular maintenance is carried out by the Ethiopian Highway Authority. The coffee region of Ethiopia in the south and south-west are better connected with Addis Ababa, the country's commercial centre. All coffee producers, private and governmental, own coffee storage and warehouses in Addis Ababa. The 890 km long Addis Ababa-Assab road is regularly used by coffee trucks.

The port of Assab can handle over 1 m metric tons of goods annually. When compared with Massawa, when Eritrea was part of Ethiopia for example, Assab's services were considerably higher (see figures I and II). Cargoes loaded and unloaded in Assab (1984) were over 2 m tons whereas in Massawa it was just under 500,000 tons. The registered tonnage of ships called and departed (1994) were over 2,500,000 tons in Assab and just over 500,000 tons in Massawa. Therefore, Ethiopian dependency on Assab will continue. However, the facilities at Assab and Massawa are less developed when compared with Djibouti. Nevertheless, Eritrea has as of late managed a major rehabilitation project for Massawa and Assab with the assistance of the World Bank. According to the EIU: 'A major rehabilitation project for Massawa and Assab ports is due to get underway in April 1996. Financed with another concessional World Bank credit, it aims at the extensive rebuilding of the two parts...the overall cost of the scheme which is due to run until 2004 is set at $35 m, of which the bank is expected to provide $20 m and the government $5 m...the project is scheduled to cover new cargo handling equipment, staff training and environment improvement.'[9]

The development of new cargo handling equipment at Assab will be to Ethiopia's advantage, as Ethiopia's imports of petroleum products, chemicals and manufacturing goods are expected to increase. However, according to the *UN Statistical Yearbook*, and as quoted by *Africa South of the Sahara*, the 1991 import and export valuation shows a decrease.

Nevertheless, according to the 5-year plan launched by Ethiopia in 1996, future economic growth appears positive. Elements like non-monetary gold are expected to increase. Coffee is the main export and hides and skins exports are projected to increase within the coming five years. Therefore, Ethiopia's dependence on Assab will increase.

FIGURES I AND II

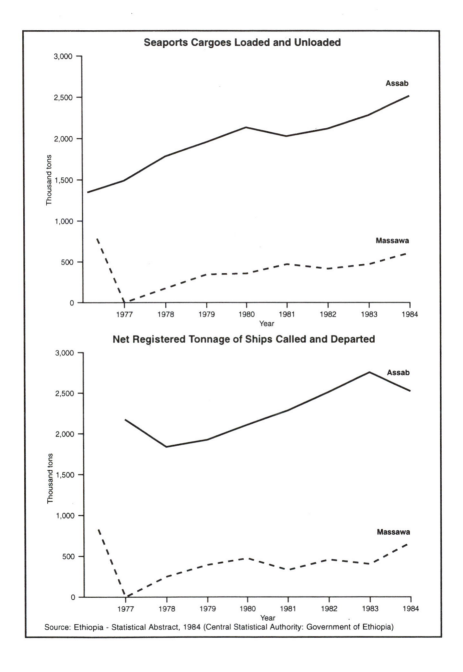

Source: Ethiopia - Statistical Abstract, 1984 (Central Statistical Authority: Government of Ethiopia)

TABLE 4

**ETHIOPIA'S IMPORTS** (US$ '000)

|  | 1989 | 1990 | 1991 |
|---|---|---|---|
| Mineral fuels, lubricants, etc. | 107,933 | 128,082 | 50,192 |
| Petroleum products | 107,847 | 128,073 | 50,134 |
| Crude petroleum oils | 86,451 | 12,892 | 29,148 |
| Refined petroleum products | 19,855 | 13,224 | 20,543 |
| Chemical and reacted products | 170,533 | 108,810 | 72,753 |
| Basic manufactures | 148,167 | 172,897 | 76,327 |
| Machinery & transport equip. | 338,402 | 427,255 | 210,482 |

**ETHIOPIA'S EXPORTS** (US$ '000)

|  | 1989 | 1990 | 1991 |
|---|---|---|---|
| Food & live animals | 323,446 | 181,978 | 126,325 |
| Vegetables & fruits | 11,186 | 25,881 | 6,292 |
| Fresh or simply preserved veg. | 10,193 | 25,256 | 3,724 |
| Coffee, tea, cocoa & spices | 296,061 | 132,864 | 117,169 |
| Crude materials except fuels | 91,466 | 76,329 | 32,311 |
| Rawhides, skins & fur skins | 65,942 | 60,776 | 25,068 |
| Non-monetary gold | N.A. | N.A. | 21,348 |
| (excluding ores & concentrates) | | | |

Source: *UN Statistical Yearbook* and *Africa South of the Sahara* (1996)

## The Djibouti Outlet

The Ethiopia-Djibouti railway (*Chemin de Fer*) was founded in 1908 during the reign of Emperor Menelik II with the financial and technical assistance rendered by the French government. It was jointly owned by the then colonial power, France, and what is now the Republic of Djibouti. Since its foundation the 780 km track of which 681 km is within the Ethiopian territory remains the main artery that transports Ethiopia's export and import merchandise.

Much of Ethiopia's trade passes through Djibouti and the port has also enhanced it's status and was declared a free port in 1981. In 1990 the Ethiopia-Djibouti railway handled freight traffic of 100 metric tons and 957,000 passengers.[10] In the late 1970s and mid-1980s much of Ethiopia's imports and exports went through the port of Djibouti.

TABLE 5

**Djibouti's Imports 1991**
(in m Djibouti francs)

| | |
|---|---|
| France (former colonial power) | 9,954 |
| Ethiopia | 3,154 |
| Japan | 2,739 |
| Italy | 2,469 |
| Saudi Arabia | 1,920 |

Source: *Africa South of Sahara* (1996) p.12

FIGURE III

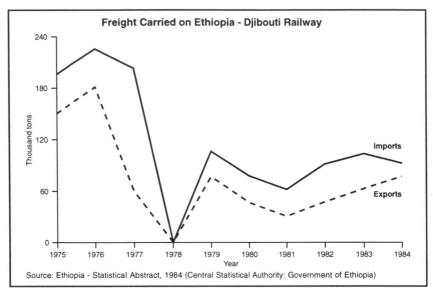

Source: Ethiopia - Statistical Abstract, 1984 (Central Statistical Authority: Government of Ethiopia)

Ethiopia and Djibouti are economically interdependent. Ethiopia exports food items and vegetables to Djibouti and in 1991 Ethiopia was the second exporting country to Djibouti. (see figure III).

In 1981 Ethiopia and Djibouti signed a new railway agreement and in 1985 the Ethiopia-Djibouti inter ministerial committee agreed to grant 'autonomous status' to the railway company, in order to enhance its profitability. The rolling stocks are old. Getting new ones and rehabilitating some of the dilapidated ones requires money. With the help of the European Union the work began in 1986. Further financial assistance came from the EU in 1993.

Due to security problems along the railway such as derailments and mechanical failures in 1995/96, the amount of cargo carried by rail between Djibouti and Ethiopia has declined from 60 per cent of total cargo to around 7 per cent.[11]

In 1992, France, the former colonial country, earmarked $8 m towards the modernisation of the railway and port facilities. Once the work is completed the chances for Ethiopia to increase her export and import needs would be improved.

**Conclusions and Recommendations**

Ethiopia as a land-locked country depends on Eritrea and Djibouti for her outlet to the sea. The 'free transit' agreement with Eritrea and the joint ownership of the Addis Ababa–Djibouti railway could ease Ethiopia's anxiety. Even if Ethiopia's economy expands extensively, without access to the sea it would be meaningless. According to Cervenka:

> While the level of economic development of a particular land-locked state might not be much different from that of a coastal state (in some instances it might be higher), the geographical isolation from the sea reduces its political options and subordinates its economic growth to that of its neighbours to a much greater degree than is the case of a coastal state, however poor.[12]

In order to avoid future isolation and confrontation, Ethiopia should pursue a positive and economically viable policy with her neighbours. In today's world, regional co-operation and the creation of economic goals are seen as positive ways forward. The US, Canada and Mexico Free Trade Zone is a case in point. Ethiopia should adopt these trends of economic and commercially viable policies. Ethiopia as a geographically disadvantaged country would benefit by pursuing regional co-operation. Ethiopia, Eritrea and Djibouti could form a nucleus for the Horn of Africa region. Currently, Uganda, as one of Africa's land-locked countries is spear-heading the reactivation of the East African Economic Community (EAEC), which collapsed in 1977. For example, the Economic Community of West African States (ECOWAS), the Common Market of Eastern, Central and South Africa (COMESA) and the South African Development Council (SADC) are positive steps forward.

Therefore, the creation of an Ethiopia, Eritrea and Djibouti Economic Co-operation Body (EEDEC) is a positive step forward. Mutual economic co-operation, free trade and commercial zones, common currency and joint development strategies along their common boundaries are some of the policies that appear viable and pragmatic. Common foreign and defence policies are also additional and positive ingredients. This kind of regional identity based on mutual respect and understanding are not only desirable but prerequisites for any land-locked country like Ethiopia.

## NOTES

1. Peter J. Taylor, *Political Geography of the Twentieth Century: A Global Analysis* (London: Belhaven Press 1995) p.36.
2. Arnold Toynbee, *A Study of History, Vol. II* (Oxford: OUP 1935) pp.360–5.
3. Seven Rubinson, *The Survival of Ethiopian Independence* (Addis Ababa: Addis Ababa University Press 1978).
4. Mesfin Wolde Mariam, *An Introductory Geography of Ethiopia* (Addis Ababa: Addis Ababa University Press 1972).
5. Ibid.

6. The Economist Intelligence Unit (EIU), *Country Report: Ethiopia, Eritrea, Somalia and Djibouti* (London: EIU, 1st quarter 1996).

7. Ibid.

8. Gerbre Hiwet Tesfagiorgis, *Emergent Eritrea* (Trenton, New Jersey: Red Sea Press 1994).

9. J. Pickett, 'Ethiopia: Economy', in *Africa South of the Sahara* (London: Europa Publications Ltd. 1996) p.393.

10. Ibid.

11. Ibid.

12. Zdenek Cervenka, *Land-locked countries of Africa* (Oslo: The Scandinavian Institute of African Studies, Uppsala 1973) p.19.

# African Land and Access Corridors

## IEUAN Ll. GRIFFITHS

A land corridor is a means whereby a state obtains access to the sea, a river, lake or an otherwise detached piece of territory. To achieve effective control the state seeking access has to extend its sovereignty over the land corridor by international treaty. Without land corridors of access some states would be land-locked, isolated or without access to a perceived natural artery of communication. A land corridor of access should be, but is not always, capable of carrying a major transport route. The corridor is normally, but not always, long and narrow. It often lies between two or more other sovereign states, though sometimes it divides one other state into two parts. Land corridors of access are manifestations of 'grand' geo-politics and the way that they fill the agendas of some modern states demonstrates that that particular art form is not dead despite many obituaries.

Careful study of the contemporary political map of Africa reveals only two obvious extant land corridors. Both are long and narrow, one containing modern transport arteries in the form of a railway and a paved road and the other not. Relict land corridors can be found fossilised on current political maps at a sub-national level. Others are to be found only on maps of an earlier period because they have long disappeared. Some land corridors have become sovereign states in their own right. Many would-be African land corridors are merely putative, representing no more than attempts to achieve, or claims to, sovereignty over access which has never succeeded. Study of these failures gives fascinating insight into African international affairs.

Politically the many land corridors of Africa may be divided into 'colonial' and 'independent'. The significance of the division is the locus of the decision making, the imperial metropole for the 'colonial', the independent states or quasi-independent states of Africa itself for the 'independent' The division is not strictly historical because some 'independent' attempts to create corridors of access pre-date colonial corridors. It is not even a matter of before and after the basic political map of Africa was set because some 'independent' corridors were thwarted by those drawing up the map. In general 'colonial' corridors were successfully created, if not always effective in achieving their original purpose, whilst attempts at creating 'independent' corridors have generally failed.

The dictum that the alignment of land boundaries is largely a matter of history did not apply to colonial Africa whose political map was newly created and imposed from the outside largely in the thirty-year period 1885–1914. The boundary lines were drawn with little or no knowledge of, or attention to, African history or indeed to African human geography. Africa at the beginning of 'the scramble' was to Europeans largely a blank outline map on which they sketched in their few coastal possessions. Exaggerated and often inappropriate attention was paid to features of physical geography which were subsequently often found to have been wrongly perceived or mapped in the first place. The mountains, lakes and rivers 'discovered' by the intrepid Victorian explorers were disputed by arm-chair geographers. These dubious scant 'facts' did not inhibit the partitioners.

Where complete ignorance of physical features was admitted, parallels, meridians, other straight lines and even arcs of circles were adopted. The Europeans argued and made bi-lateral agreements with each other, which were reasoned within their own context. They assumed the luxury of not having to take local human conditions into account except in the most marginal way. Africa's off-the-shelf network of fifty thousand miles of inter-colonial, now international, boundaries were agreed between the European powers according to a set of rules themselves drawn up and interpreted exclusively by those powers.

Surprisingly the only corridor of access to the sea created during the European scramble for Africa was the Congo (Zaire) river corridor agreed in principle at Berlin in 1885 but later whittled down in size. It has survived as a narrow funnel of Zairean territory giving on to a short 35km Atlantic coastline. Thus Africa's second largest state has a seaboard shorter even than that of continental Africa's smallest state, the Gambia. Very small in relation to the vast area of inland Zaire, it even bisects what is now the sovereign state of Angola. It is truly a corridor of access despite the fact that the river is not navigable from the ocean beyond Matadi. Today the corridor carries a railway and surfaced road from Matadi to Kinshasa the capital city at the entrance to the great inland river basin most of which comprises the modern state of Zaire.

Access to the Congo basin was the very issue which caused the European powers to meet at Berlin in 1884–85 at the Conference to lay down the ground rules for the European 'scramble for Africa'. Discussion began with the river Congo, the course of which had only recently (1877) been traced by H.M. Stanley who, alone of the great explorers, was present at the Berlin Conference. Stanley had returned to open up the Congo on behalf of Leopold II, King of the Belgians and his International Association of the Congo (IAC). By 1884 the IAC was prepared to claim recognition of its right to rule the Congo basin as an independent state on the basis of hundreds of treaties concluded with local African chiefs. This recognition was sought from the European powers. But Portugal held historic rights to the west African coast including the Congo estuary and its navigable reach from the sea and sought to have them confirmed in a treaty with Britain in February 1884. The claim was disputed in a storm of protest from the other European powers and Portugal proposed an International Conference to consider the whole question of Congo. From these beginnings the Berlin Conference materialised. Under Chapter I, Article I of the General Act of the Conference of Berlin signed by the European powers in February 1885, the Congo basin became a designated free trade area.[1] The river basin, 'its embouchures and circumjacent areas' were generously defined and extended to the Indian Ocean between the mouth of the Zambesi and 50 North.

Leopold II obtained recognition first for his IAC and later for the Congo Free State *(Etat Independant du Congo).* Even before the Berlin Final Act was signed Leopold's negotiations with Germany (Treaty, 8 November 1884), Great Britain (12 December 1884), France (Treaty, 5 February 1885) and Portugal (Treaty, 14 February 1885) gained recognition for the IAC but limited the territory of the Congo Free State to less than either the Free Trade area or the river basin as defined in the Final Act. France agreed a boundary of 'The River Chiloango from the ocean to its northernmost source'.[2] The corridor was further narrowed when Portugal reluctantly agreed to give the Congo Free State access to the sea but stubbornly held on to what became the Angolan enclave of Cabinda between the Chiloango and a point just north of the Congo estuary and to the south bank of the Congo estuary itself.

The post-World War II discovery of significant oil resources on and off the Cabinda coastline make Portugal's determination to retain the enclave a shining example of the virtue of keeping what you hold to numerous states in Africa pressured to make 'sensible' adjustments to the often arbitrary boundary lines drawn by the Europeans. The eastern boundary of the Congo Free State was set at 300 East and Lake Tanganyika.

The Congo (Zaire) river runs through the corridor but is navigable from the ocean only to Matadi about 80 miles (130km) from the sea. The navigable course of the Congo was divided between the Free State and Portugal with Noqui (Nokki) the highest Portuguese station on the south bank of the river about 5 miles (8km) west of Matadi. A little above Matadi there are rapids in the river which are the first in a series of such obstacles, rapids, cataracts and waterfalls, which extend for over 250 miles (400km) to the point where the river exits from Stanley Pool near Kinshasa (Leopoldville). Above Matadi the Congo river is entirely within Zairean

territory for about 150 miles (240km) before again becoming an
international boundary, this time between Zaire and the (former French)
Congo on the north bank.

Access to the main Congo basin had to be by means other than the river.
Stanley put the imperative graphically to the Comite de l'Association
Internationale du Congo in 1882:

> I declared that the Congo Basin was not worth a two-shilling piece in
> its present state. To reduce it into profitable order, a railroad must be
> made between the Lower Congo and the Upper Congo, when with its
> accessibility will appear its value.[3]

Stanley first cut a wagon road around the rapids from Vivi on the north
bank, opposite and a little above Matadi, to Stanley Pool. Later he made a
road from Matadi on the south bank, away from French territorial claimants
led by De Brazza, to Leopoldville (Kinshasa) on the south bank of Stanley
Pool. Work on a railway began in 1890, the first train reaching Leopoldville
from Matadi in March 1898. It was a considerable, and costly, engineering
achievement although the end result was only a low capacity, narrow gauge
(2'6', 0.76m) track of tight curves (197ft, 60m) and steep gradients, 249
miles (400km) in length. It cost almost £2.5 million and about 2000 lives,
including 43 Europeans, and was soon inadequate for the needs it was
designed to serve.[4]

Between 1927 and 1932 the railway was upgraded and realigned. The
Cape gauge of 3'6' (1.67m) was adopted, wider curves were introduced
(656ft, 200m), the maximum height above sea-level was reduced from
2448ft (746m) to 2220ft (677m) and the route length shortened to 229 miles
(366km).[5] The new alignment encroached on Portuguese territory near
Matadi so a territorial exchange was made between Belgium and Portugal
(Convention of July 1927, ratified March 1928) whereby 1 sq.mile (3
sq.km) needed for the railway was exchanged for the *Botte de Diolo* (480
sq.miles, 1243 sq.km) at the south-western corner of the Congo on the route
of the Benguela railway then under construction.[6]

Despite these improvements, and the post-independence construction of
a surfaced road, the Kinshasa/Matadi corridor has not proved adequate for
the external trade of Zaire. The main reason is that the internal source of
Zaire's bulk mineral exports is in remote Shaba (Katanga), reached by the
Cape railway in 1910. A railway from Lubumbashi (Elisabethville) to Ilebo
(Port Francqui) on the Kasai River, a distance of 980 miles (1578km), was
opened in 1928. Ilebo and Kinshasa are connected only by river (526 miles,
840km), for a railway planned and even surveyed has never been built. The
intention is demonstrated in the choice of Cape gauge for the
Matadi/Kinshasa railway. The Ilebo line is in effect an extension of the Cape

railway. The great distance, costly transhipment and low capacity of the Lubumbashi/Ilebo/Kinshasa/Matadi route has discouraged its intensive use. Following closure of the Benguela Railway through Angola to Lobito (from 1975) most of Zaire's copper exports have been routed along the spinal railway via South Africa rather than the Kinshasa/Matadi corridor.

The other colonial corridor of access to be found on the political map of Africa is the Caprivi Strip (Zipfel), a 286 mile (458km) long, narrow finger of land from northern Namibia eastwards to the Zambesi River.

Named after the then German Chancellor, the Strip was determined in principle by the Anglo-German Agreement of 1890:

> It is understood that under this arrangement Germany shall have free access from her Protectorate [Namibia] to the Zambesi by a strip of territory which shall at no point be less than twenty English miles in width.[7]

The treaty does not state why Germany wanted access to the Zambesi. It had been known that the river was not navigable since Livingstone had 'discovered' the Victoria Falls in 1855. The Strip is also cut by two large rivers, the Cubango (Okavango) and the Cuando (Linyanti or Chobe), with large areas of seasonally impassable swamp making access along it to the Zambesi extremely difficult. It may have been seen by Berlin-bound German diplomats as a geo-political thrust towards the then undefined German sphere in East Africa to cut the British Cape to Cairo axis and was perhaps the beginning of the German *Mittel* Afrika concept which survived until the Second World War. The Caprivi Strip temporarily disappeared in 1915 when occupied by British Forces from Rhodesia and administered as part of Bechuanaland (Botswana). In 1929, at the request of the League of Nations Mandatory power, South Africa, it was returned to South West Africa (Namibia). Any strategic role for the Caprivi Strip remained unfulfilled until 1965–1990 when white South Africans used it as a first line of defence for the apartheid state against incursion from black Africa. The South Africans built military bases and roads in the strip. The Caprivi Strip remains a sore thumb on the political map of Africa, fossilised in the way of African boundaries, but taken very seriously by Namibians who no doubt think of Cabinda and hang on to what they hold. In 1964, before independence, Botswana claimed it.[8] Since Namibia's independence (21 March 1991) there have been two boundary disputes in the Caprivi Strip, one with Zambia[9] and one with Botswana.[10]

A less obvious colonial corridor of access on the political map of Africa is the 'road to the north'[11] between the western border of the Transvaal and the Kalahari Desert. As early as 1883 Cecil Rhodes perceived this corridor as vital to:

the whole future of this Colony. I look upon this Bechuanaland territory as the Suez Canal of the trade of this country, the key of its road to the interior.[12]

Rhodes became obsessed with the strategic importance of the corridor to the Cape Colony, the territory which came to bear his name, his Cape to Cairo 'dream'[13] and British imperial interests. Fearful of being cut off from the interior by Boer expansion westward in the tiny republics of Stellaland and Goshen linking with a possible German thrust from Namibia, Rhodes kept the road open by a show of imperial military strength and skilful diplomacy with the local Boers, the Transvaal Boers, the Cape government, the British government, the missionary lobby and local Africans. It was along 'the road to the north' that the settler Pioneer Column trekked to found Fort Salisbury (Harare) in 1890, and along the same route the umbilical 484-mile (775km) Mafeking (Mafikeng)/Bulawayo railway was built in 1896–97 to counter the threats to Rhodesia posed by the Ndebele 'rebellion' and the rinderpest pandemic. The British used the corridor during the Anglo-Boer War of 1899–1902 to bring supplies and troops in via Beira. Between 1966 and 1975 with its northern extension to the Kazangula ferry it achieved prominence as an escape route from the apartheid state. Today it is the most densely populated part of Botswana where towns on the Kalahari fringe are linked by modern infrastructure partly of imperial/colonial strategic origin.

The Germans negotiated two more land corridors of access in Africa, both with the French to give access to the Obangui and Congo rivers from the German colony of Kamerun.

It was part of the Franco-German Convention of November 1911 which in return gave France a free hand in Morocco.[14] These corridors are not familiar features on the political map of Africa because they disappeared at the Treaty of Versailles in 1919, the territory being restored to *Afrique Equatoriale Française*.

Two other minor access corridors briefly graced the political map of the eastern Congo in deals between Belgium and Britain. One in May 1894 gave the British a 25km (15.5 mile) wide corridor for the Cape to Cairo railway to run between Lake Tanganyika and Lake Edward. Because of German opposition the lease was annulled a month later. The other, the 25km (15.5 mile) wide Mahaqi Strip, gave Belgium access to Lake Albert in 1910 but was made redundant by a boundary change which gave Belgium the whole of the western shore of Lake Albert in 1915.[15]

Though short lived, these corridors indicate the importance attached to such geo-political manifestations by the European powers at the time. The 'scramble for Africa' was an expression of the rivalry between the European powers played out with someone else's land almost as a strategic board game.

'Independent' corridors of access are those corridors where the driving force for their creation came from an independent, quasi independent or non-colonial, power. These are the corridors of those trying to get out, for example, land-locked states seeking sovereignty over their access to the sea. As the locus of decision making is internal to Africa they are very different from colonial corridors which result from external, metropolitan-based, geo-political decision making. As Africa by 1980 had fourteen independent land-locked states, then as many as in the rest of the world, it is not surprising that there have been several attempts by such states to create corridors of access to the sea. However, the process long pre-dates the European de-colonisation of Africa in the second half of the twentieth century suggesting that it is a phenomenon found wherever and whenever the condition of land-lockedness existed. On the other hand generally it has not been successful, perhaps reflecting the inherent weakness of land-locked states. Where a corridor of access has been created the independent state has been massively aided and abetted by an imperial power whose interests were also served by the land-locked state winning sovereignty over a corridor of access to the sea.

The only land-locked state in Africa to achieve sovereignty over its access to the sea was Ethiopia. Its land corridor of access, Eritrea, was barely recognisable as such for it is over 600 miles (960km) 'wide' and at the critical point only 40 miles (65km) 'long'. The scramble for Africa left Ethiopia land-locked but an independent African Empire free from European colonial rule. It was blocked from direct access to the sea by four European colonial territories: British Somaliland, French Somaliland, Italian Somaliland and (Italian) Eritrea. The Italians attempted to conquer Ethiopia but were defeated at the Battle of Adowa in 1896, the only decisive long-term defeat of a European power during the scramble. In 1935, a more militant Fascist Italy with a modern army was back in Ethiopia, with the connivance of Britain and France already on the path of appeasement. In a short, brutal Abyssinian Campaign the Italians conquered Ethiopia causing the Emperor, Haile Selassie, to flee. For the first time in the modern era Ethiopia and Eritrea were under one political administration, the short-lived Italian East African Empire (1936–41).

In five years Haile Selassie was back in Addis Ababa as head of an independent state and a British Military Administration was installed in the former Italian colonies of Eritrea and Somaliland.[16] A Four Power Commission (Britain, France, Soviet Union and the United States) could not agree on Eritrea's future. The problem passed to the United Nations (UN) who set up a Commission which also could not agree. The matter was debated at the UN and in December 1950 Resolution 390A was passed to the effect that from September 1951 Eritrea was to become an autonomous territory federated with Ethiopia. The terms of the UN Resolution were abused by Ethiopia which systematically set about turning federation into full union. Unsupervised elections saw the installation of a puppet government in Asmara and in 1961 a contrived vote in the Eritrean Assembly gave full union with Ethiopia.[17]

Behind the scenes diplomatic activity had been intense but Ethiopia would not have won the day had it not been for the super-power support of the United States. At the first Four Power Commission the United States had argued for partitioning Eritrea and giving the southern coastal area to Ethiopia with the express purpose of giving Ethiopia access to the sea. The second (UN) Commission rejected partition so the United States then framed Resolution 390A, the preamble to which refers to Ethiopian claims on Eritrea:

> based on geographical, historic, ethnic and economic reasons, including in particular Ethiopia's legitimate need for adequate access to the sea.

Ethiopia fitted into the cold-war global strategy of the United States as a strong ally in the Horn of Africa with ports on the Red Sea littoral. The pay-off came in 1953 when a Defence Pact was signed between the United States and Ethiopia which lasted over twenty years until the overthrow of Haile Selassie in 1974.

Gaining Eritrea was very much a Pyrrhic victory for Ethiopia because it sparked a bitter, costly and often deadlocked, guerrilla war for thirty years from 1961. That was resolved only with the overthrow of Ethiopia's Marxist dictator Mengistu in 1991. In May 1993 Eritrea gained its full independence and Ethiopia reverted to its earlier status of a land-locked state. Access to the sea is by rail through independent Djibouti and by tarred road to the southern Eritrean port of Assab as well as to Djibouti. Ethiopia's former broader-than-long sovereign corridor of access to the sea is now a totally separate political entity.

Independent states in Africa attempting to gain access to the sea are not recent phenomena but were evident in the nineteenth century. When the Boers trekked away from British rule on to the South African high veld in the late 1830s they were concerned about gaining access to the sea free from British control. One early party of trek-Boers under Trichardt eventually made their way to Lourenco Marques (Maputo), whilst a much larger party under Retief went to Durban. This was the beginning of a cat and mouse game played by the British with Boers by seizing Durban and the Boer Republic of Natalia in 1845, annexing St.Lucia Bay in 1846 and later annexing Zululand (1887) and Tongaland with Kosi Bay (1897) to prevent the South African Republic (Transvaal) achieving independent access to the sea. The Boers were also offered access to the sea by the British on condition they joined a Customs Union with the British colonies, but the price they felt was too high (Griffiths, 1989). In 1894 the Transvaal Boers did acquire a rail outlet to the sea independent of the British but the port of Lourenco Marques was in Portuguese territory. There is still evidence of the Boer drive to the sea on the internal political map of South Africa in the form of a long tongue of the Transvaal province extending eastwards from the eastern Transvaal high veld between Swaziland and Natal province. This relict land corridor today carries an excellent tarred road (R29) throughout its length but ends 40 miles (65km) from the Indian Ocean beyond the Lebombo mountains.

That great geo-political strategist and Empire builder, Rhodes, was also involved in a quest for access to the sea in southern Africa. As Prime Minister of the Cape province, he was instrumental in thwarting Kruger's attempts to gain access to the sea for the Transvaal. At the same time, as the founder of Rhodesia, he attempted to gain access to the sea at Beira for his new colony. He sent his agents to buy or to bully the Portuguese into granting him a corridor of access but with no success.[18] He was thwarted by the British government anxious to maintain the territorial integrity of the Portuguese possessions in Africa to prevent them falling into the wrong (that is German) hands. It is an example of local settlers and colonists losing out to the perceived imperial interest and shows how different matters of this kind can be when viewed from different geographical perspectives, metropolitan London and, in this case, land-locked Rhodesia. Rhodes won the right to build a railway from Beira but not sovereignty over a land corridor. Again the local African-based interest (albeit a white settler one) lost out to the imperial, metropolitan interest.

Since the ending of the colonial era in Africa there have been several claims, mainly from land-locked states, for corridors of access to the sea. None has succeeded, and most have been no more than verbal claims not followed up by action. In this category is the irredentist-type claim President Banda of Malawi made to the Niassa province of Mozambique which lies between Lake Malawi (and Malawi) and the sea. In 1968 he claimed in a speech that:

> Malawi's boundary to the south is the Zambesi river...[and] the boundary to the east is the Indian Ocean.[19]

The claim was made when Mozambique was still a Portuguese colony and has not been pressed in any way over the following twenty-five years.

President Amin of Uganda also planned an access corridor. He:

visited Israel twice in July 1971 seeking armaments for his plan to invade Tanzania and seize the north of the country across to the Indian Ocean port of Tanga to give him an outlet to the sea.[20]

Israel did not respond but Amin continued to worry away at the problem of access to the sea without success for some years.[21] It is ironic that a significant factor in Amin's military defeat by Ugandan dissidents and the Tanzanians in 1979 was Kenya's decision to close the border, denying Amin access to the sea and the petroleum products needed to keep his tanks on the battlefield.

Algeria is not land-locked but would like direct access to the sea from the rich iron ore deposits around Tindouf tucked away in a remote western corner of the country. Tindouf is about 345 miles (550km) from the Western Sahara port of La'youn but about 480 miles (770km) from the Algerian railhead at Bechar which is itself about 435 rail miles (700km) from the Mediterranean coast. It has been suggested that Tindouf has been a consideration in Algerian support for the POLISARIO of Western Sahara in their fight for self-determination against Morocco who now occupy and operate the Western Saharan phosphate mines and the port of La'youn. It is not clear whether Algeria's aim was to acquire an Atlantic seaboard or merely to build a mineral railway direct to the port of a friendly neighbour.

One land corridor of recurring strategic importance, but not under the sovereignty of the land-locked state, is the Beira corridor, from the Mozambique port to Mutare (Umtali) in land-locked Zimbabwe (Rhodesia). This was the corridor over which Rhodes failed to gain sovereignty in the 1890s. A railway was nevertheless constructed to serve Rhodesia by 1900, and after the second World War a tarred road and an oil pipeline to serve the Umtali refinery were built along the route. When in November 1965 the Smith regime in Rhodesia made its unilateral declaration of independence (UDI) the Royal Navy blockaded the port of Beira. The oil pipeline was closed and traffic along the corridor much reduced. Following Mozambique independence the corridor was closed to Rhodesian traffic in March 1976 until Zimbabwe achieved independence in April 1980. Though heralding a resurgence of traffic along the corridor it soon became vulnerable to attacks from the South African-backed Renamo in the Mozambique civil war. Zimbabwe had to deploy troops to keep the land corridor open to protect its own external trade which it did not wish to be routed via a hostile South Africa and in support of its long-standing ally the FRELIMO government of Mozambique.[22] The issue of the corridor ever becoming a sovereign part of Zimbabwe has not been raised.

The nearest a modern African land-locked state has come to achieving a land corridor to the sea is Swaziland in the early 1980s. White South Africa, concerned about the infiltration of ANC guerrillas across its borders, tried to create a *cordon sanitaire* by forcing on to its neighbour states 'Defence Pacts', the most publicised of which was the Nkomati Accord with Mozambique in 1984. Less well known is a secret accord with Swaziland of February 1982. Under these accords the African National Congress (ANC) were to be limited to diplomatic representation only in Swaziland and Mozambique with no guerrilla camps or staging posts. As an inducement to Swaziland to agree, the South Africa regime proposed a 'land deal' whereby Swaziland would acquire the KaNgwane 'homeland' the people of which are mainly ethnic Swazi. Also thrown in was Ngwavuma which lies between Swaziland and the sea and contains the potential port of Kosi Bay. Although the deal involved the people of these South African 'homeland' areas they were, of course, not consulted in any way. The land-deal broke down because the South African government was challenged in the courts over the legality of giving Ngwavuma away. It had previously given the territory to the 'self-governing' homeland of KwaZulu though it had never been part of historic Zululand. The courts upheld the Zulu claim, in effect telling the South African government it could not give away again something it had already given even if the original recipient was not an independent state. The removal of Ngwavuma ended the deal. Swaziland did not want KaNgwane without Ngwavuma, that is without access to the sea.[23]

In this case access to the sea was a greater incentive than the irredentist dream of uniting all ethnic Swazis under one political unit. There had been drawbacks to pursuing the irredentist path: the population of the KaNqwane homeland exceeded that of Swaziland and included many who were not ethnic Swazi. They had not been consulted by the South African regime over the proposed deal and many protested against it. But access to the sea had been a real prospect though much investment would have been needed in harbour works. The potential port at Kosi Bay had briefly been a Boer objective in the 1890s. Plans had been drawn up for a railway through the Lebombo range and across the Pongola river and the sandy wastes of Ngwavuma to Kosi Bay.

## Conclusion

There is only one functioning land corridor of access in Africa, that of Zaire, from Kinshasa to the coast. It is quite inadequate in fulfilling the purpose for which it was created; to serve the needs for access of the Congo (Zaire). Other corridors, for example the Caprivi Strip and the Transvaal Pongola 'tongue', may be found on current maps but lead nowhere in particular, certainly neither to navigable rivers nor to the sea. Some corridors have disappeared with political change, many have been no more than a gleam of ambition in some politician's eye. However, the corridor of access is a significant feature in the political geography of Africa. It has been from 1837 when the trek-Boers staked their claim to Durban, to the present when the extreme right-wing Boers put forward their proposals for a separate Volkstaat comprising roughly those constituencies which voted for the Conservative Party in the last all-white election plus a corridor of access to the sea at Richards Bay.[24] The point of access was presumably chosen, rather than the more historically correct Kosi Bay, for the practical and financial reasons of it being an existing port complete with rail access from the proposed Volkstaat.

Also in 1993, Ethiopia allowed Eritrea to claim its independence and resigned itself to being land-locked once more. It could be argued that Eritrean independence marks a new maturity in African geo-politics with Ethiopia not only allowing the Eritreans to exercise the right of self-determination but also forfeiting sovereignty over their own access to the sea. However, it was the thirty-year secessionist war that clearly demonstrated to all but the most bigoted of Ethiopian imperialists the futility of trying to hold the corridor by force, and in any case Assab was never the main port for Ethiopian trade. Even after the tarred road was built from Addis Ababa it could not compete with the road and rail link to Djibouti which was always French dominated and unaffected by the Eritrean war.

As long as Africa has fifteen land-locked states, whether or not their trade is interfered with by border closures on the part of the seaboard neighbours, there will always be aspirations by land-locked states to attain sovereignty over a land corridor of access to the sea. On the other hand, there is virtually no possibility of any land-locked state achieving this, not least because the land-locked states are almost invariably weaker than their seaboard neighbours. Where they are not, in the case of Ethiopia/Djibouti, an imperial power (France) stands as guarantor, serving its own perceived strategic interests. In the case of Zimbabwe/Mozambique long-standing friendship between the two governments (which could change) prevents Zimbabwean military control of the Beira corridor developing into any claim for sovereignty. The new Boer claim of access to the sea, no matter how unlikely, and in Europe Russia's claim to access to the Black Sea, no matter how wrapped up with irredentist claims, keep access corridors a live issue in the contemporary international politics of Africa and the world. Old-fashioned geo-politics is far from being a dead issue.

## NOTES

1. E. Hertslet, *The Map of Africa by Treaty* (London: HMSO 1909) pp.468–72.
2. Ibid., p.564.
3. H.M. Stanley, *The Congo and the Founding of the Free State Vol. 1* (London: Sampson Low, Marston, Searle and Rivington 1885) p.463.
4. UK Naval Intelligence Division, *The Belgian Congo* (London: HMSO, Geographical Handbook Series 1944) pp.457–9.
5. John R. Day, *The Railways of Southern Africa* (London: Barker 1963) p.131.
6. Ian Brownlie, *African Boundaries: a Legal and Diplomatic Encyclopedia* (London: Hurst 1979) pp.511–12.
7. E. Hertslet, *The Map of Africa by Treaty Vol 3* (London: HMSO 1909) p.902.
8. ARB, *African Research Bulletin*, Vol.1/1 (London: January 1964) p.4.
9. Ibid., Vol. 28/11 (November 1991) p.10332.
10. ARB, *African Research Bulletin*, Vol.29/5 (London: May 1992) p.10565 and Theo-Ben Gurirab, 'Status Report on Kasikili Island' (Windhoek, Republic of Namibia, Ministry of Foreign Affairs 1995).
11. J.A.I. Agar-Hamilton, *The Road to the North* (London: Longmans 1937).
12. F. Verschoyle Vindex, *Cecil Rhodes, His Political Life and Speeches 1881-1900* (London: Chapman and Hall 1900) p.62.
13. Lois A.C. Raphael, *The Cape to Cairo Dream: a Study in British Imperialism* (New York: Columbia University Press 1936).
14. E.D. Morel, *Ten Years of Secret Diplomacy: an Unheeded Warning,* 2nd ed. (London: National Labour Press 1915) p.160.
15. UK, Naval Intelligence Division, *The Belgian Congo* (London: HMSO, Geographical Handbook Series 1944) p.204.
16. K.C. Gandar Dower, *The First to be Freed* (London: HMSO, Ministry of Information 1944)
17. Ieuan Ll. Griffiths, *The Atlas of African Affairs* (London: Routledge and Johannesburg: Witwatersrand University Press 1993) pp.110–13.
18. Ian Colvin, *The Life of Jameson*, Vol. I and Vol. II (London: Arnold 1922) pp.148–70.
19. ARB, *African Research Bulletin* Vol. 28/11 (London: September 1968).
20. David Martin, *General Amin* (London: Faber and Faber 1974) p.161.
21. B.W. Langlands, 'On the dangers of relevance in political geography: some reflections upon experience as adviser on the Kenya-Uganda boundary to President Idi Amin of Uganda', (Unpublished seminar paper, 1978).
22. Jose Smith, 'The Beira Corridor' in *Geography*, 73/3 (1988) pp.258–61.
23. Ieuan Griffiths and D.C. Funnell, 'The Abortive Swazi Land-Deal' in *African Affairs* 90/358 (1991) pp.51–64.
24. The Guardian, 9 July 1993.

# Afghanistan:
# the Geopolitics of a Buffer State

## KEITH MCLACHLAN

Afghanistan is land-locked. It is topographically a divide both north and south and east and west by virtue of the mountain knot of the Hindu Kush. Afghanistan has politically acted as a buffer zone[1] between Russia or the USSR in the north and the contiguous power/powers of the Indian subcontinent, Iran and the Persian Gulf. This paper will examine the background to the nature of Afghanistan as a land-locked state and its role as a buffer in the so-called 'great game' of international geopolitics. The hypothesis under review is that Afghanistan represents a mountain fortress, virtually a residue of tribal territories and geographical fastnesses, which the Russians, Persians and British in India were never able to control. The country may also be looked upon as an exclusion zone from which rival great powers sought to exclude each other. Afghanistan was therefore in many ways a classic buffer-state throughout much of the nineteenth century and possibly until 1947 when the British withdrew from India. The persistence of Soviet-American rivalry in Afghanistan between 1960 and 1973 gave an illusion of a continuing buffer role for Afghanistan in that period.

## Geography

Afghanistan takes its name from the Persian 'land of the Afghans', though Afghans only in the sense of population of Pathan origin account for about half of the 17 million population of the country. The country covers some 653,000 square km and has no independent access to the Arabian Sea from which it is separated by some 500km respectively between Iranian Baluchestan and Pakistani Baluchestan. In the south, Afghanistan has a border of approximately 1,850km with Pakistan, including some 275km along the Wakhan strip (or pan-handle). In the north, the frontier with the CIS is 1,675km. The Pakistani and CIS borders lying against Wakhan are separated by a short 55km stretch of Afghanistan's frontier with the Peoples Republic of China. To the west, Afghanistan has a 525km frontier with Iran.

Afghanistan is a mountainous country. It is one of enormous geographical diversity. More than half of its territory is above 2000 metres

MAP 1

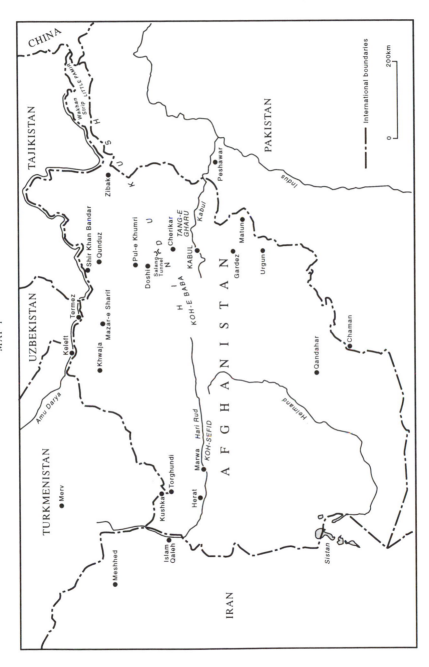

and most of the remainder above 1000 metres in altitude. Its topography is dominated by the Hindu Kush range of mountains, which has its greatest heights of more than 6000 metres in the Little Pamir in the east in the vicinity of Wakhan. Heights of 6411 metres are attained north of Sarqez. The range diminishes in altitude to the west to 4572 metres above Kabul. Thereafter the principal ranges of the Koh-e Baba and the Koh-Sefid (Safid Koh) drop towards the Hari Rud and the Iranian frontier. Four great river systems derive from and drain the central mountain core of the country, namely the Hari Rud in the north west, the Helmand of the south west, the Kabul River in the south and the Oxus (Amu Darya) in the north. Other than the Kabul Darya, the river valleys are peripheral and/or physically confined. The Hari Rud valley above Marwa, for example, is no more than a narrow defile through high mountain walls, while the Amu Darya lies, except east of Qunduz, on the absolute topographic rim of and separate from the mountains.

The climate of Afghanistan is one of extremes and considerable variety of microclimates. Climate is influenced by high altitudes together with the continental position of the country. The higher mountains of the east are permanently snow-covered and the considerable areas above the 2500 metre contour suffer from long winters of six months or so. In the intermediate mountain basins, such as the one in which Kabul is located, the growing season is made short for agriculture through the severity of night temperatures in a diurnal range of as much as 24°C. Average winter temperatures in Kabul give a maximum of 8°C and a minimum of -20°C. Rainfall is mainly in the winter months between November and May, much as snowfall. Kabul receives an average of 285 mm/year. Most of the south receives less than 100 mm/year. Summers are hot in the valley areas, averaging 22°C. In Kabul the average summer maximum is 40°C and the minimum 16°C. The bad-e sad-o-bist ruz (wind of 120 days) blows a hot blast across the west of the country in early summer, creating a hazard for farming activity.

## Land-lockedness

Afghanistan is more extremely land-locked than the 500 or so kilometres that separate it from Chah Bahar on the Gulf of Oman in south eastern Iran indicate. Despite Iranian promises that there would be a great development of both the port facilities at Chah Bahar and the road and rail infrastructure between the Afghan border in Sistan and the coast at the time of the 1973 border settlement, little was accomplished at least for the Afghans before the coming of the Iranian revolution in 1979 and the invasion of Afghanistan in that same year by the USSR. Thus, the access by the

Afghans via Iran to the Gulf of Oman/Arabian Sea is extremely poor through rugged country over third rate roads. There are no rail links through Iran to Afghanistan.

The surface transport connection with Pakistan is better but only marginally so.[2] From Afghan territory through Quetta it is more than 700km to the port of Karachi. The Peshawar route, the principal one from Kabul and central Afghanistan, travels 1500km to reach the same port. The road system in Pakistan is good and there are also railheads leading from points below the Afghan border which can be tapped into. The Pakistani rail system is for the most part old-established and in its northern extensions slow and not always reliable. Breaks of bulk for goods coming from Afghanistan generally make road transport more useful for the transit of goods.

In the north, Afghan borders with the CIS and China carry inherent physical difficulties quite apart from the matter of political factors. The break-up of the USSR has meant the creation of a multiplicity of international boundaries between Afghanistan and the land and sea outlets, which will inevitably hinder any use of the northern routes. In any case, St Petersburg, the nearest though only seasonal port in Russia, lies at a distance of 2000km from the Afghan frontier. The exit for Afghanistan through China has little to recommend it at the present time since time and cost of freight across some 3500km to Canton are extremely high even assuming a willingness by the Chinese to give unimpeded access for Afghan goods to their transport systems.

## The Factor of History:

It has been argued that the poverty of access by routeways in Afghanistan to the southern borders as defined by the Durand Line[3] was deliberate policy by the British in India as a means of deterring any Russian military drive to the south.[4] Certainly, there was a continuing poverty of roads between the Afghan southern frontier and the centre, while roads of the northern area were equally badly developed. Given the state of internal insecurity in Afghanistan and its depressed economic condition, prospects for railway and road construction were in any case very limited, though British antipathies against transport development as argued by Ispahani were a natural concomitant of Afghanistan being a buffer zone.

The rulers of Afghanistan were no less opposed to transport developments. It is believed with some justification that 'This barrier on communications represented part of the price they (the Afghans) paid for their independence and the realisation, in practice, of the buffer-state concept.'[5] In addition there was the undeniable need of regional rulers to keep their own local fortresses well distanced from any demanding central authority or aggressive neighbour within Afghanistan.

In British India there was a strong expansion of roads and rail systems in the border area once the Durand Line was selected as the official Indian/Afghan border in 1893. Even so, the communications system by the end of the British period, still the basis of transport facilities inside Pakistan, terminated at Torkham and Chaman, the residual links into Afghanistan being represented at that time by 'nothing but fair-weather tracks, unmetalled, and no railways.'[6] Transport in the border areas at that time was slow and expensive because of the hostile terrain and lack of security. Afghanistan was thus effectively isolated by distance and topography in close alliance with political obstructiveness by the British in India.

This position changed in the period beginning during World War II. There was a major thrust to improve internal communications within Afghanistan, the first effort designed to modernise the road between Kabul and Peshawar begun by the Government of Afghanistan in the 1940s by driving a road down the Kabul River through Tang-e Gharu. In the post-war period, during the years of Soviet-American rivalry in Afghanistan, both external powers expressed their competition through road building schemes. The main part was taken up by the USSR. A high grade highway was driven from Shir Khan Bandar on the Amu Darya via Pul-e Khumri to Doshi and thence via the treacherous but none the less all-weather Salang Tunnel, opened in 1964, through the Hindu Kush to Cherikar and Kabul. Mazar-e Sharif was connected to Kabul through a road from Pul-e Khumri and to the USSR principally via Termez. The USSR also constructed the road from the frontier at Kushka via Torghundi to Herat, a magnificent but scarcely used road until the invasion of 1979. The Herat-Qandahar road, also built with Soviet aid, continued the road which then linked with the Pakistan frontier at Chaman on an American-built highway. Similarly, the USA, in association with Iran, constructed the Islam Qaleh to Herat road. While the latter did connect Afghan and Iranian road systems and provided fairly reasonable all-weather access to Meshhed and the Iranian plateau, it had poor linkages to the Persian Gulf. The final connection in the Afghan road building programme was the 520km Qandahar to Kabul highway. In practice the road construction undertaken by USSR provided a great loop of highway through the main settled areas of Afghanistan and connected them with the Soviet highway system to the north. The USA tried to tap into this new circular network and defeat perceived Soviet strategic objectives by laying down spur roads to the new highway from the territories of its CENTO[7] allies, Iran and Pakistan.

The extent to which these new road systems reduced Afghanistan's land-lockedness is debatable. The easy outlets from the country provided by the new highways were above all to the north into the USSR at enormous distances from warm water sea ports. Political predilections of Afghan government after the *coup d'état* of 1973 were also for linkages to the USSR which reinforced an orientation northwards. To the south the great loop of road from Herat through Qandahar to Kabul provided, other than the crossing at Chaman, only four spurs running southwards – Gardez, Matun, Urgun and the Gomal River area, none of which were formally joined up with the Pakistani road systems across the international border.[8] The road connection with Iran, though sufficient to stimulate projects for bulk exports of Afghan livestock from Herat to the states of the Persian Gulf in the early 1970s[9], was of little general use in joining Afghanistan with Iran's southern ports.

It can be argued that the construction of roads by rivals engaged in a struggle for political influence would inevitably maximise the military objectives of those powers rather than serve the interests of the Afghans. The strategic connections made to Islam Qaleh on the Iranian border by the Americans and the scarcely used concrete highway from Herat to Torghundi are admirable examples of this problem. There must also be a strong suspicion that the Afghan government looked at the new roads above all as a means for knitting together the country for domestic political purposes. In all, therefore, whatever the mixture of motivations might have been, the modern transport network did little to diminish the country's difficulties as a land-locked state.

Land-lockedness in Afghanistan is also a manifestation of the country's poor endowment of natural resources and low level of economic development. The motivations for breaking down Afghan isolation, for mobilising capital and technology to overcome the natural hazards and difficulties of access to the country are generally lacking. The economic structure of the country is ill-developed, a problem exacerbated and extended by the Soviet invasion from 1979 and, subsequently, the protracted civil war. A depressed agriculture accounts for more than 50 per cent of national income (GDP). Manufacturing, government utilities such as electricity supply and hydrocarbons, principally natural gas, make up 28.5 per cent of GDP. Agricultural development is impeded by a mediaeval structure of ownership, strong reliance of self-sufficient/low yielding pastoral activities and particularly by shortages of water for irrigation. Most industry is extractive and concerned with natural gas, which is two-thirds consumed inside the state or exported to the north. The trade sector is ill-developed and more transactions are made informally through smuggling activities than through officially registered channels.

Levels of per capita income are extremely low at approximately $220 (1988). Growth of the economy has been negligible for some years beset by drought, invasion and the restrictive activities of local tribal leaders. Agricultural production expanded at an average of only 0.7 per cent annually between 1980 and 1985, for example. The potentially cultivable area is put at 14 million ha. but a mere 8 million ha were totally under all forms of cultivation each season before 1979. At that time 2.6 million ha. was actually irrigated and by 1991 this had diminished to 1.0 million ha. Of existing cropped land, half is given over to wheat, a basic commodity but of low value. Cotton is grown in small qualities at Mazar-e Sharif.

Livestock is the mainstay of the rural economy. It accounts for 75 per cent of farm value-added and 80 per cent of agricultural exports. There was a catastrophic decline in livestock numbers during the war against the USSR in which cattle numbers fell by 56 per cent and those of sheep and goats by 65 per cent. Exploited mineral resources include salt, barytes, copper, gypsum and construction materials but none so far are thought to exist in prolific quantities worth development for export. The scale and commercial importance of the discovery of iron ore in the Koh-e Baba have yet to be determined.

TABLE 1

CONTRIBUTIONS TO NATIONAL INCOME (GDP), 1989/90
(PER CENT)

| Sector | Contribution |
|---|---|
| Agriculture | 52.6 |
| Mining & manufacturing | 28.5 |
| Construction | 5.8 |
| Trade | 7.9 |
| Transport/communications | 3.5 |
| Other services) | |
| Net foreign trade) | 1.7 |
| Total | 100.0 |

*Source*: IBRD, Da Afghanistan Bank, Kabul, 1993

Only natural gas has attracted commercial investment from outside. Natural gas was discovered in 1960 and developed at Khwaja Gogerdak in the north east, producing 2.5 billion cubic metres by the mid 1970s. Production in 1988 was officially put at 3.0 billion cubic metres. A 92km gas pipeline was constructed to Keleft on the Amu Darya and an 82km line to Mazar-e Sharif to provide fuel and power for a new industrial complex close to that city. Shows of crude oil have so far been non-commercial. It is remarkable that the only raw material attractive to the outside world – natural gas – brought immediate development of a transport system to tie Afghanistan to, in this case, the USSR. The almost total lack of analogous transport links suggests the validity of the hypothesis that isolation as measured by the poverty of the transportation network persists for good economic as well as political reasons.

## Afghanistan as a Buffer State

Afghanistan is generally represented in the literature as a classic buffer-state constructed between imperial Russia and the British in India. The reality of blocks of territory being retained as buffers between rival rulers and empires is an old one, perhaps going back to pre-Roman times[10] and certainly to the time of the partition of Charlemagne's empire in the ninth century.[11] The definition of the term 'buffer-state' is dated to the late nineteenth century and was first recorded in 1883 in the *Oxford English Dictionary*. A recent edition suggests that a buffer-state is 'a neutral state lying between two others and serving to render less possible hostilities between them',[12] which is a useful working definition. The literature on buffer states has been developed over some years by geographers and others *inter alia* such as Partem,[13] Prescott[14] and Spykman.[15] The use of the buffer state concept has been criticised in recent times for being eclectic and unintegrated into a general theory of political geography.[16]

The application of the idea of a 'buffer-state' to Afghanistan was well established by the end of the eighteenth century by which time the Russians were already felt in British India and in London to harbour imperial designs on the Indian sub-continent.[17] In 1809 the British had begun to formulate relations with the rulers in Kabul in which Afghanistan was to be used as a military bulwark against the Russians and their French allies. Russian and Persian threats against Herat in particular in 1837 gave a further impetus to British strategic demands that Afghanistan remain neutral territory as part of the defence of India.[18] Further encroachment by Russia on the Persian Empire throughout the nineteenth century added to the perception[19] that Afghanistan should be retained as a *cordon sanitaire* against an ultimate and unthinkable face to face confrontation between Russia and Great Britain in Central Asia.

The British position was shared by the Russians who also preferred to obviate any expensive and inconclusive military engagements with the British after the experiences in the Crimean war. Thus by 1844 the Russians had begun to offer a neutral zone for British consideration.[20] In 1873 a British-Russian agreement was reached between Lord Granville and Prince Gorchakov for the establishment of a barrier of small neutral states to separate the two empires. The British and Russian sides settled but slowly to the idea of Afghanistan as a buffer-state, distracted by suggestions from strategists in New Delhi that Great Britain should have a forward policy in which key defensive sites would be selected from which India could be held against possible Russian incursions. In fact the British did take possession in a number of important mountain passes in the Indian north west but were never successful in taking permanent control of core sections of Afghan territory. Russian advances in Central Asia continued through the nineteenth century. Russia took Merv in 1884, Penjdeh in 1886 and the north sub-Pamir region in 1896. But they were careful not to trespass beyond this limit. In 1885 Russia acquiesced in a beginning of the delimitation of the international borders of Afghanistan.

The close association of the acceptance of fixed national frontier for Afghanistan with its successful role as a buffer-state became clearer during the latter part of the nineteenth century. The Russian occupation of Merv in 1884 was the final turning point, drawing as it did a British ultimatum that any further advance would bring war, after which the two sides began a protracted demarcation of frontiers. By 1907 the British and the Russians generalised their agreement (the St. Petersburg Convention) on the division of political influence in Central Asia to include Iran, Afghanistan and Tibet.[21]

It can be argued that Afghanistan remained as an acknowledged buffer-state in the nineteenth century sense for only a few years, perhaps between 1884 and 1947. Within a technical or legal definition it perhaps was a buffer-state for the brief period 1907–47. Certainly the role of Afghanistan in the 'great game' in a traditional sense[22] was ended shortly after World War II, when the British withdrew from the Indian sub-continent in 1947.

Among historians and political analysts there tend to be two forms of accepted wisdom on Afghanistan's role as a buffer-state. The first suggests that Afghanistan positively opted through its rulers in the nineteenth century for international isolation. Adamec[23] (1974) took the view that the main objectives of the Afghan leaders were the preservation of national independence and territorial integrity. Defensive isolationism gave the country the opportunity to manage its own internal affairs by denying both the British and the Russians a monopoly of power as they played out their rivalry for domination of the region.[24] Afghan policy in the period 1880–1919 can be described as a policy for isolation, designed to run a political alliance with the British in India in opposition to the Russians. The stance against Russia was, it is believed, not given hard form and was never articulated as an aggressive policy so that Kabul could retain a kind of equilibrium between the powers thereby enabling the country to remain independent.

Bilgrami suggested that the amirs of Afghanistan played an admirable role by trading on the fears of both Russia and Great Britain so that they could retain independence.[25] This source conceded, however, that Great Britain and Russia could have partitioned Afghanistan with little difficulty had they chosen to do so. It is also possible to believe that Afghanistan was an active player in perpetuating the 'great game'. Ghaus claimed that the amirs of Afghanistan were successful in enforcing a form of peace and stability within their country and in doing so they helped to prove that the territory within the buffer-state was indivisible if equilibrium was to be maintained between Russia and Great Britain.[26] The isolationist content of Afghan policy developed as a countermove to the British forward policy for intervention in the domestic affairs of Afghanistan.

The arguments of Adamec and historians of similar views take the premise that isolationist policies served Afghanistan well until 1907 when the Anglo-Russian agreement was arranged, which gave respective spheres of influence to the two great powers in the region at large. From that time, the Afghans were forced to look for a third party as a lever against the two great powers. Germany was a natural choice given its growing challenge to the established imperial interests throughout the world. Afghanistan had a measure of success in expanding its relations with Germany though this was never adequate to act as a base for a united confrontation against the resident powers. At the same time, Germany became a partner in the economic development of Afghanistan. This move reinforced the ability of the Afghans to retain an independent political life. The process of economic development and political amity with Germany did not square with a policy of isolationism and Adamec[27] contended that Afghanistan switched at this stage from isolationism to neutralism.

A second school of accepted wisdom has been created mainly by historians from the West which argues that Afghanistan was merely a pawn in the great game with no room for initiatives of its own. Wilber,[28] Taussig[29] and Hyman[30] are representative of this style of analysis. Roucek suggested that Afghanistan was the paid retainer of the imperial power on the basis of the subsidy paid by Great Britain to the Amir Abdur Rahman Khan after 1880 in return for which the British took over management of the foreign policy of Afghanistan.[31] Wilber offers a less extreme view of Afghanistan, accepting that the country was not completely controlled by external forces and gained an element of autonomy from its isolationist stance. He concedes none the less that it was the foreign powers who remained the arbiters of Afghan independence.[32] Taussig[33] argued that the British and Russian aim, inferentially one that was achieved, was to keep Afghanistan as a buffer-state within an economic and political vacuum. Taussig also had little patience with the suggestion that the Afghan amirs had scope for independent manoeuvre, making the point that it was the powers who kept the country 'without a railway, undeveloped and an effective turnstile barring the spreading of each other's spheres of interest.'[34]

This latter interpretation of Afghan history in the nineteenth century is supported by Hyman.[35] For him Afghanistan became a buffer-state by virtue of British inability and perhaps one might add lack of strategic commitment to hold the country down despite a series of military campaigns on its territory. Finally, Great Britain adopted a view that 'A policy of either military occupation of Afghan strongholds or of indirect rule (must be) abandoned in favour of upholding Afghanistan as a buffer state – "an elastic substance placed between the unyielding fabric of colonial sovereignties (which) could bend and bounce in a way that the defined boundaries of colonies could not".'[36]

Balancing the realities among these various interpretations of events is not easy, given the ideological slant of many commentators, the understandable nationalism of Afghan historians and the poverty of the Afghan archives, not to mention the difficulties of access to what documentary evidence does exist within them. However, it is denied by few analysts that Afghanistan did act as a buffer-state during periods of the nineteenth century and in the early twentieth century. There is a consensus too that the 'great game' was much devalued in the period after the creation of the Russo-British agreement on spheres of influence of 1907. Even so, Lord Curzon, the British foreign secretary, remained excitable on the matter of Russian propaganda and influence against the British in Iran and Afghanistan into the 1920s.[37]

Certainly, as Louis Dupree has suggested[38] Afghanistan was the 'land of the mud curtain', where the country, like its fortified villages, could be set up against outsiders and which, no sooner breached, was rebuilt. Isolation was a natural form of existence and defence for the Afghan rulers. But is must be admitted that this policy entirely suited the great powers and accorded with their need to impose a buffer status on the country. It was the great powers themselves who established Afghanistan's borders to lines of their own convenience. The setting up of the Durand Line as the preferred northern boundary of Pakistan in 1893 is a good example of this treatment,[39] where large tracts of territory were incorporated into Pakistan despite Afghan counter-claims.

Perhaps the contention[40] that Afghanistan was made by its terrain to be a natural buffer-state has validity. The idea is reinforced by consideration of the fact that those British rulers of India persuaded of a Russian threat to their position picked the Hindu Kush out as the line at which to hold the expanding Russian empire long before Russian absorption of territory left Afghanistan as a residual zone between the Russian and British Indian armies. At the same time, the mixed ethnic, religious and tribal groups in the Afghan area reacted to pressures from the two great powers by consolidating behind a single national flag to form an albeit ill-fused nation in the twentieth century.[41]

## The Linkage Between Land-lockedness and the Role of Afghanistan as a Buffer-state

In Afghanistan there is possibly an operation of special circumstances in which the application of the concept of buffer-state to the country is reinforced by the fact of the national territory being land-locked. Afghanistan's designation as the 'Switzerland of the East'[42] is the analogy which gives support to this contention.

Being land-locked, Afghanistan was created as the inevitable client to Russian and British patrons. For, without transit routes through Russia and India, Afghanistan was trapped behind its isolationist mud wall without choice or scope for real initiative in the management of its own affairs. Similarly, land-lockedness meant that Afghanistan had no choice in its selection of its allies. Third parties – i.e. states other than Great Britain and Russia – sought as allies by the Afghans were at a severe disadvantage in the political games of Central Asia. The role of Germany in the period after 1910 is instructive in this context. The Germans did work hard to establish themselves in Afghanistan as an adjunct of their new links with Persia. But, as Professor Yapp has put it, 'Too much should not be read into this activity, however. Important as trade with Germany was to the Northern Tier, it was of little value to Germany. And Germany was still unwilling to be drawn into political commitments to the states of the region; their help might eventually be useful but she was not going to quarrel with the USSR and Britain for the sake of them.'[43] It might be surmised that an important part of Germany's diffidence arose from the problems of access to Afghanistan, which was only through adjacent and unreliable countries.

Being land-locked, Afghanistan was very much at the mercy of conspiracy, treaty or tacit arrangement between the neighbours between which it was a buffer-state. The Russo-British division of spheres of influence in Central Asia in 1907 demonstrated the reality of this assertion. In the coastal state of Iran the USSR and Great Britain had to deploy force during the First and Second World Wars to get their way in the teeth of local nationalist sentiment and a pro-German tendency in government policy. In Afghanistan, which was land-locked and which had both similar nationalist sentiments and a pro-German orientation, an invasion at that time was never necessary since it could be controlled at its borders.

The case for Afghanistan as a buffer state after 1947 is weak. Afghan concerns were woven increasingly into the contest with Pakistan for sovereignty of the Pushtun territories of the erstwhile North West Frontier province. In doing so the country in 1950 was put under retaliatory constraints in moving goods in transit to and from Pakistani ports. Thus, as soon as the Government of Afghanistan attempted to play an active role in international politics and to take the Soviet side in the cold war,[44] a situation which replaced the great game after 1945, its quality as a diplomatically weak land-locked country was exploited by its southern neighbour.

The development of diplomatic and commercial relations with the USSR was rapid and all-pervading. Only US activities in aid-giving in the late 1960s and early 1970s[45] offset this pattern of Afghan-Soviet co-operation.[46] The *coup d'état* of 1973 against the rule of Zahir Shah by Daud Kahn led to further political instability and the overthrow of Daud Khan in 1978 when the People's Republic of Afghanistan was set up with close ties with the USSR. At this stage in Afghanistan's political life, the role as a buffer state was entirely put aside. The entry of Soviet troops into Afghanistan on December 27 1979 opened a new tragic phase in the country's history, the ramifications of which persist to the present time and which continue to preclude the country acting as a buffer state.

## Conclusions

Afghanistan appeared to lose its buffer role and its virtues of natural defence through isolation in the period after the second world war, particularly in 1947 with the independence of Pakistan. At that stage Afghanistan ceased to be a buffer between British and Soviet spheres of influence signified by the eruption of local territorial disputes between Afghanistan and Pakistan. It is remarkable, however, that the Soviet invasion and its sad human consequences[47] proved to be a transitory phase and that the USSR, like the previous British, Iranian and Russian invaders before them[48] were forced into ignominious withdrawal. In the 1990s the 'tyranny of terrain remains a stubborn reality'[49] in Afghanistan. The country was made more accessible than formerly thanks to extensive road building and, since 1980, fragmented internal political authority. It is none the less an area which repels rather than attracts. Its strategic significance is as a negative zone where external powers intrigue but find it difficult put down roots. In that sense, Afghanistan might have lost its dubious reputation as a buffer state in the context of the Anglo-Russian 'great game', but might now be caught in a form of stasis in which it still separates international communities rather than unites them. It will continue to act as a grim topographic divide between the steppes of Central Asia and the Indian sub-continent. If only in that sense, Afghanistan will persist as a zone denying the land-locked states of Central Asia access to the warm waters of the Persian Gulf and Indian Ocean.

NOTES

1. The definition of a buffer zone by specialists in geography and geopolitics can be summarised as '…a small political or administrative unit located between and separating two larger opposing powers.' G.L. Ingalls, 'Buffer states: outlining and expanding existing theory' in J. Chay and T.E. Ross (eds), *Buffer States in World Politics* (Boulder, Colorado: Westview Press 1986) p.233.

2. The Afghan-Pakistani border was closed to traffic in the period 1961–63, for example.

3. M.Z. Ispahani, *Roads and Rivals: the Politics of Access in the Borderlands of Asia* (London: I.B. Tauris 1989) pp.97–8.

4. Ibid, pp.94–6.

5. O. Caroe, *The Pathans, 550 BC–AD 1957* (London: Macmillan 1965) pp.538–9.

6. Ibid, p.541.

7. CENTO (Central Treaty Organisation) was a military and economic alliance which comprised Turkey, Iran, Pakistan and the United Kingdom with the USA as an active non-territorial partner. See R.H. Magnus, 'International organisations in the Persian Gulf' in A.J. Cottrell et al. (eds), *The Persian Gulf States* (Baltimore: Johns Hopkins 1980) pp.179-81.

8. Caroe, p.549.

9. The Herat Livestocks Development Project was sponsored by the FAO-UN. See Ercon, *Hydrogeological Investigation of the Hari Rud Valley* (Bracknell: UK Ministry of Overseas Development 1974).

10. J. Chay and T.E. Ross, (eds) *Buffer States in World Politics* (Boulder, Colorado: Westview Press 1986) pp.16–19.

11. Ibid.

12. *The Shorter Oxford English Dictionary* (Oxford: OUP 1980) p.248.

13. M.Partem, 'The buffer system in international relations', *Journal of Conflict Resolution*, 27 (1983) pp.3–26.

14. J.R.V. Prescott, *Geography of Frontiers and Boundaries* (London: Hutchinson 1967) pp.46–7.

15. J.Spykman, 'Frontier, security and international organisation', *Geographical Review*, 32 (1942) pp.436–47.

16. S.D. Brunn and K.A. Mingst, 'Geopolitics' in , M. Pacione (ed.) *Progress in Political Geography* (London: Croom Helm 1985) p.57.

17. J. Chay and T.E. Ross 'Introduction' in *Buffer States in World Politics* (Boulder, Colorado: Westview Press 1986) p.1. '…the term *buffer state* is relatively recent, probably first being applied by the British in 1883 to refer to Afghanistan.'

18. A.S. Khan, 'Tribes and state in Waziristan' in R.T. Tapper (ed.) *The Conflict of Tribe and State in Iran and Afghanistan* (London: Croom Helm/St.Martin's 1983) pp.192–5.

19. That the perception lacked reality is a serious contention. A. Verrier, 'Francis Younghusband and the great game' in *Asian Affairs*, 23/79/1 (1992) pp.35–6.

20. A.P. Thornton, 'The reopening of the "Central Asian question" 1864-69' in *History*, N.S. 41 (1956) p.122.

21. A. Saikal, 'Iranian foreign policy 1921-1979' in P. Avory, G. Hambly and C. Melville (eds), *Cambridge History of Iran*, Vol.7 (Cambridge: CUP 1991) p.427.

22. G.N. Curzon, *Persia and the Persian Question*, Vol.1 (London: Cass 1966) p.3.

23. L.W. Adamec, *Afghanistan's Foreign Affairs to the Mid-twentieth Century: Relations with the USSR, Germany and Britain* (Tuscon, Arizona: University of Arizona Press 1974) p.324.

24. Ibid.

25. A.H. Bilgrami, *Afghanistan and British India, 1793-1907: A Study in Foreign Relations* (New Delhi: Sterling Publishers 1972) pp.274–8.

26. A.S. Ghaus, *The Fall of Afghanistan* (London: Pergammon-Brassey's 1988) pp.1–17.

27. op.cit.

28. D.N. Wilber, 'Afghanistan, independent and encircled' in *Foreign Affairs*, 31/3 (1953) pp.486–94 and D.N. Wilber, 'Afghanistan: A neutral in orbit' in *United Asia*, 11/6 (1959) pp.514–18.

29. H.C. Taussig, 'Afghan Neutralism' in *Eastern World*, 15/12 (1961) p.11.

30. A. Hyman, *Afghanistan under Soviet Domination, 1964-81*, (New York: St.Martin's Press 1984).
31. J.S. Roucek, 'Afghanistan in geopolitics' in *Eastern World* 17/12 (1963) pp.14–17.
32. Wilber (1959) p.514.
33. Taussig, p.11.
34. Ibid.
35. Hyman, pp.38–9.
36. Hyman, p.39.
37. M. Yapp, '1900-1921: The last years of the Qajar dynasty' in H. Amissadeghi, (ed.) *Twentieth Century Iran* (London: Heinemann 1977) pp.21–2
38. L. Dupree, *Afghanistan*, (Princeton: Princeton University Press 1973) p.249.
39. Ispahani, pp.97–8.
40. 'Buffer states owe their existence to....hostile environments', T.E. Ross, 'Buffer states: A geographer's perspective' in J. Chay and T.E. Ross (eds) *Buffer States in World Politics*, (Boulder: Colorado 1986) p.14. Also, 'Afghanistan's establishment as a buffer state was assisted by its physical geography', D.B. Jenkins, 'The history of Afghanistan as a buffer state' in J. Chay and T.E. Ross p.186.
41. L. Dupree, 'The mujahidin and the muhajerin' in B. Huldt and E. Jansson (eds) *The Tragedy of Afghanistan* (London: Croom Helm 1988) p.21.
42. Roucek, p.14.
43. M. Yapp, *The Near East since the First World War* (Harlow: Longman 1991) p.387.
44. Afghanistan in 1954 accepted economic and military aid from the USSR. In 1955 the Soviet leaders Bulganin and Khrushchev visited Kabul when the 1931 Treaty of Neutrality and Mutual Non-aggression was renewed. The USSR took the part of Afghanistan in its dispute with Pakistan over the Pakhtunistan issue.
45. The American University, *Area Handbook for Afghanistan* (Washington D.C.: US Government Printing Office 1973) pp.348–9.
46. Some Chinese, German, British and other aid was also mobilised by the Government of Afghanistan but, though the quality of work done was excellent in many cases, its impact was small and confined to specific regions or single development projects.
47. B. Huldt and E. Jansson, pp.121–261.
48. R. Greaves, 'British relations with Great Britain and British India 1798-1979' in P. Avery, G. Hambly and C. Melville (eds) *Cambridge History of Iran* (Cambridge: CUP 1991) p.393.
49. Ispahani, p.2.

# Land-locked Central Asia:
# Implications for the Future

## SARAH J. LLOYD

The Central Asian republics of Kazakhstan, Kyrgyzstan, Tajikistan, Turkmenistan and Uzbekistan cover an area of approximately 4 million square kilometres. Kazakhstan alone is roughly four-fifths the size of India, with a total area of 2,717,300 square kilometres. The natural barriers which encompass this vast territory include great mountain ranges such as the Tien Shan or Heavenly Mountains in the east, the Pamirs in the south-east and the Altai range in the north-east. In the west, the Caspian Sea provides a border between Central Asia and the Caucasus. The expansive steppe in the north, with its extreme continental temperatures, combined with the Kara Kum and Kyzl Kum deserts, in the central and southern regions, have consistently been an obstacle to penetration throughout history.

Beneath this great land mass lies a wealth of natural resources. Since Central Asia's independence, almost all of the major international oil companies have been scrambling to carve out a niche in one of the last frontiers and lay claim to a portion of the region's enormous energy reserves. Kazakhstan alone has proven reserves larger than those of Norway and the UK taken together.[1] In 1993, the American company Chevron agreed to invest $20 billion to develop the giant Tengiz and Korolev fields in Kazakhstan, which are estimated to contain 9 billion barrels of recoverable oil and 380 billion cm of gas.[2] Analysts have estimated that the Tengiz field could produce 700,000 barrels of crude daily, worth $10.5 million a day at current world prices.[3] In terms of natural gas, Turkmenistan's total indicative resources are estimated at 14 trillion cubic metres, while identified reserves amount to 3 trillion cubic metres, equalling 10.9 per cent of world gas supplies.[4] The region is also endowed with substantial amounts of precious and non-ferrous metals, including gold, silver, platinum, chrome, lead, zinc, copper and uranium.[5]

Unlike the neighbouring Caucasian republics, where there was a strong nationalist thrust towards independence, the Central Asian republics were eager to remain within the Soviet Union. Hence, they found themselves unprepared politically, economically and psychologically for their independence which came in 1991 with the demise of the USSR. Since then, these fledgling countries have been struggling to create the necessary

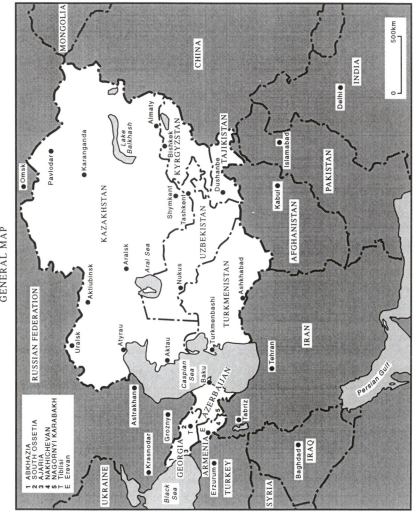

GENERAL MAP

apparatus to run modern nation-states. In so doing, it has become apparent to the Central Asians, for the first time in their recent history, that the need to have independent access to the sea is vital for their future economic development.

This paper will initially examine the development of the region's trade and transport infrastructure from an historical perspective and the impact that it has had on the evolution of the Central Asian economies. The purpose of doing so is twofold: first, to give an understanding of the degree to which these economies were distorted by imperial domination, which has accentuated the extent of their dependence on Russia; and second, to draw attention to a new trend towards re-establishing pre-Soviet trade and transport routes which, if successful, will counterbalance Russia's stranglehold on exports. The latter half of the chapter will focus on more recent economic developments, particularly in the energy sector, as well as the transport options that are currently open to these republics. It will be shown that the Iranian route to the sea is one of the most viable alternatives to Russia for most of Central Asia and as such, its influence in the region is likely to increase in the near future.

## Pre-Tsarist Trade

For centuries, overland trade routes between east and west traversed the vast expanse of Central Asia, creating what is known as the 'Silk Roads'. Alongside silk and other commercial goods travelled new ideas, making these routes a channel for interaction among societies. The thriving cities which developed became famous centres for learning, trade, religion, and the arts. By the sixteenth century, the golden age of the Silk Roads gradually came to an end when the empires at the centre lost their strength and control over eastern trade. Although sea routes had always existed as an alternative to the Silk Roads, they had been considered more perilous and less reliable. However, during the fifteenth and sixteenth centuries they increasingly gained importance and consequently led to the severe economic decline of the cities along the Silk Roads. Samarkand, which had been at the crossroads of several routes, was uninhabited from the 1720s to the 1780s.[6]

By the end of the eighteenth century the three khan dynasties of Bukhara, Kokand and Khiva had emerged, offering the region a certain degree of stability. Although they had developed an organised administrative apparatus, their frontiers were fluid and often disputed. Persia contested the regions of Khorasan and Herat with Khiva and Afghanistan, while the latter disputed Balkh, Gissar, Kulyab, Badakhshan and the Pamir vilayets with Bukhara[7] (see Map 1).

Despite the decline of the Silk Roads, access to the sea was not vital for

100

MAP I

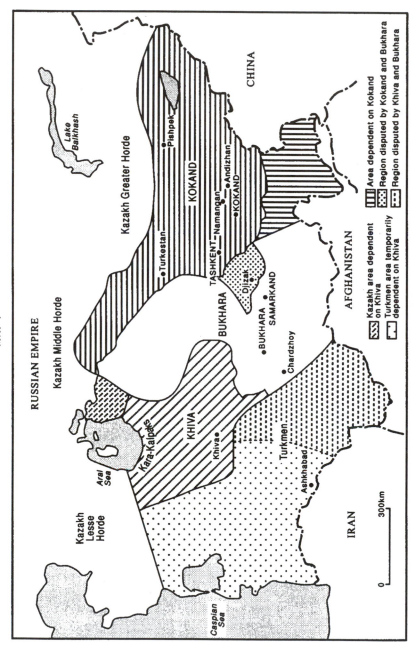

sustaining the economies of the khanates. Internal trade in the region was well-developed and based primarily on reciprocal exchange between nomads, semi-settled communities and urban populations. External trade was mainly conducted with neighbouring Afghanistan, India, Persia and Russia. Imports from Afghanistan included shawls, pottery, metal goods, wool, karakul, tea, indigo and some manufactured goods from British India; from India came green tea, muslin, indigo, some English cottons, sugar, metal goods and books; Persian exports included dyes, Mashhad cottons, pepper, saltpetre, silver, Islamic books, nuts and contraband opium. Russia exported iron pots and pans, sugar, paper, tin, fur, mercury, candles, paraffin and manufactured goods and textiles.[8] The khanates in turn, traded goods such as camel hair cloth, satin, silk materials, velvet, carpets, gold, horses and mules. Throughout the eighteenth century there was a steady growth in trade between Moscow and Central Asia which was a precursor to a more concerted move towards annexing the region in the following century.[9]

## Russian Expansion

In the mid-1700s, Russia's eastern frontier consisted of 'lines' which were defined and held by military posts that were extended with each territorial annexation. Russian penetration into Central Asia commenced in the Kazakh steppe, which was divided between three hordes or *zhuzi*. The territory of the Great Horde was south-eastern Kazakhstan, while the Middle Horde controlled the central regions and the Little Horde governed the northern and western lands.[10] The Russians took advantage of the internecine fighting among the hordes by directly annexing the steppe, which was then supported by a strong military presence and the construction of new fortified lines deep within Kazakh territory. The traditional pastures and herding routes used by the Kazakh nomads were cut off, while thousands of Russian and Ukrainian settlers migrated southward from Siberia to cultivate the steppe. Kazakhstan came under complete Russian domination with the envelopment of Chimkent in 1864[11] (see Appendix I).

Once the Kazakh lands were subjugated, Russia advanced its military campaign towards the three neighbouring khanates. One by one they fell under Russian control. Kokand was defeated in 1866 and subsequently annexed in 1876, while Bukhara and Khiva became protectorates in 1868 and 1873, respectively. Thereafter, the Russian armies turned their attention towards Transcaspia, where they met with strong resistance from the Turkmen tribes. The region was conquered in 1885 after a bloody confrontation.

### Extension of the Russian Railway System

The development of an efficient transport network was instrumental in securing the final conquest and retaining physical control over Central Asia. Until 1880, the primary mode of Russian transportation was by camel and horse. Inhospitable terrain along with scarce water supplies posed a formidable problem for military deployments. According to one account, such expeditions consisted of 'only a caravan or train, following no regular route, always suffering from want of water or fuel and liable at each halt to have its horses and camels driven away and consequently to be deprived of its means of advancing.'[12] The commencement of the series of Russian campaigns against the Turkmen in 1877, and the disastrous defeat of Lomakin at the Akhal Tekke fort of Geok Tepe in 1879, led the Russians to build one of their main arteries in Central Asia, the Transcaspian railway.[13] The implications that it had for the region were foreseen by Lord Curzon, when he wrote: 'The construction of the railway means the final Russification of the whole Turkoman steppes from Khorasan to Khiva and from the Caspian to the Oxus.'[14]

Ironically, the Transcaspian railway was used not only as a means for military conquest but also as a pilgrim route for the indigenous inhabitant. Shiite pilgrims from both western Persia and the provinces of the Caucasus used the railway and the Ashkabad-Kuchan road to reach the sacred city of Mashhad. It also became a popular mode of transportation for the first half of the journey to Mecca for the Sunni Muslims from Bukhara, Samarkand and further east. Between 1887 and 1888 the number of such pilgrims using the railway increased from 6,000 to 10,000.[15]

This railway, along with a line which ran from Samarkand to Tashkent to Andhijan and another, connecting Merv to Kushk on the Afghan frontier, contributed not only to the subjugation of the region, but also posed a threat to British strategic interests (see map 2). The natural barriers which divided the British and Russian spheres of influence had been overcome. Although the Russians assured the British in the Gortchakov-Granville agreement of 1872–73 that they did not have designs on Afghanistan, knowledge of General Skobelev's detailed plans of invasion and attempts to initiate direct trade connections with the Punjab and Kashmir worried the British. They began a counter-campaign of road and rail building, for it was conceded that if the Russians took Afghanistan, they would become dominant in the region.

*Economic Integration with Russia*

Expansion of the railway system into Central Asia also brought economic benefits to Russia. Towards the end of the nineteenth century Russia's need for a steady supply of raw cotton became pressing. The country's textile industry was ranked fourth in the world, after Britain, USA and Germany.[16] Hitherto, Russia's raw cotton had been supplied by Egypt, India and the

103

MAP 2

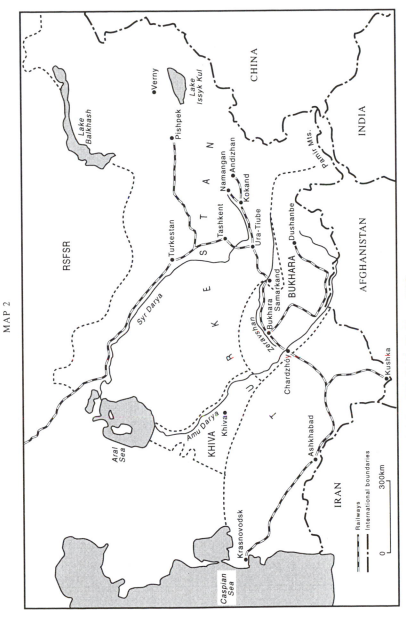

*Source:* based on a map in Istoriya Uzbekskoy SSR, Vol. 1. (Tashkent, 1995)

United States. However, the disruption in supplies resulting from the American Civil War caused the Russians to search for more politically and economically secure sources. Cotton was already grown in Bukhara, Khorezm and the Ferghana Valley and, with the construction of the Transcaspian railway, it became cheaper to import it from these peripheral territories than from traditional sources. It was estimated that cotton grown in Central Asia could be purchased at fourpence a pound, whereas imported cotton from Egypt, India or America was procurable at an average price of sevenpence a pound.[17] Aware of the economic benefits of such an arrangement, Russian colonial authorities embarked on a scheme to increase cotton cultivation in the region by restructuring its agricultural sector. Irrigation was expanded and vast tracts of land, previously devoted to traditional food crops, were displaced to accommodate the growing demand for cotton. The following tables illustrate the dramatic increase in cotton exports from Central Asia to Russia during this period.

TABLE 1

RAW COTTON EXPORTED TO RUSSIA FROM BUKHARA
(in puds*)

| 1880 | 1890 | 1915 |
|------|------|------|
| 410,000 | 1,359,099 | 2,624,000 |

*1 pud = 36.1 pounds

Source: Mary Holdsworth, Turkestan in the 19th Century (Oxford: Soviet Affairs Study Group, 1959), p.20

TABLE 2

RAW COTTON EXPORTED FROM KHIVA TO RUSSIA
(in puds)

| 1885 | 1889 | 1900 | 1905 | 1910 |
|------|------|------|------|------|
| 50,000 | 150,000 | 320,000 | 450,000 | 600,000 |

Source: Holdsworth, p.25

TABLE 3

RAW COTTON USED IN RUSSIAN TEXTILE UNDERTAKINGS
(in puds)

|  | 1897 | 1900 |
|------|------|------|
| From Central Asia (including Bukhara, Khiva & Ferghana) | 4,110,000 | 4,483,000 |
| From Egypt | 2,472,000 | 1,819,000 |

Source: Holdsworth, p.30

TABLE 4

TOTAL COTTON FREIGHT CARRIED BY TRANSCASPIAN RAILWAY

(in puds)

| 1888 | 1889 | 1890 | 1891 | 1892 | 1893 |
|------|------|------|------|------|------|
| 873,092 | 1,470,503 | 2,673,267 | 2,626,110 | 3,026,518 | 3,588,025 |

Source: Holdsworth, p.20

The economic integration of Central Asia with the imperial economy was facilitated by a deliberate policy to exclude foreign, primarily British, trade from the region. In 1881 most European products were systematically excluded from Central Asia, while heavy duties were placed on Indian products imported through Afghanistan.[18] These restrictions were reinforced by prohibitive customs regulations (see Appendix II). In an effort to dominate the Afghan market for manufactured goods and gain a political foothold there, the region was exempted from the tariffs that Russia imposed elsewhere. This led to the progressive expulsion of British and Indian manufactures from the Afghan markets. Another result of Russia's policy was that the volume of trade between Russia and Central Asia began to rise towards the end of the 1800s and to rise steeply from 1895, when Bukhara was included in the Russian customs boundary.[19]

*Development of Alternative Transport Routes*

To avoid exorbitant tariffs on goods transiting Afghanistan, alternative trade routes were established by Indian and Bukharan merchants. Indian merchandise (chiefly green tea) was shipped to the ports of Bandar Abbas or Bushire and then transported along Persian caravan routes to Ashkabad where it was taken by the Transcaspian railway to Bukhara.[20] This route was made feasible, in part, because of Russian designs on controlling trade in Khorasan. In order to attain this goal, the Russians constructed a military road from Ashkhabad over the Kopet Dagh to the Persian frontier. Due to the Persians' failure to complete their portion of the road, only a mountain track descended to Quchan and the high road to Mashhad. However, this route, together with the Transcaspian railway, superseded two of the three main caravan routes into Khorasan – the Azerbaijan route via Tabriz, Tehran and Shahrud and the Astrabad or Shahrud routes from the Caspian.[21] Eventually Russia gained a stranglehold on trade in Khorasan, which was one of the wealthiest and most fertile province in Persia. A Foreign Office report on Russian trade in 1887 gave the following account:

Traders from Khiva, Bokhara, Tashkent, Persia, and even Asia Minor, are said to have made considerable purchases of Russian cotton goods at the

Fair of Nijni Novgorod in 1887, instead of, as formerly, supplying themselves with English productions, which they obtained through Batoum, Asia Minor, and Persia. The closing of Batoum as a free port, the abolition of the transit trade across the Caucasus, and the construction of the Transcaspian Railway have undeniably resulted in the acquisition of new markets for Russian manufacturers in the far East, to our clear disadvantage. According to the report of the Governor of the Transcaspian region, the sale of Russian goods is not only yearly increasing in Persia (especially at Quchan, Bujnurd and Meshed), but is driving British goods out of the neighbouring Afghan territory, as, for instance, out of Herat. Bokhara is reported to be replete with the products of Russian manufacture. The Russian diplomatic agent there states that English goods are not able to compete with Russian products, and that English prints are rarely to be met with at present in Bokhara. Native dealers of the Caucasus, and Turkish Armenia are reported to have also become large purchasers of Russian manufactured goods. Great Britain, which formerly enjoyed almost the monopoly of the trade in most of these parts, is now receding there, commercially, into the background. The Governor-General of Turkestan confirms the report of his colleague of the Transcaspian region as to the increasing demand for Russian goods in Central Asia.

Russian merchants' eagerness to exploit further Persian and Indian markets provided the impetus to improve access to the sea and the rudimentary transport routes. High transit costs, partially resulting from the risks involved in traversing the perilous terrain, caused an upward spiral effect on the price of their merchandise, which in some cases was doubled or tripled.[22] Fearful of British plans to acquire railroad concessions from Naser ed-Din, the Russians forced the Shah into giving them exclusive rights over all such concessions for a five year period commencing in 1889.[23] Although Russia planned a number of roads and railways in north Persia, few were ever realised as a result of military considerations. 'The Russian military thought it best to 'keep Persia completely without railroads'; if this became impossible for political reasons, they suggested the most useful route would run from Tehran to the Caucasus.'[24]

## Central Asia Under the Soviets

Under the Soviets, expansion of the Russian transport network played an instrumental role in the development of their statehood, particularly in the dissemination of their ideology and the creation of their command economy. After World War I, the Soviets embarked on an aggressive programme to consolidate their communication systems. Rural areas were linked by intricate road networks and inter-regional railways expanded. The peripheral republics of Central Asia became fully integrated into the USSR's infrastructure with the completion of the Turk-Sib railway in 1930 which connected the Trans-Siberian railway with the Central Asian network.[25] Once incorporated into the Soviet Union, the Central Asian economies became so intertwined with the other republics, that the wider possibility of mercantile contacts with their former trading partners was hardly explored until the late 1980s.

## Distortion of the Central Asian Economies

During the early Soviet period, one of the chief accusations levelled against the Tsar's economic policy in Central Asia was that it had transformed the area into a 'cotton appendix of Russia' (Lenin), just as British policy in Egypt was also directed at pushing cotton production at the expense of grain.[26] However, in the 1930s the Soviets adopted a similar policy towards the region, which transformed it into a specialist supplier of raw cotton. Such a policy did not secure the all-round development of productive forces in Central Asia; but rather converted it into a specialised (agricultural) component and incorporated it into a wider inter-regional system of the division of labour.[27]

The government initially encouraged indigenous cotton producers to expand the areas under cultivation by offering high procurement prices (see Table 5).[28] The result was dramatic. By 1937, only two years after the policy was initiated, the production of raw cotton in Uzbekistan rose to 1,522,000 tons – nearly three times the pre-revolution peak – and yield per hectare was at an all time high of 1.6 tons.[29] With the exception of World War II and a brief period in the late 1950s, cotton output in the region continued to increase well into the early 1980s (see Table 6).[30] In 1983, Uzbekistan alone produced almost as much cotton as the entire United States.[31] By this time, Central Asia was producing approximately 95 per cent of the USSR's cotton and cotton fibres, 15 per cent of its vegetable oils, 100 per cent of its machinery and equipment for cotton growing, more than 90 per cent of its cotton gins, a large quantity of looms, and equipment needed for irrigation.[32] Expansion of cotton production also enabled the former Soviet Union to become one of the world's leading exporters of cotton.[33]

The incentives offered to producers to induce them to increase cotton production eventually led to a shift in cropping patterns. The major shift was away from grains. In particular, rice – despite the fact that rice was the major component in the local diet. In 1913 about 75 per cent of the sown land in Central Asia consisted of grain and only 15 per cent cotton. By 1965 the share of grain had fallen to 41 per cent and that of cotton had risen to 36 per cent.[34] (see Tables 7, 8 and 9). Although this shift meant higher returns for producers, it caused the region to become increasingly dependent on

TABLE 5

ALL UNION

(average procurement prices in roubles per ton)

| | 1955 | 1956 | 1958 | 1960 | 1962 | 1964 | 1965 | 1966 | 1967 | 1970 | 1975 |
|---|---|---|---|---|---|---|---|---|---|---|---|
| Grain | 47.9 | 55.0 | 60.3 | 62.2 | 72.3 | 72.3 | 89.7 | 98.2 | 103.0 | 97.2 | 111.8 |
| Cotton (raw) | 362.9 | 366.0 | 337.4 | 343.8 | 343.8 | 394.7 | 442.4 | 442.4 | 452.0 | 555.0 | 583.6 |
| Meat | 518.3 | 589.2 | 1041.1 | 1104.0 | 1353.8 | 1437.1 | 1589.7 | 1853.5 | 1873.6* | 2278.0 | 2385.1 |
| Milk | 88.2 | 97.2 | 117.6 | 117.6 | 126.9 | 133.0 | 148.5 | 153.9 | 156.0 | 191.9 | 215.1 |

UZBEKISTAN

| | 1955 | 1956 | 1958 | 1960 | 1962 | 1964 | 1965 | 1966 | 1967 | 1970 | 1975 |
|---|---|---|---|---|---|---|---|---|---|---|---|
| Grain | - | - | - | - | - | - | 157.8 | - | - | 157.0 | 172.2 |
| Cotton (raw) | - | - | - | - | - | - | 435.6 | - | - | 539.8 | 544.0 |

TAJIKISTAN

| | 1955 | 1956 | 1958 | 1960 | 1962 | 1964 | 1965 | 1966 | 1967 | 1970 | 1972 | 1973 |
|---|---|---|---|---|---|---|---|---|---|---|---|---|
| Grain | - | - | - | 63.5 | - | - | 99.5 | - | 144.4 | 126.5 | 148.8 | |
| Cotton (raw) | - | - | - | 378.6 | - | - | 490.7 | - | 613.0 | 586.9 | 614.8 | |

Source: The figures for 1965, 1970 and 1975 are calculated by dividing the payments by quantities shown in NK SU 60, NK Uz. 60 and ST 50. For 1967 the data are from V.R. Boev, Zakupochnye Tseny i Chisty i, Dokhod Kolkhozov Moscow 1969. For 1953 to 1967 indices are available in A.N. Malafeyev, Istoriya Tsenoobrazovaniya v SSSR (1917–1963), Moscow 1964. Absolute prices have been found by applying these indices to the 1967 prices shown in Boev, op cit. Khan and Ghai, p.23.

* The figure for 1967 in Boev, op cit is assumed to be the price for cattle in liveweight which we have converted to slaughterweight (liveweight = 1.56 times slaughterweight).

TABLE 6

COTTON HARVEST IN CENTRAL ASIA

(quintals per hectare*)

| | 1961–65 | 1966–70 | 1971–75 | 1976–80 | 1981–85 | 1986–88 |
|---|---|---|---|---|---|---|
| Uzbekistan | 21.9 | 25.1 | 28.5 | 29.4 | 26.7 | 24.7 |
| Kyrgystan | 20.6 | 23.5 | 27.6 | 28.3 | 19.1 | 23.9 |
| Tajikistan | 24.2 | 27.1 | 30.7 | 30.7 | 29.8 | 28.8 |
| Turkmenistan | 17.8 | 23.9 | 23.1 | 22.4 | 21.4 | 19.6 |
| Kazakhstan | n.a. | n.a. | 26.6 | 27.0 | 23.3 | 25.2 |

Source: Narodnoye Khozyaystvo of Central Asian Republics, various years; USSR, TsSu Narodnoye Khozyaystvo Sssr, various years, Goskomstat, 1988, p.151.

* 1 quintal = 100kg

agricultural imports from other republics. This was illustrated during World War II, when the Germans occupied much of the food-surplus areas in the European half of the USSR, making it impossible to supply food to cotton-growing and other industrial crop areas. This led to a marked increase in subsistence farming, especially in the sowing of grain, which in turn caused the production of cotton to fall in 1943 to only 32 per cent of the pre-war level.[35] Yet despite this experience, the policy of increasing cotton production resumed in the post-war era, as did the region's dependence on imported foodstuffs. In 1972, products of the food industries composed almost a fifth of all inter-regional imports into Uzbekistan. At the same time, such products represented only a negligible portion of Uzbekistan's inter-regional exports.[36]

With the population of Central Asia growing at a rapid pace, the import of foodstuffs was not sufficient to meet local demand. Uzbek food stores, for example, experienced even greater shortages of meat, cheese, fresh fruits and vegetables than other government stores in many parts of the USSR.[37] According to official statistics there was one third less meat sold at retail prices in Uzbekistan; one third less milk, and far fewer consumer goods, both in quantity and variety.[38]

TABLE 7

CHANGES IN THE STRUCTURE OF SOWN AREAS: CENTRAL ASIA 1930–1979

|  | per cent of Sown Area (in 1930) | | | | |
|---|---|---|---|---|---|
|  | 1930 | 1940 | 1960 | 1970 | 1979 |
| Grain | 58 | 62 | 40 | 44 | 44 |
| Technical crops | 30 | 30 | 42 | 54 | 58 |
| Cotton | 25 | 26 | 39 | 52 | 56 |
| Potatoes & vegetables | 2 | 2 | 2 | 3 | 4 |
| Fodder crops | 7 | 14 | 27 | 25 | 34 |
| Other | 3 | 1 | 2 | 2 | 2 |
| Total | 100 | 109 | 113 | 129 | 142 |
| irrigated | n.a. | 83a | 91 | 98 | 120 |

*Source*: Sotsialisticheskoi Stroitelstvo, Moscow, 1934; NK SSSR 1975; NK SSSR 1979; Selskoe khozyaistvo SSSR, Moscow, 1971.
a  Refers to 1950

TABLE 8

AGRICULTURAL OUTPUT: CENTRAL ASIA, 1928–1979
(in '000 tons)

|  | 1928 | 1940 | 1960 | 1970 | 1979 |
|---|---|---|---|---|---|
| Grain | 1879 | 1637 | 1666 | 2299 | 4889 |
| Cotton | 708a | 1846 | 3837 | 6449 | 8089 |
| Vegetables | n.a. | 432 | 584 | 1348 | 3226 |
| Meat | 129a | 175 | 380 | 457 | 606 |
| Wool | 13.3a | 16.6 | 59.4 | 68.0 | 81.1 |

*Source*: 1928 – *Sotsialisticheskii spravochnik SSSR*, Moscow, 1928, pp.178–227; 1940 – *NK SSSR 1975*; 1960–70 – *Selskoe khozyaistvo SSSR*, 1971; 1979 – *NK SSSR 1979*.
a.  Excludes Kyrgystan

TABLE 9

PRODUCTION OF COTTON AND GRAIN IN UZBEKISTAN
(area under cultivation in '000 hectares)

| Harvest | 1913 | 1938 | 1950 | 1965 | 1978 |
|---|---|---|---|---|---|
| Cotton | 423.5 | 917.2 | 955 | 1549.9 | 1824.0 |
| All cereals | 1521 | 1452.7 | 1371 | 1252.6 | 1194.5 |
| Only rice | 161 | 80.4 | 52.8 | 55.3 | 94.2 |

*Source*: Rywkin, p.65; *Narodnoe Khozyaystvo Uzbekskoi SSR v* 1978 g. *Statisticheskii ezhegodnik*, Tashkent, Uzbekistan, 1979, p.92.

Industrial development in Central Asia was originally undertaken by the Soviets more as a commitment to ideology than for sound economic reasons. Given the poor distribution of natural resources, the distant location of markets and alternative uses of capital within the USSR, there can be little doubt that economic rationality played a marginal role in industrial planning for the region. Inspired by Lenin, the Soviets promoted a policy of economic egalitarianism, which included industrial development of the 'backward' regions. The purpose of this policy was to raise the level of these regions to equal that of the more developed republics.[39]

Prior to the October Revolution, Central Asia was a purely agrarian and cattle-breeding area, with only a few cotton and silk mills. As a result, during the first two five-year plans, capital investment was devoted primarily to building an industrial base and expanding the region's infrastructure. The process of industrialisation continued at a significant pace until the late 1930s, when there was a sharp decline in industrial output. This downturn was temporary, for during World War II many industrial enterprises from the European part of the USSR were evacuated to Central Asia. Equipment from more than 100 industrial plants (in toto or in part) was shipped to Uzbekistan alone: metallurgy, coal industry, machine building and others.[40] In Uzbekistan, this provided the basis for 47 new industrial enterprises, more than half of which were located in and around Tashkent. This development transformed Tashkent and the contiguous territory into the largest industrial complex in Central Asia.[41]

Relocation of many of the industries after the war, coupled with a decrease in investment led to a marked decline in industrial output towards the end of the 1950s. Recovery from this slump came with Khrushchev's new system for territorial economic administration called *sovnarkhozy* (1957–1965). This was the only period in Soviet history when national regions were given a real opportunity to control their own economies. Although Moscow still exercised oversight, the Central Asian *sovnarkhoz* independently managed many aspects of the region's economy and used its authority to expand the industrial base.[42] Even after the abolition of the *sovnarkhozy* (1966–1970), growth in the industrial sector continued as a result of investment programs initiated during that period. However, during the mid-1970s industrial output declined sharply and has continued to do so up to the present. In purely economic terms, achievements in the industrial sector in Central Asia were remarkable given the low base from which it developed. Yet, without large sums of capital investment, subsidies and the imported skilled workforce, it is doubtful that such rapid progress would have occurred.[43]

**Sovereignty or Continued Dependence?**

Despite the decline in agricultural and industrial output from the mid-1970s onwards, the economies of Central Asia were kept afloat through government subsidies. Unexpected independence and the subsequent collapse of the reciprocal credit and payment systems forced these nascent states to scramble for hard currency to obtain previously subsidised goods and services from other republics. Diplomatic ties with potential donor countries were promptly established and a campaign to attract foreign interest was initiated. Using their geographical proximity to Iran and the fact that the majority of the population in the region is Muslim (albeit Sunni as opposed to Shiite), the Central Asian states raised the spectre of Islamic fundamentalism. This, coupled with the publicity the Kazakh government gave to its nuclear capability, caused great anxiety among many Western strategists. On an economic level, the region's vast energy reserves became a focal point for international oil companies which could not ignore the 'unexplored frontier' or what some have called 'the next Kuwait'.[44]

Given the distorted economies of these land-locked states, it is unlikely that they will achieve economic growth without the development of their energy resources. Although Kazakhstan and Turkmenistan have the potential to become net exporters of oil and gas, at present they are not self-sufficient in oil products. This is a result of being locked into an integrated system controlled by Russia, which is currently responsible for over 90 per cent of oil and 75 per cent of natural gas production in the former Soviet Union (FSU).

*General Structure of the Oil Sector*

Since Kazakhstan was the second largest producer of crude oil and condensates in the FSU, with 532,000 b/d and 90,000 b/d respectively, it is worth briefly examining a few aspects of the integrated nature of its oil sector to illustrate some of the problems the republic is facing in its quest to exploit its energy resources.[45]

One of the fundamental problems with the structure of the Kazakh oil sector is the lack of co-ordination between its production and refining capabilities. Although there are three refineries in the republic, only one, in Atyrau (formerly Guryev), is situated in the western part of the country where the majority of the oilfields are located. Therefore, a large percentage of Kazakh crude must be piped to European Russia to be refined. In the eastern half of the country, where the main consuming market is located, the refineries in Chimkent and Pavlodar are supplied primarily with crude from Siberia.[46] This structure has been reinforced with an agreement between Kazakhstan and a new Russian oil company called the Siberian Far East Oil Company (Sidanco). According to its terms, the latter will supply crude feedstock to Pavlodar in exchange for Kazakh crude delivered to the Saratov refinery in Russia.[47] In April 1995, Lukoil followed suit by offering to deliver Siberian crude to Pavlodar and Chimkent in exchange for Kazakh feedstock supplies to its Volgograd refinery.[48]

Since the break up of the Soviet Union, Russian crude supplies from Siberia to Kazakhstan's eastern refineries have been unreliable, causing the refining industry to enter a severe recession (see Table 10). In 1991, Russia supplied 14 m tonnes of oil to Kazakhstan. Three years later, this figure plunged to 4.5 m tonnes, while products output fell from 18 m t/y to 11.8 m t/y.[49] In October 1995, Russia suspended crude supplies to the Pavlodar refinery on the grounds that Kazakhstan had used up its 1995 export quotas, causing the plant to slash its runs by 50,000 b/d.[50]

TABLE 10:

KAZAKHSTAN REFINERY THROUGHPUT 1991–1995
(in barrels per day)

| Plant | 1991 | 1992 | 1993 | 1994 | 1995 |
|---|---|---|---|---|---|
| Pavlodar | 143,343 | 129,018 | 103,616 | 65,868 | 60,150 |
| % change | n/a | -10.0 | -19.7 | -36.4 | -8.7 |
| Chimkent | 125,876 | 120,986 | 99,697 | 74,492 | 72,180 |
| % change | n/a | -3.9 | -17.6 | -25.3 | -3.1 |
| Atyrau | 91,805 | 88,200 | 93,411 | 95,941 | 84,210 |
| % change | n/a | -3.9 | 5.9 | 2.7 | -12.2 |
| Total | 361,024 | 338,203 | 296,726 | 236,301 | 216,540 |
| % change | n/a | -6.3 | -12.3 | -20.4 | -8.4 |

Source: *EBRD in Kazakhstan* (Internal EBRD Publication, September 1996)

Even before the collapse of the USSR, this integrated structure caused Kazakhstan to be in the ironic position whereby it was unable to meet domestic demand for gasoline and diesel – the country's two largest export products and a major source of earnings. Statistics for 1990 show that after domestic production of 72,600 b/d of gasoline, there was a net deficit of 14,200 b/d, while consumption of 117,900 b/d of diesel outstripped production by 27,000 b/d.[51] With the refining industry currently in the midst of a recession, this deficit has undoubtedly increased.

Since Kazakhstan can no longer rely solely on imports from other FSU states to meet domestic demand, there is a possibility it will turn to neighbouring Xinjiang, China, where there is a growing surplus of gasoline and diesel. In 1991, Xinjiang's production of gasoline averaged 32,800 b/d, while local consumption averaged 18,300 b/d and production of diesel averaged 31,000 b/d whereas local consumption was 20,400 b/d.[52] With the recent completion of the rail connection between Urumchi and the border town of Druzhba, the likelihood of Kazakhstan importing refined products from Xinjiang has increased. This connection has also meant that Xinjiang's traditional markets for its surplus, Shaanxi and Sichuan, are more distant and less profitable than the Kazakh market.[53]

During the Soviet era, Central Asia received its oil and gas imports by way of a credit system. However since then, this system has collapsed, causing enormous payment arrears and the development of a barter trade. As most of the FSU states have been unable to pay their debts, a situation has arisen whereby the producing countries have begun to decrease or even cut supplies to former trading partners. In March 1994, Uzbekistan reduced deliveries of natural gas to Kazakhstan by 25 per cent in response to the republic's payment arrears, which amounted to $900 million.[54] In February the same year, Turkmenistan suspended gas supplies to Ukraine which had a debt of $154.1 million for gas supplied in 1994 and an unpaid bill for 1993.[55] The two countries eventually reached an agreement in which Turkmenistan supplied gas in return for food shipments and other consumer goods. Such barter agreements have consistently been used for oil and gas transactions between Central Asia and Russia. For example, in 1993, Uzbekistan provided 544,000 tonnes of cotton fibre, one third of its total harvest, in return for 4 million tons of oil, 150,000 tons of petrol, 700,000 tons of fuel and 71,000 tons of diesel oil from Russia.[56] However, as the legal systems of these countries have yet to accommodate such arrangements, there are currently no provisions which would ensure compensation when a deal falls through. This was illustrated when Russia reduced its oil exports to Turkmenistan by 650,000 tons after the breakdown of a barter agreement involving the exchange of 1.5 million tons of crude for Turkmen cotton. The oil earmarked for Turkmenistan was then sold to markets outside the FSU.[57]

*Current Export System*

As noted earlier, the role of the Central Asian states as part of a command economy meant that their transportation system, including pipelines, was directed towards, and controlled by, Russia. The lack of an independent export system to world markets is arguably the greatest obstacle to developing the region's energy resources. Although a number of international oil companies are engaged in developing the region's oil and gas fields, the pipeline facilities have been poorly maintained and will have to be upgraded before they can handle any increase in production. As a consequence, Moscow has imposed strict quotas on exports. In 1993, Russia limited Turkmenistan's gas exports to the West to 8.2 bn cubic metres, instead of the agreed 11.3 bn cubic metres.[58] In Kazakhstan, Chevron increased the production capacity of the Tengiz field to 90,000 b/d, yet Russia limited its crude throughput to only 65,000 b/d.[59]

These restrictions have led to the development of swap arrangements with both Russia and Iran. In the case of the Tengizchevroil joint venture, crude has been supplied to Russian refineries in return for Urals blend down-loaded at Novorossiysk, Russia's main oil exporting port on the Black Sea.[60] As the Central Asian republics are eager to increase their bargaining power *vis-à-vis* Russia, they have begun to look to their southern neighbour as an alternative outlet to world markets. On May 11 1996 a deal was signed between Iran and Kazakhstan whereby Kazakh crude would be shipped across the Caspian Sea to refineries in northern Iran as payment for oil sold on Kazakhstan's behalf at Kharg Island.[61] Such an arrangement is mutually beneficial since northern Iran currently depends on crude shipments from the country's southern fields. In addition to this exchange system, Turkmenistan and Kazakhstan have also begun to ship limited amounts of oil through Iran using its rail and road facilities. In December 1994, Kazakhstan transported 3,600 tonnes of crude across the Caspian Sea to the Iranian port of Bandar Nowshahr, where it was then taken by rail to Bandar Janoubi, on the Gulf of Oman, for export to Europe.[62] Two months later, the Dutch company, Larmag, bought a 3,200 tonne consignment of oil at the Turkmen port of Cheleken which was also shipped to Bandar Nowshahr. From there, it was unloaded into trucks and transported to Bandar Khomeini on the Persian Gulf.[63]

Russia's stranglehold on export routes to the world market has also enabled it to set high transportation tariffs. The proposed tariff for use of an upgraded pipeline from the Tengiz field to Novorossiysk is estimated at $3.25 per barrel (in 1993 prices).[64] According to one analyst, 'Chevron believes that the commercial rates proposed as tariffs are simply too high. Chevron argues that these need to come down; Russia argues that this would cost it $100m a year in lost transit revenues and that, over the prospective life of Chevron's 40-year agreement for developing Tengiz crude, this would cost it $4bn.'[65]

Recognising the profits to be made from these duties, other states have tried to follow suit by demanding dollar transit fees for inter-republic use of pipelines. In response to Turkmenistan's request of hard-currency payments for gas in 1993, Uzbekistan demanded transit fees of $1.50/mcm for Turkmen gas passing through its 430 km pipeline, while Kazakhstan wanted $2.80/mcm for gas travelling along its 860 km section.[66]

Russia's ability consistently to put obstacles in the path of foreign companies, whether it be through quotas, high transportation tariffs, taxes or laws, has given it a foothold in several major deals. A recent example is Gazprom's entry into the Karachaganak project. In 1992, British Gas and Agip won the exclusive rights to negotiate a development contract for the giant Karachaganak field, which has an estimated 16 trillion cf of gas reserves and 2.4 billion cm of condensates.[67] Two years later, British Gas and Agip were obliged to sign over 15 per cent of their shares in the field to Gazprom.[68]

*Pipeline Options*

A number of lines are currently being studied for the combined export of Central Asian and Azeri oil, which may generally be categorised as traversing either Russia, Georgia, Turkey or Iran. Almost all of the considered routes have serious drawbacks, whether they be political, economic or logistical, making the issue extremely sensitive and complex. Although a detailed discussion of each line is beyond the scope of this chapter, attention will be given to a few aspects of the main routes which are being proposed.

In 1992, Russia, Kazakhstan and the Oman Oil Company established the Caspian Pipeline Consortium (CPC) to construct a 1,500 km pipeline from the Tengiz field to the Black Sea port of Novorossiysk. However, financing for the $1.5bn project had been uncertain since Chevron refused to join the CPC. Chevron was offered 25 per cent of the shares, but in return was expected to cover the full cost of the pipeline's construction.[69] The consortium was reorganised in April 1996 and now includes: the governments of Russia, Kazakhstan and Oman; Russia's Lukoil and Rosneft; Kazakhstan's Munaigaz; British Gas; Agip; Chevron; and the Oryx Energy Company. The Russian company Transneft will construct the pipeline.[70] With the possibility of Gennady Zyuganov's Communist Party coming to power, project financing is unlikely to be concluded until after the Russian elections. Once that hurdle is overcome, the consortium will still be left with the problem of reaching the Mediterranean. Turkey has already stated that it will not allow any more heavy tanker traffic to pass through the congested Bosporous.[71] This, in turn, has forced Russia to examine other routes.

One of the alternative schemes that Russia has shown an interest in is the proposed $700m Trans-Balkan pipeline. This project calls for the laying of a 42-inch pipeline which would run 270–300 km from Bulgaria's port of

Bourgas to an export terminal on the Greek coast at Alexandroupoulis.[72] Once this line is completed and port facilities upgraded, Caspian crude could be shipped across the Black Sea from either Tuapse or Novorossiysk to Bourgas and then onto European markets. As with the CPC line, financing for the project has yet to be finalised, although it is anticipated that the European Union will offer loans and grants to cover half of the costs, while the other half would be financed privately.

There are several other proposed pipeline routes that also have the problem of shipping oil through the Bosporous. They are primarily those that would traverse Georgia and terminate at the Black Sea ports of either Batumi or Poti. The first phase of one proposal, designed by Brown & Root, envisages a 30-inch pipeline which would run 650 km from the Tengiz field across the Caspian Sea to Makhachkala, the capital of Daghestan. A 300 km pipeline would then be built connecting Makhachkala to Tbilisi, where the oil would be exported along an existing line to Batumi.[73] (see Map 3) The logistics of building such a route are formidable. The pipeline would have to cut through the steep and perpetually snow-capped Caucasus mountains. The heavy equipment needed to achieve this task would be dependent on a Georgian military road, which is the only north/south passage through the mountains.[74] As the political situation in Georgia is volatile, protection of the pipeline and equipment would have to be considered. The mountains are often controlled by warlords and militias, who have been known to levy 'taxes' at will and are prone to siphon crude from the pipelines for local refineries. The second phase of the project consists of building another 30-inch pipeline that would transit 1,100 km from Tbilisi to Ceyhan, Turkey. The oil would then be piped through existing facilities to the port at Yumurtalik. The estimated cost for the entire Brown & Root scheme is $2.6 bn.[75]

Although this scheme for Tengiz crude has been put on the back burner for the time being, a route through Georgia has been accepted by the Azerbaijan International Operating Co. (AIOC) for the export of early oil from the Azeri, Chirag and deep-water Guneshli fields. The project, which includes laying 180 km of new pipeline and building loading facilities at Supsa, will cost an estimated $250 million,[76] which is likely to be raised by the consortium members. As a result of Russian pressure, the AIOC has also adopted a 1,250 km route via Grozny and Tikhoretsk to Novorossiysk. Despite a recent attack on a gas pipeline in Chechnya, the Russians have assured the AIOC of the pipeline's security. It is anticipated that the majority of the 100,000 b/d of early oil will be transported through this route after the flow is reversed and a section of new pipeline is built. The AIOC has yet to decide on a route for the fields' main production of 700,000 b/d.

MAP 3

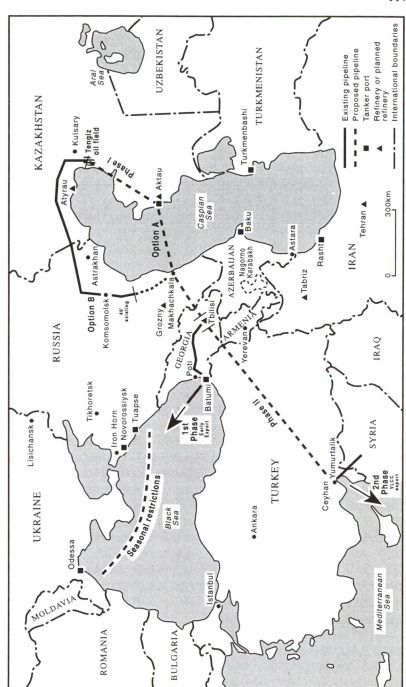

Existing pipeline
Proposed pipeline
Tanker port
Refinery or planned refinery
International boundaries

0        300km

As noted earlier, Iran has already been used as a transit route for limited shipments of Caspian crude, demonstrating that it is one of the safest and most direct routes to the sea. Contrary to its Caucasus counterparts, the country enjoys a certain amount of political stability, enabling it to guarantee the security of oil shipments. For the transportation of larger volumes of crude, the Caspian port of Bandar-e Anzali would need to be connected to the rest of the country's pipeline network. This is quite feasible since the distance between the two is only 100 km.[77] Yet, in order to handle greater exports, the pipelines would undoubtedly have to be upgraded and in some cases the flow reversed. Although this may be costly, the Iranian route has the additional advantage of easy access to both eastern and western markets. The Islamic Republic is currently lobbying for the construction of a pipeline that would be connected to the existing Iraq export pipeline in Turkey, giving Iran and by proxy, the Central Asian states, both a sea and land route to European markets.[78]

Despite the apparent benefits the Iranian route has to offer, the US government has made it quite clear that co-operation with Iran is not an option for American oil companies. After the State Department stopped a billion dollar oil development contract between Conoco and Iran, President Clinton signed an order prohibiting US companies from participating in Iranian oil and gas projects.[79] Now Congress is debating a sanctions bill which would punish *any* company giving significant help to Iran or Libya in developing their energy reserves. Foreign companies not complying with the bill could be subject to restrictions on trade with the US and a ban on loans from American banks.[80] Although European politicians are threatening to take the matter to the World Trade Organisation, the possibility of such sanctions has caused a number of companies to put off further negotiations. The Italian oil company Ente Nazionale Idrocarburi (ENI) and Argentina's Bridas have already expressed a desire to participate in a proposed gas pipeline which would stretch from Turkmenistan through Iran and onto Turkey.[81] However, the $8bn line which would carry 15–25 bcm per year to the European market is unlikely to be built in the near future if the bill is passed.[82]

Turkmenistan has actively been seeking alternative routes for its gas since the Russian quota system caused a dramatic decrease in production and hard currency earnings.[83] Within three years production plunged from 88 bn cubic metres to a mere 35.8 bn cubic metres. (see Table 11) Besides the southern route via Iran, Turkmenistan has been examining various eastern routes in conjunction with a number of US oil companies.

One of the most ambitious projects is a 7,000 km gas pipeline stretching from Central Asia through the oil and gas fields in China's Tarim Basin to the port at Shanghai. The Japanese trading company, Maiubeni and the American oil company, Mobil have agreed to back a feasibility study of the

TABLE 11

TURKMENISTAN'S GAS PRODUCTION
(billion cubic metres)

|                   | 1991 | 1992  | 1993 | 1994 |
|-------------------|------|-------|------|------|
| Production        | 88.0 | 55.69 | 65.2 | 35.8 |
| Domestic demand   | 9.0  | 6.0   | 9.0* | n.a. |

\* Estimated from mid-year date

*Source: Petroleum Economist*

proposed line which is also supported by the World Bank and the UNDP. The ¥1 trillion ($11bn at current prices) line is to carry 20m tonnes of natural gas to the markets of the Far East and South East Asia by the year 2004.[84] The logistics involved in such an endeavour are formidable. Apart from the sheer size of the project, surmounting the natural barriers, which include the Tien Shan mountains and the Taklamakan desert, would require great tenacity.

A more modest route eastward, which has interested Gazprom, Delta Oil of Saudi Arabia and the US company, Unocal, envisages the construction of 1,400 km of pipeline to transport 20bn cubic metres of gas from the Turkmen field of Sovetabad across the northern regions of Afghanistan to a gas plant in the town of Sui, in the Baluchistan province of Pakistan.[85] However, like the proposed routes through the Caucasus, security of this $3bn pipeline would not be guaranteed given the political unrest in Afghanistan and the tribal warlords of Baluchistan.

Since the economic future of Central Asia depends on the development of its energy resources, it is imperative that a decision on a pipeline route (or routes) is promptly made. The growing presence of Russia's oil companies in what were previously foreign ventures, together with its tight grip on domestic and external exports, have diminished the Central Asians' ability to negotiate for alternative pipeline routes. However, the US State Department has announced that it would challenge Russia's stranglehold on oil exports and its domination of the 'near abroad', in order to ensure the independence of these republics and to protect US corporate interests.[86] Although Russian activities in the region may be detrimental to the Central Asians, it is unlikely that the US will take measures against it, particularly when Russian actions in the region coincide with the US foreign policy agenda. An example of such a case, is the recent signing of a 'friendship pact' between Russia and Turkmenistan, whereby the latter was given access to Gazprom's gas pipelines in exchange for a pledge not to export gas to the south (i.e. Iran), eliciting no response thus far from Washington.[87]

### Regional Co-operation in Transport and Trade

The proposed extension of the pipeline system to surrounding countries exemplifies one area in which the Central Asian republics are attempting to re-establish links with their neighbours. During the Soviet era, it was necessary to sever the peripheral regions' external contacts in order for the concept of a Soviet national identity to become deeply rooted in the population's mindset. Hence, for over seven decades almost all of the communication between Central Asia and its borderlands was conducted through Moscow. Now these nascent republics are actively courting their neighbours on cultural, religious and economic bases. Their objectives are primarily to redefine their national identity, which was completely associated with Soviet ideology, and to establish a counterbalance to Russian influence by gaining access to regional and international markets.

### *The Economic Co-operation Organisation*

One of the main bodies currently promoting regional integration is the Economic Co-operation Organisation (ECO), which came into existence as a successor to the Central Treaty Organisation (CENTO). The latter was initially part of a US containment policy in the 1950s and 1960s that centred on the acquisition of strategic and political access by the US and its denial to the Soviet Union.[88] CENTO members, which included Turkey, Pakistan and Iran, were encouraged to form a land cordon to prevent the Soviet Union from gaining access to warm water ports.[89] In return, they were accorded American military and economic resources. Ironically, one of the ECO's goals is to establish land corridors from the FSU republics to warm water ports.

Although the ECO was established in 1985, its activities were fairly limited until the collapse of the Soviet Union, when its members were suddenly faced with several new bordering nations that had the potential to threaten regional stability. The member states needed to quickly adjust to the new political reality and the ECO provided an ideal forum for the development of joint strategies towards Central Asia and Azerbaijan.[90] Contrary to the idea that the members were vying for power in the region following the USSR's demise, they were actually swift in advocating a policy of Cupertino. After only one year of independence, the five fledgeling states of Central Asia, along with Azerbaijan and Afghanistan, were formally inducted as members of the ECO. The organisation's objectives included the expansion of trade, development of commercial and financial institutions, co-operation in transportation services, extension of tourism and the consolidation of cultural and spiritual ties.[91] Speaking on the economic goals of the ECO, the former Prime Minister of Pakistan, Nawaz Sharif proclaimed:

The aspirations of 300 million people who share a common heritage and culture have been realised... Together our nations can build a prosperous and vibrant society. The ECO should embark on a comprehensive strategy for co-operation. The most important and dynamic mix seems to consist of massive investments in infrastructure and the encouragement of the private sector which can bring together resources and act as a multiplier for development.[92]

At the moment the major stumbling block for a number of ECO projects is the 'massive investment' needed for their realisation. The economies of all of the member states are either fragile or faced with a considerable debt burden which has prohibited them from contributing large sums to these projects. Hence, the achievement of complete economic integration between the ECO members is unlikely to occur in the near future.

*Transportation Options: The Iranian Route*

Out of all of the ECO members, Iran is in the best geographical position to offer the land-locked Central Asian states access to international markets. As noted earlier, routes through Iran are currently being used for the shipment of limited supplies of petroleum. Yet, with the above mentioned political drawbacks, it is questionable whether or not Iran will become the main highway for oil exports. On the other hand, it is highly probable that Iran will provide arterial routes for other commodities headed for the region, as was the case in the nineteenth century.

In order to secure this position as a main thoroughfare, the Islamic Republic has been making great strides towards improving its rail, road and shipping facilities. The railway system has recently been extended with the completion of a 700 km line from Bandar Abbas to Bafq. The country's southern port is now linked to Turkey and Azerbaijan via the Bafq–Tehran–Tabriz line, which is connected to the north-western stations of Razi and Jolfa.[93] In May 1996, the Iranian rail network was joined to the Central Asian system. Iran began construction on a 165 km railway connecting the holy city of Mashhad to the border town of Sarakhs over three years ago. (see Map 4) Turkmenistan, which shares a 600 km land border with Iran, simultaneously started work on a 150 km rail spur from Tedzhen to Sarakhs.[94] Theoretically passengers and cargo are now able to travel from Bandar Abbas to the Central Asian capitals and then onto China, via the Druzhba connection at the Kazakh border. There are also plans to construct a 350 km line from Kerman to Zahedan, which would facilitate rail shipments from Pakistan.

Presently, the Iranian road network is the primary means of transporting cargo bound for Central Asia. Travel time from Bandar Abbas to

MAP 4

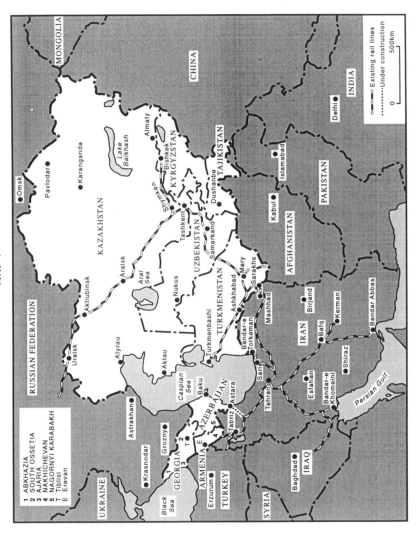

Ashkhabad is estimated at 15 to 16 days via the Damghan–Mashhad–Quchan–Bajgiran–Gaudan road, which is roughly the same route that Russian, Persian and Indian merchants used in the late 1800s.[95] This highway has recently been shortened with the completion of a new road that runs from the northern town of Damghan across the Kavir desert to the southern towns of Mo'alleman and Jandaq.[96] The Islamic Republic has also begun to take steps towards improving facilities for foreign transit truckers. Terminals are to be built which would provide the drivers with mechanical services, administrative aid for transit documentation and recreational facilities. They are to be established in the regions of Bazargan, Urumiyeh, Tabriz, Ardabil, Rasht, Astara, Semnan, Shahrud, Azadshahr, Yazd, Neka and near the Turkmenistan border.[97] Despite these improvements, one of the main disadvantages of using Iranian highways is the 17 tonne limit for trailers as opposed to the 21 tonne limit in Russia.[98]

Although most western countries tend to ship their cargo to the ports at Riga and Arkangel, the transit fees for the use of the old Soviet rail system are becoming prohibitive, encouraging exporters to seek other alternatives. The cost for the transportation of 20 ft. containers to Central Asia can be as much as $2,000–$3,000 more than the Iranian route.[99] Since Russia has a stranglehold on the FSU transportation system, transit fees can be set at monopoly rates. The Iranian tariffs are substantially lower for the reason that international freight is primarily transported by truck.

Iran's low transit fees, geographical position and relative stability have enticed neighbouring Asian and Far Eastern countries to use this route to access Central Asian markets. In April 1995, India, Iran and Turkmenistan signed a trilateral transit agreement which was aimed at increasing the volume of Indian exports to the region via Iran.[100] Currently, Indian vessels use Georgian or Ukrainian ports to get to Central Asia. This route takes approximately a fortnight in shipping time, whereas to reach Bandar Abbas from Bombay takes a mere three days.[101] In order to accommodate larger volumes of cargo, Iran has constructed a new port near Bandar Abbas which has full container holding facilities with a capacity of 10 million tonnes.[102] Pakistan has already used the Iranian route as an alternative to the one through war-torn Afghanistan for the transportation of a consignment of cotton purchased from Turkmenistan.[103] Indonesia, Malaysia, the Philippines, Brunei and Thailand have also voiced their readiness to transit Iran.

While the Iranian highways and railroads are being expanded, the Caspian Sea is serving as an important interim transportation link. Iranian goods, such as appliances, processed foods and textiles are currently shipped from Bandar-e Turkoman, in the Mazandaran province, to the Turkmen port of Turkmenbashi (formerly Krasnovodsk). In turn, Turkmenistan has been sending carpets and handicrafts to Iran.[104] With respect to international trade, both Uzbekistan and Turkmenistan are utilising this sea route for imported goods arriving at Iranian ports on the Persian Gulf. The cargo is transported across Iran to Bandar-e Turkoman, where it is shipped to the terminus of the Transcaspian railway at Turkmenbashi.[105]

As a result of the resurgence of Islam in Central Asia, Iran is once again becoming a stepping stone for pilgrims bound for Mecca. In May and June of 1993, approximately 50 Turkmen pilgrims used the above mentioned Caspian service to reach Tehran, where they boarded an international flight headed for Saudi Arabia.[106] Although this number is modest in comparison to the thousands transiting Iran in the 1800s, it is significant in that the Iranian route is considered a relatively inexpensive and safe way to reach Mecca.

### The Pakistani Route

There are two proposed routes through Pakistan which the Central Asian republics are considering using to access the sea. The first route stretches approximately 3,400 km from the Kazakh capital of Almaty, through the Kyrgyz capital, Bishkek to Kashi (Kashgar), in China's Xinjiang Uighur Autonomous Region. From there, goods would be transported south by the Karakoram highway to Islamabad where they would be taken by rail to Karachi.[107] Although the four countries signed an agreement in March 1995, establishing trade along this highway, it is unlikely that international exporters will send their cargo via this arduous route. Freight forwarders are reluctant to use transit routes through northern Pakistan due to the prevalence of banditry.[108] The other route to Karachi is equally hazardous. It entails building a $600 million rail link from the Turkmen town of Kushka, through the Afghan cities of Herat and Kandahar, to Quetta in Pakistan, where it would connect with the rest of the country's railway network. If built, this railroad would have the same drawbacks as the proposed gas pipeline through Afghanistan, i.e. lack of security.

### The Chinese Route

As noted earlier a rail connection between Kazakhstan and China has already been made at the border town of Druzhba. This line, which was started in 1956, has attracted Japanese interest, as it is a potential short-cut to European markets. In April 1995, Japan offered Kazakhstan a low-interest loan worth $78 million for improving the railway's facilities as well as technological and management assistance.[109] It has been estimated that once the facilities are updated, products from Xinjiang, such as coal, will be able to reach Europe in less than a week. Conversely, the line has already been used to transport Kazakh goods to Lianyungang seaport on the Yellow Sea. Although this line goes some way towards re-establishing the ancient Silk Road, it is unlikely to be used for international traffic in the near future. However, it has been instrumental in facilitating trade between China and the Central Asian republics. Since the break-up of the Soviet Union, China has become Kazakhstan's main hard currency trading partner. Exports to China in 1992 were up by 258 per cent on the previous year to $227.8 million, while imports were up by 189 per cent to $204.4 million (see tables 12 and 13).[110] Trade between the two increased by 64 per cent in the first half of 1995, over the same period in 1994, while the volume of cargo transported by rail doubled.[111]

TABLE 12

DESTINATIONS OF KAZAKHSTAN'S EXPORTS
(outside the CIS)*

| (% of total) | 1990 | 1991 | 1992 |
|---|---|---|---|
| China | 2.58 | 4.72 | 15.30 |
| Bulgaria | 3.35 | 0.60 | 1.20 |
| Czechoslovakia | 7.52 | 3.60 | 4.20 |
| Cuba | 3.35 | 0.68 | 1.50 |
| Hungary | 3.89 | 4.00 | 1.30 |
| Poland | 4.16 | 2.01 | 3.20 |
| Romania | 5.90 | 1.28 | 0.30 |
| Belgium | 3.88 | 5.45 | 1.00 |
| Germany | 4.03 | 4.31 | 8.00 |
| Greece | 2.24 | 4.79 | -- |
| Netherlands | 12.79 | 8.31 | 3.50 |
| UK | 1.29 | 0.16 | 6.10 |

* CIS is the Commonwealth of Independent States

*Source*: Kazakhstan Goskomstat, 1993

TABLE 13

SOURCE OF KAZAKHSTAN'S IMPORTS
(outside the CIS)

| (% of total) | 1990 | 1991 | 1992 |
|---|---|---|---|
| China | 3.69 | 15.11 | 43.60 |
| Bulgaria | 2.30 | 0.92 | 0.40 |
| Czechoslovakia | 3.11 | 1.84 | 0.60 |
| Cuba | 21.18 | 19.71 | 6.20 |
| Hungary | 2.31 | 3.60 | 5.80 |
| Poland | 11.09 | 4.33 | 1.70 |
| Romania | 1.99 | 0.53 | 1.00 |
| Germany | 12.49 | 6.57 | 4.00 |
| Italy | 3.59 | 0.51 | 0.50 |

*Source*: Kazakhstan Goskomstat, 1993

As a result of this new rail link, and the opening of several cross-border roads, China has also become a major trading partner for the other Central Asian republics. Trade between China and Kyrgyzstan has burgeoned to such an extent that some believe the latter's economy will be completely dominated by China before the end of the decade.[112] China's main exports are consumer goods, such as food, clothing, and electronic products while it imports industrial commodities, like mineral fertilisers, copper, and sheet steel. It has encouraged this trade with Kyrgyzstan by extending credits worth $5.7 million.[113] Bilateral trade with China has also flourished in Tajikistan despite the civil war. It increased from $2.7 million in 1992, to $4.4 million in the first four months of 1993.[114] With respect to Uzbekistan, by the end of 1992, China was its leading trade partner outside the FSU.[115]

Although these cash-strapped republics are keen to do business with their neighbour, such extensive economic relations with China has had a Damoclean effect on them. A large number of Chinese tradesmen have crossed the border on the pretence of business and have proceeded to buy property and settle down. Out of fear of economic subjugation, Kazakhstan has introduced new visa procedures to limit the number of Chinese entering the country.

## Conclusion

Since the breakdown of the Soviet command system, Central Asia has been suffering from severe economic dislocations. A heavy reliance on trade with the FSU republics (see Table 14) and subsequent disruptions in supplies have led to acute shortages in almost every sector. With regard to transportation, unreliable shipments of spare parts, equipment, fuel and rolling stock from Russia, Belarus and Ukraine have meant that road and rail facilities are functioning far below capacity.

TABLE 14

UZBEKISTAN'S EXTERNAL TRADE
(million roubles)

|                | 1989   | 1990   | 1991   | 1992    |
|----------------|--------|--------|--------|---------|
| Total imports  | 14,158 | 14,662 | 21,475 | 191,885 |
| FSU            | 12,046 | 11,864 | 17,766 | 162,246 |
| Foreign        | 2,112  | 2,798  | 3,709  | 29,639  |
| Total Exports  | 10,169 | 9,351  | 19,535 | 50,518  |
| FSU            | 8,542  | 8,169  | 17,339 | 123,136 |
| Foreign        | 1,628  | 1,182  | 3,709  | 27,382  |

Source: Europa World Yearbook 1994

In an effort to free themselves from Russia's grip and break this economic decline, the Central Asian republics have re-established relations with neighbouring countries. The latter have not only begun to fill the gap in inputs and skilled labour, previously supplied by other FSU republics, but have also offered Central Asia, for the first time in recent history, independent access to world markets. Yet, before transit routes through neighbouring states can be considered viable alternatives to Russia, Central Asia's own transport network will have to be upgraded and extended which is unlikely to occur without funding from international agencies. Of the transit options currently available to these republics, the Iranian one is probably the most advantageous. In addition to its geographical location and relative stability, the investment required for linking the country's infrastructure to Central Asia is relatively minor compared to the other options.

Although Central Asia can decrease its reliance on Russia, by establishing other trading partners and transit routes, it will not be able to sever its dependence and achieve real economic growth without developing its energy resources and establishing alternative pipeline routes. Each of the routes under consideration will require substantial foreign investment. Despite the apparent advantages the Iranian route has to offer, this investment is unlikely to be forthcoming as a result of the current political situation. The Turkish and Georgian routes are both costly and suffer from a lack of security. In addition to these drawbacks, oil shipments using the latter route would have to pass through the congested Bosporous thereby increasing the potential for an ecological disaster. Russia has already shown that it is able and willing to limit oil throughput from this region and will bully Central Asia into opting for the Russian route in the long-term. If the Central Asian states were to succumb to Russian pressure, they would soon revert to their former status as a Russian appendage. Given its growing presence in Central Asia's energy sector and its stranglehold on exports, Russia is unlikely to release its grip on the region without the involvement of a third party which is prepared to and is capable of exercising its political leverage.

## APPENDIX I.

**Prince Gortchakov's circular of November 9, 1864 to the British Government on Russia's Programme in Central Asia**[116]

*'The position of Russia in Central Asia is that of all civilised States which are brought into contact with half-savage, nomad populations, possessing no fixed social organisation. In such cases it always happens that the more civilised State is forced, in the interest of the security of its frontier and its commercial relations, to exercise a certain ascendancy over those whom their*

*turbulent and unsettled character makes most undesirable neighbours.*

*First, there are raids and acts of pillage to be put down. To put a stop to them, the tribes on the frontier have to be reduced to a state of more or less perfect submission. This result once attained, these tribes take to more peaceful habits, but are in their turn exposed to the attacks of the more distant tribes.*

*The State is bound to defend them against these depredations, and to punish those who commit them. Hence the necessity of distant, costly, and periodically-recurring expeditions against an enemy whom his social organisation makes it impossible to seize. If, the robbers once punished, the expedition is withdrawn, the lesson is soon forgotten; its withdrawal is put down to weakness. It is a peculiarity of Asiatics to respect nothing but visible and palpable force; the moral force of reason and of the interests of civilisation has as yet no hold upon them. The work has then always to be done over again from the beginning.*

*In order to put a stop to this state of permanent disorder, fortified posts are established in the midst of these hostile tribes, and an influence is brought to bear upon them which reduces them by degrees to a state of more or less forced submission. But some beyond this second line, other still more distant tribes, come in their turn to threaten the same dangers, and necessitate the same measures of repression. The State thus finds itself forced to choose one of two alternatives – either to give up this endless labour, and to abandon its frontier to perpetual disturbance, rendering all prosperity, all security, all civilisation an impossibility, or, on the other hand, to plunge deeper and deeper into barbarous countries, where the difficulties and expenses increase with every step in advance.*

*Such has been the fate of every country which has found itself in a similar position. The United States of America, France in Algeria, Holland in her colonies, England in India – all have been irresistibly forced, less by ambition than by imperious necessity, into this onward march, where the greatest difficulty is to know where to stop.*

*Such, too, have been the reasons which have led the Imperial Government to take up at first a position resting on one side on the Syr-Darya, on the other on the lake of Issyk-Kul, and to strengthen these two lines by advanced forts, which, little by little, have crept on into the heart of those distant regions, without, however, succeeding in establishing on the other side of our frontiers that tranquillity which is indispensable for their security.*

*The explanation of this settled state of things is to be found, first, in the fact that between the extreme points of this double line there is an immense unoccupied space, where all attempts at colonisation or caravan trade are paralysed by the inroads of the robber tribes; and, in the second place, in the perpetual fluctuations of the political condition of those countries where Turkestan and Khokand, sometimes united, sometimes at variance, always at war, either with one another or with Bokhara, presented no chance of settled relations, or of any regular transactions whatever.*

*The Imperial Government thus found itself, in spite of all its efforts, in the dilemma we have above alluded to, that is to say, compelled either to permit the continuance of a state of permanent disorder, paralysing to all security and progress, or to condemn itself to costly and distant expeditions leading to no practical result and with the work always to be done anew; or, lastly, to enter upon the undefined path of conquest and annexation which has given to England the Empire of India, by attempting the subjugation by armed force, one after another, of the small independent States whose habits of pillage and turbulence, and whose perpetual revolts, leave their neighbours neither peace nor repose.*

*Neither of these alternative courses was in accordance with the object of our august master's policy, which consists not in extending beyond all reasonable bounds the regions under his sceptre, but in giving a solid basis to his rule, in guaranteeing their security, and in developing their social organisation, their commerce, their well-being, and their civilisation....'*

## APPENDIX II.

### Customs Regulation in Russian Turkestan in May 1889[117]

I.    All imports from other parts of the Russian Empire, and all merchandise and products from Bukhara, Khiva and China are admitted free of customs duties into Russian Turkestan, with the exception mentioned in III.

II.  The importation of Anglo-Indian, Afghan, Persian, Turkish and Western European goods not enumerated in III., and also of powder and warlike stores, is forbidden.

III.  The following articles may only be imported on payment of duty as set forth:-
   1)  Precious stones, real and imitation, pearls, garnets, and unworked coral at 4 roubles 8 kopecks per pud.
   2)  Laurel leaves and berries at 2 r. 21k. per pud.
   3)  Spices at duties varying between 5 r. and 24 r. per pud.
   4)  Sugar products, mainly confectionery and preserves, at 1 r. 65 k. per pud.
   5)  Tea at 14 r. 40 k. per pud.
   6)  Indigo at 6 r. per pud.
   7)  Boots and shoes of Indian leather at 1 r. 19 k. per lb.
   8)  Muslin at 1 r. per lb.
   9)  Coral, worked and threaded, at 6 r. 72 k. per lb.

**Selected Provisions from a 1889 Decree for the Establishment of a Special Customs Service in Transcaspia**
I.  European, Anglo-Indian, and Persian goods, brought by land from abroad into the Transcaspian province are subjected to an *ad valorem* duty of 2 ½ per cent.

II.  Goods passing through the custom house at Uzun Ada for European Russia or the Caucasus are to pay the full European tariff, deducting the amount already paid under I.
   Later the same year, an official proclamation was issued declaring that all goods from Persia will be allowed free transit through Transcaspia if sent via Uzun Ada and Baku; a privilege which had previously been concede to Persian trade passing through the Caucasus.

## NOTES

1.  Mojgan Djamarani, 'Who might realign with OPEC?', *Petroleum Review* (March 1994) p.136.
2.  On May 3, 1996 the US company Mobil acquired 25 per cent of the Kazakh government's stake in the joint venture.
3.  Steve LeVine, 'High Stakes' in *Newsweek* 125/16 (17 April 1995) p.10.
4.  John Odling-Smee, *IMF report: Turkmenistan* and British Embassy Commercial Department, *Turkmenistan, The Economy and Commercial Opportunities* (December 1992) p.3. Based on an annual production rate of 80bn–90bn cm, Turkmenistan's reserves/production ratio is approximately 35 years. Jean Christophe Fueg, 'The Gas Industry of the Southern FSU', *Petroleum Economist* (1995) p.36.
5.  Uzbekistan maintains the largest gold mine in the world, which produces 50 tonnes of ore annually, while Tajikistan contains the world's largest known silver deposits.
6.  John Obert Voll, 'Main Street of Eurasia', in *Aramco World* 39/4 (July–August 1988) p.6.
7.  Mary Holdsworth, *Turkestan in the 19th Century* (Oxford: Soviet Affairs Study Group 1959) p.2.
8.  Ibid., p.15.
9.  Ralph S. Clem, 'The Frontier and Colonialism in Russian and Soviet Central Asia', in Robert A. Lewis (ed.) *Geographical Perspectives on Soviet Central Asia* (London: Routledge 1992) p.31.
10.  The role of these tribal federations are still significant in present day Kazakh consciousness and politics.
11.  Clem, p.31.
12.  Mahnaz Ispahani, *Roads and Rivals, The Politics of Access in the Borderlands of Asia* (London: I.B. Tauris & Co. 1989) p.91.
13.  The Russians captured Geok Tepe in a truculent and bloody campaign in 1881.

14. Hon. George Curzon, *Russia in Central Asia in 1889 and the Anglo-Russian Question* (London: Longmans, Green, and Co. 1889) p.275.
15. Ibid., p.99.
16. Holdsworth, p.19. Some 6,000,000 spindles and 200,000 power looms, of which 3,728,336 and 109,810 respectively were located in the Moscow region.
17. Curzon, p.278.
18. Ibid., p.280.
19. Holdsworth, pp.18–19.
20. Curzon, p.99.
21. Ibid., p.287
22. Ispahani, p.38.
23. Ibid. The Shah later extended this privilege until 1917.
24. Ibid., p.39. The Russians did complete a road connecting Qazvin to the Bay of Anzali in October 1899.
25. Although the administration for the Central Asia railway was based in Tashkent, the primary functions of the system, such as management and pricing, were controlled by Moscow.
26. Michael Rywkin, *Moscow's Muslim Challenge* (London: Hurst and Company 1982) p.47.
27. Alistair McAuley, *Soviet policy and Economic Development in Central Asia.* A paper that was delivered to the Turkish Area Study Group's Autumn Symposium on the Turcophone Peoples of Soviet Central Asia: Economic and Social Development (27 November 1981) p.12.
28. The actual procurement prices for the 1930s and 1940s are not available.
29. Azizur Rahman Khan and Dharam Ghai, *Collective Agriculture and Rural Development in Soviet Central Asia* (London: Macmillan Press 1979) p.22.
30. Statistics for the late 1970s and early 1980s are questionable due to the cotton scandal which included falsification of production figures.
31. Ibid., p.76.
32. Boris Rumer, *Soviet Central Asia: 'A Tragic Experiment'* (Boston: Unwin Hyman 1989) p.28.
33. Ibid., p.76. According to data for 1983, the largest producer in the world was China, followed next by the USSR, with the USA in third place.
34. Khan and Ghai, p.26.
35. Alec Nove and J.A. Newth, *The Soviet Middle East, A Model for Development?* (London: George Allen and Unwin Ltd. 1967) p.60.
36. Leslie Dienes, *Soviet Asia, Economic Development and National Policy Choices* (London: Westview Press 1987) p.124.
37. Nancy Lubin, *Labour and Nationality in Soviet Central Asia* (London: Macmillan Press 1984) p.180.
38. Ibid.
39. Rumer, p.21.
40. Ibid., pp.53–4.
41. Ibid., p.54.
42. Rumer, p.56.
43. The need to import skilled labour was primarily the result of an inappropriate strategy towards industrialisation. One significant factor which the Soviets overlooked when initiating their policy of economic equalitarianism, was the indigenous population's deeply rooted aversion to industrial occupations. According to an Uzbek scholar 'industrial work among indigenous inhabitants of pre-revolutionary Turkestan was avoided by all but the lowest strata of society – even if other types of work in which they engaged may have been equally arduous. Before the Revolution it was characteristic that the main contingent of indigenous personnel working (in the oil industry in the Ferghana Valley) was from the poorest levels of the peasantry, who for many years had worked in large land holdings of the bie.' This trend continued after the Revolution, for only the most deprived classes entered the fuel or heavy industrial sectors. Nancy Lubin, *Labour and Nationality in Soviet Central Asia* (London: Macmillan Press 1984) pp.206 and 208.

44. The reason for this analogy is primarily due to Kazakhstan and Turkmenistan's low level of domestic consumption relative to their energy reserves.
45. Sino-Kazakh 'Petroleum Trade Could Take Off', *Petroleum Economist* 60/1 (January 1993) p.33.
46. Ibid. Chimkent and Pavlodar have a processing capacities of 6.5 m t/y and 7.5 m t/y respectively. Pavlodar is completely dependent on Siberian oil because no other line feeds the plant, while the refinery at Chimkent is fed with crude supplies from Siberia and the Kumkol field in central Kazakhstan. In recent years, Kazakhstan has tried to substitute some of the Siberian blend with the more viscous crude from Kumkol. However, 'if the Kumkol crude input exceeds 30 per cent of total throughput at any one time, oil will congeal in the system causing wastage and eventually, technical breakdown'. Valera Belousov and Isabel Gorst, 'Refineries bond with Russia', *Petroleum Economist* 62/7 (July 1995) p.3.
47. 'Carving up the Oil Industry', *Petroleum Economist* 62/1 (January 1995) p.31. Sidanco was founded in 1994 and is an amalgam of three western Siberia producers – Purneftegas, Kondpetroleum and Vanyoganeftegas – and two refineries at Saratov and Angarsk in eastern Siberia. It should be also noted that Kazakhstan is planning to expand its refining and processing facilities, with the help of foreign investment, to a level which would make the country self-sufficient. In 1992 a Japanese consortium won a tender to design and construct a new refinery at Mangistau to process heavy Buzachi crude. Currently only one refinery in the FSU is able to handle the production of this crude.
48. Belousov and Gorst, 'Refineries Bond with Russia' *Petroleum Economist* 62/7 (July 1995) p.3. Under a swap arrangement, Russia delivered 137,000 b/d of crude to Kazakh refineries in 1995 in return for 58,800 b/d of Kazakh crude. In separate deals, Kazakhstan sold a further 88,000 b/d to Russia. 'Kazakhstan; Refinery Runs Rise as Russian Crude Supplies Resume', *Nefte Compass* 5/1 (4 January 1996) p.8.
49. Ibid.
50. 'Kazakhstan; Refinery Runs Rise as Russian Crude Supplies Resume', *Nefte Compass* 5/1 (4 January 1996) p.8.
51. Sino-Kazakh 'Petroleum Trade Could Take Off', *Petroleum Economist* 60/1 (January 1993) p.33.
52. Ibid.
53. Ibid.
54. Dun & Bradstreet, *Country Risk Reports, Uzbekistan* (April 1994) p.20. In March 1995, Uzbekistan decreased gas supplies to Kazakhstan from the required 750,000 cubic metres per hour to 450,000. It also cut off gas supplies to Tajikistan in response to an unpaid debt of $142 million. *Summary of World Broadcast* (24 March 1995), SUW/0376 WD/4 .
55. *Radio Free Europe/Radio Liberty Daily Report*, No. 36 (22 February 1994) p.3.
56. Sarah Lloyd, 'Dipendenza e sottosviluppo nell'Asia centrale' in *Politica Internazionale* 4 (October–December 1993) p.60.
57. 'Kazakhstan', *Petroleum Economist* 60/6 (June 1993) p.76.
58. Jean Christophe Fueg, 'The Gas Industry of the Southern FSU', *Petroleum Economist* (1994) p.24. In addition to decreasing Turkmen gas exports, the Russians have effectively blocked a two year old contract to supply Turkmen gas to a German customer. Derek Bamber 'Russia insists on a Slice of the Action', *Petroleum Economis 62/3* (March 1995) p.14.
59. 'Kazakhstan', *Petroleum Economist* 62/3 (March 1995) p.41. Kazakhstan and Russia reached an agreement in April 1996 whereby the former would be allowed to pump 4.5 times more than last year's quota of 1 m tonnes. According to analysts, Kazakhstan could make a profit of at least $450 m from the increased exports. 'Kazakhstan permitted to pump more oil across Russia', *Summary of World Broadcasts* (20 April 1996) SU/2591 G/1.
60. Ibid.
61. Valery Belousov and Isabel Gorst, 'Time for a New Strategy to Reap the Rewards' *Petroleum Economist* 62/1 (January 1995) p.9. A similar arrangement with Azerbaijan is currently being considered.
62. 'First Kazakh Oil Consignment Exported Through Iran', *Kayhan Havai* (21 December 1994).

63. 'First Transit Shipment of Turkment Oil Arriving', *Tehran Times* (23 February 1995).
64. John Roberts, 'Russia and the Northern Option for Caspian Crude Exports'. A paper which was delivered at a conference in London entitled 'Oil and Caviar in the Caspian: A Balance of Power or a Balance of Interests?' 23-24 February 1995.
65. Ibid.
66. *World Gas Intelligence* 4/1 (January 1993) p.18.
67. 'Azerbaijan', *Petroleum Economist* 62/4 (April 1995) p.34.
68. 'Kazakhstan', *Petroleum Economist* 62/1 (January 1995) p.34.
69. 'Kazakhstan Delays Signing Protocol for Caspian Pipeline,' *Middle East Economic Survey (MEES)* 38/25 (20 March 1995) p.A15.
70. 'Pipeline consortium brings in oil companies', *Middle East Economic Digest (MEED)* (10 May 1996) p.18.
71. There are primarily two reasons for this: firstly, a logjam would develop in the Black Sea, increasing the likelihood of accidents and ecological damage; and secondly, Turkey would like the Central Asian pipeline to traverse its territory thereby giving it another source of revenue.
72. 'Plans for Trans-Balkan Crude Pipeline Move Forward', *MEES* 38/39 (26 June1995) pp.A12–A13.
73. 'Oil Export Routes Still Up in the Air', *Petroleum Economist* 62/7 (July 1995) p.28.
74. 'Time to Talk to the Bear', *Petroleum Economist* 62/7 (July 1995) p.2.
75. Ibid.
76. 'Azerbaijan; Turkey Puts Forward Georgian Pipeline Proposals', *Nefte Compass* 5/7 (15 February 1996) p.7.
77. Ibid.
78. Ibid.
79. 'Iran', *Petroleum Economist* 62/5 (May 1995) p.55.
80. 'Politics and Oil: Rigging the Market', *The Economist* 339/7967 (25 May 1996) pp.93–4.
81. 'Italy eager to have a share in Turkmen gas project to Europe', *Ettela'at* (16 November 1994). Despite official US policy, this route is supported by Alexander Haig, the former Secretary of State under Ronald Regan, who is now closely associated with Turkmenistan's president, Saparmurad Niyazov. LeVine, *Newsweek* (17 April 1995) p.14. A number of British firms have also shown in interest in providing the construction work and equipment supplies for this line. *Summary of World Broadcasts*, (24 March 1995), SUW/0376/WD/6.
82. Jean Christophe Fueg, 'The Gas Industry of the Southern FSU', *Petroleum Economist* (1994) p.24.
83. Gas exports account for more than 70 per cent of Turkmenistan's hard currency earnings. It is also a net gas exporter. More than 40bn cubic metres per year is exported to the FSU republics while more than 10bn cubic metres used to be exported to the West. Ibid.
84. 'Maiubeni and Mobil to back World Bank Eurasian Pipeline Project', *Nihon Keizai Shimbun* (28 July 1995) p.1. Japan's Mitsubishi Corporation is promoting a similar gas project which would run from Turkmenistan across Uzbekistan and Kazakhstan to the eastern coast of China then onto Japan. The gas would be delivered to the latter in either liquefied form or through an underwater pipeline. 'Mitsubishi in Turkmenistan for talks on pipeline project', *Summary of World Broadcasts* (12 June 1995), SU/2327 G/3.
85. 'Turkmenistan and Pakistan agree to build gas pipeline', *Summary of World Broadcasts* (24 March 1995), SUW/0376 WD/6.
86. LeVine, p.12.
87. 'Time to talk to the bear', *Petroleum Economist* 62/7 (July 1995) p.2.
88. Ispahani, p.13.
89. Iraq was one of the founding members of CENTO, but withdrew from the organisation in 1958.
90. Eric Hooglund, 'Iran and Central Asia', in Anoushiravan Ehteshami (ed.), *From the Gulf to Central Asia: Players in the Great New Game* (Exeter: University of Exeter Press 1994) p.116.
91. Tahir Amin, 'Pakistan, Afghanistan and the Central Asian States' in Ali Banuazizi and Myron Weiner (eds) *The New Geopolitics of Central Asia and Its Borderlands* (London: I.B. Tauris 1994) p.244.

92. Ibid.
93. Sadrodin Moosavi, 'Rafsanjani opens economically vital Bandar Abbas-Bafq railway', *Tehran Times*, (19 March 1995). This project, which took roughly 13 years to complete, cost $600 million in hard currency and 520 billion Iranian rials. 'Bafq-Bandar Abbas Railway Complete', *Ettela'at* (10 March 1995).
94. Hooglund, p.120.
95. Interview with John Duffy from the freight forwarding company Spedition Services Ltd.
96. 'Central Asia to benefit from new Iranian highway', *Summary of World Broadcasts* (1 June 1995), SU/2318 G/1.
97. 'Transit terminals to provide facilities for foreign truckers', *Tehran Times* (12 December 1994).
98. Interview with Henk Buzink from the freight forwarding company Fransen Transport.
99. Interview with John Duffy.
100. 'India, Iran and Turkmenistan sign transit agreement', *Summary of World Broadcasts* (20 April 1995) SU/2282/ G/4.
101. 'Iranian port welcomes Indian traffic to Central Asia', *Ettela'at* (28 March 1995).
102. Ibid.
103. 'Pakistan, Turkmenistan use Iranian transit routes', *Tehran Times* (10 April 1995).
104. Hooglund, p.118.
105. .Ibid.
106. Ibid., p.119.
107. 'Transit route links Kazakhstan, Pakistan, China and Kyrgyzstan', *Summary of World Broadcasts* (13 March 1995), SU/2250 G/6.
108. Interview with John Duffy
109. 'Japan to finance Kazakh Eurasian railway project', *Summary of World Broadcasts* (14 April 1995), SUW/0379 WD/13.
110. Dun & Bradstreet, p.36.
111. 'Kazakhstan to Promote Trade with Xinjiang', Beijing Xinhau, 18 July 1995 cited in *FBIS-CHI-95-139* (20 July 1995) p.5.
112. Ross H. Munro, 'Central Asia and China' in Michael Mandelbaum (ed.) *Central Asia and the World* (New York: Council on foreign Relations Press 1994) p.232.
113. Ibid., p.233. According to Russia, a large percentage of the Kyrgyz exports are subsidised goods bought from other FSU countries and re-exported at world prices.
114. Ibid.
115. Ibid. Before the Druzbha connection was made trade was routed through the Trans-Siberian railway and the border crossing at Khabarovsk which is 3,000 miles east of Tashkent.
116. Demetrius C. Boulger, *England and Russia in Central Asia, Vol. I* (London: W.H. Allen & Co. 1879) pp.318–25
117. Curzon, pp.280–1.

# Mongolia:
# Looking to the Sea

## ALAN SANDERS

Mongolia, until 1911 Outer Mongolia and from 1924–1992 the Mongolian People's Republic, is an independent land-locked state situated in the heart of North-east Asia between Russia (the Russian Federation, RF) and China (the People's Republic of China, PRC). It extends 1,259 km from north to south, between 41 deg 35 min and 52 deg 09 min north latitude, and 2,392 km from west to east, between 87 deg 44 min and 119 deg 56 min east longitude. Mongolia's surface area of 1,565,000 sq. km and population of 2.2 million give an average density of 1.3/sq. km, although half the population is concentrated in the capital Ulan Bator (Ulaanbaatar) and a few other main towns.

The 3,485 km border with the RF runs to the west and north through high mountains, the Altai and Sayan ranges, but to the east the Hentiy and Yablonovyy chains present a less formidable barrier. The 4,674 km southern border with the PRC parallels the Mongol Altai mountains south-eastwards then dips into the Jungarian basin and south of the Gobi Altai range before winding its way through the Gobi semi-desert towards Mongolia's lowest-lying areas around Lake Buir. At its nearest point, the Zamyn-Uud/Ereen rail and road crossing, Mongolia's border is about 675 km from the port of Tianjin on the Yellow Sea coast.

For centuries the crossroads of migrating civilisations, nomadising herdsmen and international caravan routes, Mongolia gradually became isolated from the outside world under Manchu (Qing dynasty) rule from 1691 to 1911 and was bypassed by modern economic and commercial development. Soviet domination from 1921 to 1990 increased Mongolia's isolation and only partially succeeded in eliminating its backwardness. Today, Mongolia is still largely dependent on its livestock (26 million head in 1995) and mineral wealth (gold, copper, fluorspar, coal).

The Trans-Mongolian Railway provides an important link between the Trans-Siberian Railway junction at Ulan-Ude in the Buryat Republic of the RF and the rail network of northern China (Datong and Beijing). However the need to change wagon wheels at Ereen from the Russian gauge to the standard gauge used in China reduces the link's capacity. Freight movements are also hampered by the single track and obsolete equipment.

MAP

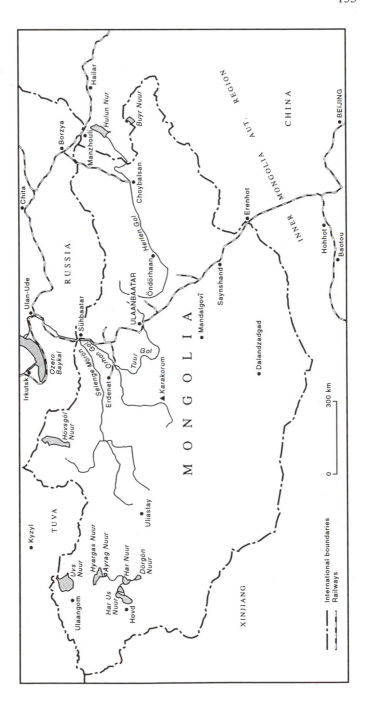

Nonetheless, Mongolia's railways carried 74 per cent of the country's freight in 1990 and almost 90 per cent in 1993.

Motor transport follows rutted routes which scar much of the open countryside, ruining the thin topsoil, punishing the vehicles and drivers and wasting time and fuel. Hard-topped roads, of which there are only about 1,200 km (1994), are limited to the main towns and the north-south corridor between Kyakhta on the RF border and Ulan Bator. A further 5,000 km or so of gravel-topped roads in various parts of the country are termed 'improved'. There is a particular lack of modern roads running east-west. Communication with outlying areas is still mostly by horse or camel. Road transport was responsible for 25 per cent of national freight carriage (in metric ton/km) in 1990, but because of fuel supply problems had declined to about 10 per cent by 1993. International road freight haulage is underdeveloped.

Despite their links with Lake Baikal and the river Angara, navigable waterways in northern Mongolia – Lake Hovsgol and the river Selenge – are only of local importance and small capacity, not serving any important population centres. Freight carried by inland waterways and by air accounts for less than one per cent of total freight carriage. The airline's equipment is obsolescent and is only now being phased out. The airfields are mostly rough strips and the few surfaced runways are too short for modern jets except at former Soviet military airfields, where they are not strong enough. However, there has been some expansion of Ulan Bator's international air links.

Since 1992 all forms of transport in Mongolia have been seriously disrupted by the irregularity of fuel supplies from Russia, the chief supplier.

## Mongolia's Cultural and Political Boundaries

Despite the difficulties caused by the economic legacy of 70 years of 'bypassing capitalism' under Soviet guidance, Mongolia has won unprecedented political freedom. Born in the collapse of communism in Eastern Europe in 1989 and the disintegration of the Soviet empire in 1991, Mongolia's new multiparty democracy produced the country's first liberal constitution in 1992. The role of Genghis Khan is being restored to an appropriate place in Mongolian history and life.

The only independent state of Mongol people, Mongolia is becoming the focus of cultural, socio-political and economic co-operation for the world's Mongol communities. It has established direct links with all three former 'Autonomous Soviet Social Republics' of the RF which are ethnically or historically Mongol: the Buryat (Buryaad, Buriat-Mongol) Republic in Siberian Russia to the north, the neighbouring Republic of Tuva (Tyva, Urianhay), and the Kalmyk Nation (Khalmg Tangkhch) on the Caspian Sea.

The Buryats came under Russian control in the 17th century. Some were converted to Orthodoxy, while others became Lamaists. The Turkic Tuvans, who were conquered by Genghis Khan and partially Mongolised, also converted to Lamaism. Tuva, which was with Outer Mongolia part of the Qing empire, came under Russian influence in the early 20th century. It declared independence as the People's Republic of (Tannu) Tuva in 1921, but was swallowed up by Soviet Russia in 1944. Khalmg Tangkhch is the post-Soviet Kalmyk Republic of Torgut Mongols (western Oirats) whose ancestors migrated through Central Asia to the river Volga in the 17th century. The Oirats also gave their name to what is now called the Altai Republic, the former Gornyy Altai district of the Russian Altai territory (*krai*).

The Buryats, Kalmyks and Tuvans make up 23, 41.5 and 60.5 per cent respectively of the otherwise predominantly Slav population of their own republics. Buryats are also concentrated in two 'autonomous districts' (*okrug*), at Aga near Chita and Ust-Orda near Irkutsk, just outside the boundaries of the Buryat Republic. The small Buryat and Tuvan communities along the northern border of Mongolia proper account for 2.5 and 1.3 per cent of the country's total population.

The largest non-Mongol ethnic group in Mongolia is formed by the Kazakhs, a Turkic tribe which accounted for some six per cent of the population at the last census. About 100,000 live in Bayan-Olgiy province (*aymag*) in western Mongolia, forming 80 per cent of the local population, and another 30,000 in neighbouring Hovd (Kobdo) province. The Kazakhs migrated into Mongolia from East Turkestan (Xinjiang) towards the end of the last century. Although they share no common border, most external links have been with the Republic of Kazakhstan (the former Kazakh SSR). Since 1991 many thousands of Mongolia's Kazakhs have found work in Kazakhstan.

To the south, Mongolia's cultural and economic contacts have been growing with the Tumet, Ordos and Chahar Mongols of the Inner Mongolia 'Autonomous Region' (AR) of the PRC through exchanges of delegations and publications and development of crossborder trade. However, these contacts are closely monitored by Han Chinese officials, to try to limit the spread of Mongol nationalism in Inner Mongolia.

In the PRC there are some 5.5 million Mongols, including 3.4 million in Inner Mongolia AR where they account for only 14 per cent of its overwhelmingly Han population. Mongolian minority tribes are to be found in Xinjiang Uighur AR – in Bayangolin and Bortala Mongolian 'autonomous prefectures' and Hoboksar Mongolian 'autonomous county' – as well as Mongolian 'autonomous counties' in the provinces of Jilin (Qian Gorlos), Heilongjiang (Dorbod), Liaoning (Fuxin and Harqin Left Wing),

Gansu (Subei) and Qinghai (Henan and Haixi), and without 'autonomy' in five more provinces.

The 1689 Treaty of Nerchinsk between China and Russia, the first international agreement made by an Emperor of China with a European power, established the eastern boundary between Chinese and Russian territory along the rivers Argun and Amur as far as the Stanovoy Mountains. Mongolia's northern border was drawn along the Sayan Mountains in accordance with the Sino-Russian Treaty of Kyakhta of 1727. The treaty's Abagaytuy (Avgayt) protocol delimited the border from the river Kyakhta eastwards to the Argun (63 markers), while the Bur (Buur *gol*) protocol delimited the border westwards (24 markers) from the Kyakhta to Shabin Dabaga (Shavinayn Davaa), a pass on Tuva's northern boundary with Krasnoyarsk *krai*. This border was extended to Kokand (present-day Uzbekistan) under the Treaty of Peking of 1860 and delimited under the Tarbagatay (Chuguchak) protocol of 1864; demarcation was completed under the 1870 Treaty of Uliassutai (Uliastay).

From 1920 Mongolia bordered to the north-east on the Far Eastern Republic, which amalgamated with Soviet Russia in 1922. From 1921–44 part of Mongolia's northern border was shared with the People's Republic of (Tannu) Tuva. In the period 1932–45 the Japanese puppet state of Manchukuo was Mongolia's eastern neighbour. Mongolia's border with Japanese-held territory extended to 1,700 km after Japan's seizure of Chahar and Suiyuan (previously parts of Inner Mongolia). Following the victory of Mongolian-Soviet forces over the Japanese army in the Battle of Halhyn Gol (Nomonhan) in August 1939, agreement on Mongolia's border with Manchukuo was eventually reached in 1942, between the Soviet Union and Japan.

Mongolia now shares its border with only two countries, the RF and PRC. The border with the RF runs from the Altai Republic in the west to the Republic of Tuva, the Buryat Republic and Chita *oblast*. The border with the PRC is contiguous with Xinjiang Uighur AR (East Turkestan Republic 1945–49), Gansu province and Inner Mongolia AR. During the Chinese 'cultural revolution' Inner Mongolia AR was truncated, and for some years Mongolia also bordered on Heilongjiang and Jilin provinces and Ningxia Hui AR.

### Kyakhta and Sino-Russian Trade

Under the 1727 Treaty of Kyakhta, Russian traders were required to move to the border from Urga (Outer Mongolia's religious centre) and Tsitsihar (Qiqihaer, in northern Inner Mongolia). The border was guarded on the Mongolian side by border posts (*karaul*) manned by Mongols with Manchu officers. Forts, posts and pickets on the Russian side were manned by Buryats, Evenkis and Russians. A Russian fort on the Kyakhta was founded as Fort Troitskiy and later renamed in honour of Savva Raguzinskiy, the Russian ambassador to China, as Fort Troitsko-Savvsk (later called Troitskosavsk, now part of Kyakhta town). Trading began there in September 1728. A Manchu official (*dzarguchei*) handled every-day border affairs at Maimachen (Maimaicheng, the Chinese trading town, now called Altanbulag), built opposite Fort Troitskiy in 1730. Initially the Russians had their commissioner from Selenginsk deal with border issues, but a border office was set up in Kyakhta in 1783 to liaise with the *dzarguchei,* control movements of people and livestock across the border and supervise trade, particularly the storage of rhubarb purchased by foreign merchants. Many of these were 'Bukharans', Siberian Uzbeks from Tomsk, Tobolsk and Tyumen, trading with the Oirats.

There was frequent wrangling over Qing demands for the return of Mongol refugees fleeing to Russia. They were wanted by the Qing for resettlement with their families in Jungaria, to fight the Oirats. There was a big increase in such refugees in 1755–58, during the anti-Manchu uprisings led by Amarsanaa in Jungaria and Chingunjav in Halh (the Mongolian heartland). In 1762 the Manchus suspended trade through Kyakhta following disagreement over customs duty and in protest at the Russians' refusal to provide a Russian text of the Treaty of Kyakhta, which they wanted to examine so as to avoid differences over the treatment of the refugees. Contraband trade developed between the border posts and was joined by lamas and local officials, some of whom were punished by the Manchus. Official trade was renewed in 1767.

By 1772 Kyakhta was the only legal trading post between Russia and China. Russian exports comprised mostly of furs (78 per cent) and leather. China exported cotton, silk and tea. After another dispute and interruption, trade increased by 70 per cent in the years 1792–1801, and by a further 50 per cent up to 1826. By the end of the 18th century tea made up 30 per cent of Chinese exports, and subsequently cotton exports declined, from 46 per cent in 1802–07 to two per cent in 1831–40. The Qing government had little interest in trade, which was permitted by the Emperor 'out of pity for the poor people of the two countries' and because the Russian Senate had requested it.

The main trading activity took place in the winter months (September to April). Russian imports were carted to Irkutsk and sledded to Makariyev on the Volga, where annual trade fairs were held (June to August) until 1817, when they moved to Nizhniy Novgorod. Trade through Kyakhta doubled in 1830–39, but the 1851 Treaty of Kuldja began to open up East Turkestan to Russian traders. Russian fur exports declined from 50 per cent in 1824–28 to 34 per cent in 1836–40, while imports of Chinese tea rose by 420 per cent in 1800–40 to account for 90 per cent of Chinese exports through Kyakhta. As Russian fabric production rose, shipments of Chinese cotton and silk fell (from 26 and 21 per cent in 1812–17 to 0.4 and 1.8 per cent in 1839–45). China was suffering from a shortage of precious metals, and tea was traded for silver articles. From 1861 restrictions on Chinese imports of gold were removed and the first caravans of gold and silver set out for Peking.

The 1860 Treaty of Peking led to the opening of a Russian consulate in Urga and the Russian customs post in Kyakhta was moved to Irkutsk. Duty-free trade (barter or cash) was introduced in the 50-verst (53.3 km) border zone. These developments led to significantly increased Russian contacts with the Mongols. The development of direct trade in livestock was necessitated by the expansion of gold mining in the Lake Baikal area. Chinese traders became increasingly active in Mongolia. Russian shops opened in Urga. A postal service began in 1862 from Kyakhta to Peking and Tianjin via Urga and Kalgan (Haalgan, Zhangjiakou), but for some time the Manchus resisted introduction of the telegraph.

Russian-Chinese trade through Mongolia fell off sharply in 1870–71 because of a cattle plague, a drop in the number of pilgrims going to Urga following the death of the Mongolian Living Buddha (Khutukhtu, Hutagt, or Bogd Gegeen), and Muslim Dungan (Hui) raids in the south-west. However, for several years in the 1880s the grain harvest in the Lake Baikal region failed, and increased prices encouraged the Mongols to sell grain in Russia. Russian livestock was pastured on the Mongolian side of the border where haymaking and timber felling were also permitted.

After the Opium War (1839–42) the Kyakhta trade was increasingly affected by the opening up of Chinese ports. Russia had only a small merchant fleet and concentrated on developing new overland trade routes into Mongolia from Minusinsk and Biysk through the valleys of the Us, a tributary of the Yenisey, and the Chuya (Chuy), a tributary of the Katun, which enters the river Ob at Biysk. Trade through Uliassutai and Kobdo gradually increased. The Chuya *trakt* or caravan route was improved in 1901–02 to take cart traffic, but otherwise goods were still carried on the backs of horses, bullocks and camels. Navigation of the Upper Yenisey was contemplated, but the numerous rapids prevented this.

With the completion of the Trans-Siberian Railway in 1894, Russia planned construction of access roads and a branch line into Mongolia. Mongolian wool was now mostly exported to western Europe through Tianjin, and the Qing authorities discussed a US plan for construction of a railway from Kalgan to Urga. The collapse of Qing rule and the first world war prevented this, but in 1916 an American-Norwegian company began transporting wool from Urga to Kalgan by lorry.

## The North-western Border and Separation of Tuva

Tuva (Urianhay) lies north of the Tannu-Ola (Tangdy-Uula) mountains at the headwaters of the Yenisey. In 1913 Russia and China issued a joint declaration that 'Autonomous Outer Mongolia comprises the regions under the jurisdiction of the Chinese *ambans* (civil governors) at Urga and Kobdo and the Chinese military governor at Uliassutai', provided that the exact boundaries of Outer Mongolia should be the subject of a subsequent conference. Urianhay was governed by the Kobdo *amban*. In 1914 however, Russia declared a protectorate in Urianhay. When China sought to put Urianhay on the agenda of the 1915 Kyakhta tripartite conference, to obtain recognition of the northern border, the Russians refused to discuss it.

The further history of Tuva during and after the Bolshevik revolution mirrored events in Mongolia. In 1924 many inhabitants of Tuva offered their allegiance to Mongolia, and the congress of the Mongolian People's Revolutionary Party the same year declared Mongolia's wish for Tuva to remain part of Mongolia. Despite objections from the Soviet representative at the congress, it resolved to set up a Mongolian-Russian commission to regulate Tuva's position.

An official Soviet history of Tuva at this time refers to various 'counter-revolutionary uprisings' and ploys 'to split Tuva from the USSR' and 'eliminate the republic's independence'. It describes the purpose of a conference in Kyzyl of representatives of the USSR, Mongolia and Tuva as 'to discuss the Mongol feudalists' aim of uniting Tuva and Mongolia'. However, the conference concluded that the 'elimination of Tuva's independence and its unification with Mongolia does not reflect the views of the basic mass of the Tuvan population'.

The Mongolians were obliged to accept the 1921 declaration of Tuvan independence, and this was confirmed in the Mongol-Tuvan friendship and mutual recognition treaty of August 1926, following which there was an exchange of diplomatic representatives. This treaty was drawn up by Soviet negotiators, who arranged for 16,000 sq. km of Darhat lands west of Lake Hovsgol belonging to Tuva to be given to Mongolia.

Another important revision of the Mongolian-Tuvan border took place in 1930, when it was moved to the alignment of the former Mongol pickets. However, the Tuvans were dissatisfied with this and in 1932 a border commission realigned the border, in some places up to 25 km inside Mongolian territory in the Tes *gol* area. The salt mine at Davst *uul*, north of Lake Uvs, was transferred to Tuva, Mongolian nomads on the border being offered free salt.

In August 1944 the pro-Soviet party and government leaders of Tuva manoeuvred the Little Hural (legislature) into adopting unanimously a resolution that the People's Republic of Tuva should join the USSR. Its admission was decreed by the Presidium of the USSR Supreme Soviet in October of that year. Tuva became an autonomous *oblast* and later an autonomous republic within the RSFSR (Russian Federation).

When Vyacheslav Molotov arrived in Mongolia to take up his post as Soviet ambassador in 1957, the Mongolian Foreign Minister Avarzad claimed that the agreement on Davst *uul* was invalid because it was unratified and had been annulled at talks with the Tuvans in 1940. Molotov had Avarzad removed and a new border agreement was signed in March 1958 which not only confirmed that Davst *uul* was in Tuva, but also redrew the Soviet–Mongolian border across the north-eastern corner of Lake Uvs. As a result, a 7 km strip of Soviet territory cut off from one another two rural districts of Uvs province (Davst and Tes *sum*) which had previously shared a 20 km boundary.

Examining the background to these events in 1990, a Mongolian journalist blamed this unsatisfactory state of affairs on 'external factors', saying: 'This is why we are optimistic about the present Soviet leadership [i.e. Mikhail Gorbachev], which has the wisdom and courage to right this injustice.' In November 1991, during a Tuvan delegation's visit to Mongolia, Mongolia and Tuva concluded an agreement on their border regime. Then and subsequently however it was agreed not to hold official talks on territorial disputes.

Following demarcation of various sections of the Mongolian–Soviet border in 1959–60 and 1977–79, further border agreements between Mongolia and the USSR were concluded in 1976 and 1980. The 1980 agreement, signed by the foreign ministers, was initially valid for 10 years and renewable for five-year periods. It provided for joint inspection of the border every 20 years, regulated responsibility for markers and required the clearing of all vegetation from the border in a five-metre strip on each side the line. A meeting of the Mongolian-Russian interstate joint border inspection commission took place in April 1992.

## Communications Developments in the Soviet Period

With the consolidation of communist rule in Mongolia in the 1920s, Soviet Russia initiated a programme for the upgrading of communications and transport. The main telegraph route ran from Irkutsk via Kyakhta to Urga (renamed Ulan Bator in 1924). Inter-governmental agreements between 1924–30 improved communications with outlying parts of Mongolia, in particular Mondy, Hatgal and Tariat in the area of Lake Hovsgol on Mongolia's northern border; Hovd in western Mongolia, linked to Kosh-Agach in Russia's Gornyy Altai (now Altai Republic); and

Bayantumen (now Choybalsan) in eastern Mongolia, linked to Ulan Bator.

In the 1970s and 1980s, Soviet technicians built radio-relay links across Mongolia from north to south and from east to west through Ulan Bator, where an 'Orbita' satellite ground station was installed. However, the Soviet period left Mongolia with a sad legacy of underdevelopment in the field of telecommunications, without trunk dialling and with only some 50,000 telephones for the whole country. This situation is gradually being rectified, with new links through Asiasat providing a modern international telephone/fax service and automatic exchanges for some Ulan Bator subscribers, and making Mongolian television available throughout the country for the first time.

One of the earliest transport agreements between the two countries (1926) permitted vessels of the Soviet-owned Selenga State Shipping Line to ply the rivers Selenge and Orhon and their tributaries in Mongolia, build wharfs and storehouses and exploit local sources of coal and timber. When the line's shore equipment was handed over to the Mongolians ten years later, the protocol noted the extreme difficulty of operations and the 'negative qualities' of the rivers, which had however been in daily use over navigable stretches of 270 km and 175 km respectively. In 1937 Mongolia leased back five wharfs at Suhbaatar, Ingettolgoy, Usun-Ser, Sharagal and Budun.

A new agreement in 1949 dealt with improvements to navigation including dredging work by the now renamed East Siberian River Shipping Line. Mostly the rivers were used for timber rafting and grain shipments, but during construction of the Trans-Mongolian (Ulan Bator) Railway equipment was transported along the Hara *gol* and Yeroo *gol* as well as the Selenge and Orhon. In 1963 the USSR agreed to promote Mongolian river shipping operations by improving navigation conditions, training crews and undertaking ship repairs at the yard in Ulan-Ude.

In 1934 the Soviets had also provided tugs and barges for operation on Lake Hovsgol between Hatgal and Hanh, the cross-border road link via Mondy with Irkutsk. Bigger ships and two 1,200 metric-ton barges were provided in 1956. Much of the freight carried on this route consisted of petrol and oil (20,000 metric tons a year). Because of concern about environmental damage, oil shipments on Lake Hovsgol were halted in the 1990s.

Construction of Mongolia's first highway, linking Ulan Bator via the Orhon valley with Suhbaatar and Altanbulag on the Soviet border, was begun in 1937 following agreement on a Soviet government loan. This main road was widened and surfaced in the 1960s and then a branch was built in the 1970s from Mongolia's second industrial town, Darhan, to the copper-mining town of Erdenet. Other roads of international importance also follow traditional routes: the old Chuya *trakt* from Biysk and Kosh-Agach to Tashanta, thence into Mongolia and terminating at Tsagaannuur, site of a large freight depot; and the Us *trakt*, from Abakan to Handgayt (Tuva) and onwards into Uvs province.

During a visit to Hovd in 1992, Mongolian President Ochirbat proposed the construction of a new 1,000 km international highway linking Kyzyl, the capital of Tuva, with Ulaangom and Hovd in Mongolia and Urumqi, the capital of Xinjiang. He emphasised the project's potential for Mongolian, Russian and Chinese economic development, but its viability is uncertain.

Passengers, freight and post were carried on Mongolia's first international air route (450 km) between Ulan Bator and Verkhneudinsk (Ulan-Ude) by a Junkers monoplane of the Soviet airline Dobrolet in 1926. After the introduction of regular airmail deliveries and customs formalities on the border two years later, additional landings were made at Altanbulag and Troitskosavsk. The single PR-5 biplane used by Aeroflot on the route from 1930–45 was a civilianised R-5 military aircraft which could carry four passengers or a metric ton of freight. It carried around 1,000 passengers and 50 metric tons of post a year until the second world war, averaging one or two return flights a day.

In the post-war period Aeroflot introduced Li-2 (converted lease–lend Dakota) aircraft and in 1952 re-routed flights to Irkutsk. In 1956 the Mongolian Ministry of People's Army and Public Security Affairs set up an air communications directorate which formed the basis of the Mongolian airline now called MIAT (Mongolian Civil Air Transport). It acquired several Soviet Ilyushin Il-14 twin-engined passenger aircraft for flights to Irkutsk and inter-provincial services, and some Antonov An-2 biplanes for local services. The development of Ulan Bator's Buyant-Uhaa airport under a Soviet-Mongolian agreement of 1961 allowed the introduction of larger Soviet Il-18 aircraft on Aeroflot's Moscow–Ulan Bator route.

Currently replacing its ageing Tupolev Tu-154 and An-2 aircraft, MIAT operates Antonov An-24 and Chinese Yu-12 twin-turboprop airliners on internal services and international routes to Irkutsk, Ulan-Ude, Hohhot and Peking, and two Boeing 727s from Ulan Bator to Moscow and Almaty.

Railway transport developments have had the greatest economic impact on Mongolia. The country's first railway was built in 1937–39, the Soviet Union providing credit for construction of a narrow-gauge line to Ulan Bator's power station from the coal-mine at nearby Nalayh. With the threat of Japanese invasion looming from Manchukuo, the Soviet Union built and operated a single broad-gauge (1,524 mm) line from Borzya on the Trans-Siberian Railway's Manchuria branch to Bayantumen (Choybalsan) in eastern Mongolia. Its length from Ereentsav (Chuluunhoroot), the Mongolian border station opposite Solovyevsk, is 268 km. From Bayantumen the Soviet

Army then built a narrow-gauge (780 mm) line 380.5 km long to Tamsagbulag, which was developed as a military base. After playing an important war-time role these lines and their equipment were handed over to Mongolia in 1956. The narrow-gauge line was abandoned, but the broad-gauge line is still in use. In June 1949 Mongolia and the Soviet Union launched the Ulan Bator Railway Joint Stock Co. to operate a 404 km single-track broad-gauge line being built to Ulan Bator from Naushki, near Kyakhta, on the Russian border. The company acquired a 120 metre strip of land along the entire track and a further 19,000 hectares for coal, timber, storage, etc., and was given the right to lay access tracks, install telegraph lines, build airstrips for aerial survey purposes, ship equipment along inland waterways and employ its own armed guards. Linking central Mongolia with the Trans-Siberian, the line went into operation in December 1950.

Under a Soviet Mongolian agreement with the PRC signed in September 1952, the Naushki–Ulan Bator line was extended to Zamyn-Uud on the Mongolian border with China, and the PRC undertook to build a standard-gauge line from Jining, north of Peking, to Erhlien (Erenhot, Ereen), opposite Zamyn-Uud. Facilities were built at Ereen for jacking up the rolling stock and switching the bogies. Regular through traffic opened with ceremonies in Ulan Bator on 31 December 1955 and at the Chinese border on 3 January 1956.

The throughput of the trans-Mongolian line (1,100 km, 35 sidings and passing loops) was initially set at 12 pairs of trains every 24 hours, but planned to double. This enormous project involved the construction of over 500 bridges, main stations in Ulan Bator and six other towns, seven diesel generating plants and associated power lines, locomotive servicing and repair depots, telephone exchanges, a hospital, housing, schools, wells and pipelines, and several building materials enterprises and road vehicle maintenance shops. In 1957 the Ulan Bator Railway employed one-fifth of Mongolia's industrial work-force.

The Ulan Bator Railway was the key to Mongolia's rapid economic development in the 1960s, even though revenue from transit freight fell off rapidly with the onset of the Sino-Soviet ideological and territorial dispute. Deliveries of heavy machinery promoted Mongolia's industrialisation; access to Eastern European markets became easier; and improvement of the transport infrastructure led to exploitation of new mineral deposits for home and foreign consumption: oil at Zuunbayan (production ceased in 1967), coal at Sharyn Gol and Baganuur, fluorspar at Bor-Ondor, copper and molybdenum at Erdenet, uranium at Marday. By 1983 mineral exports accounted for 30 per cent of all exports. High-voltage power line equipment supplied by the USSR linked the central Mongolian grid to Gusinoozersk power station in the Buryat Republic and the Siberian grid.

The economic situation has changed greatly since 1990–92, following the withdrawal of Russian military and civilian personnel and cutbacks in Russian aid, amidst the disruption caused by the collapse of command economies and tentative moves towards privatisation. From 1980–85 Mongolian transit rail freight rose from 259,200 to 1,473,800 metric tons per annum, but by 1990 it had dropped to 978,400 tons. Between 1989–92 transit rail traffic fell by 86.7 per cent, rail freight turnover by 49.4 per cent, and the amount of freight carried by rail by 39.1 per cent. The decline in rail freight traffic continued in the period 1991–93, from 2.9 billion to 2.5 billion metric ton/km. Mongolia is still dependent on this link with the Trans-Siberian Railway for all its oil and petrol supplies, which in 1990–92 were cut from 800,000 to 500,000 metric tons a year and have been further reduced since then.

However, the growing emphasis on trade with and through China has encouraged the redevelopment of Zamyn-Uud freight depot, with considerable Japanese financial assistance. Meanwhile, China has extended its standard-gauge railway line from Ereen to the depot and completed an electric power line to Zamyn-Uud, the first to link Mongolia with China's grid.

## The Southern Border and Relations with China

In view of Mongolia's history, it is perhaps ironic that Mongolia's future economic prosperity is so closely linked with China, which offers aid, trade and easier access to third markets. The bitter legacy of Qing rule, China's unwillingness for a quarter-century to recognise Mongolia's independence, China's claims (sometimes official, sometimes unofficial) on Mongolian territory, and the persecution of China's Mongols during Mao's 'cultural revolution' still cast a deep shadow on relations between the two countries.

Powerless as it was to assert its claim in the face of Soviet Russian entrenchment in Mongolia, the Republic of China did not surrender its sovereignty until after the Second World War. At the Yalta conference in February 1945 the UK and US agreed to Stalin's call for preservation of the *status quo* in Mongolia. The USSR would recognise the independence and territorial integrity of the People's Republic of Mongolia. China eventually agreed to 'recognise Outer Mongolia within its existing borders if a plebiscite confirms the people's will to be independent'. The plebiscite took place under UN auspices on 20 October, and the Mongols voted virtually unanimously for independence. The Republic of China recognised Mongolia on 6 January 1946 and established diplomatic relations in February.

After the establishment of the People's Republic of China in 1949

Mongolia was recognised by the new regime in Peking, which signed an economic and cultural co-operation agreement with Mongolia in 1952, a treaty of friendship and mutual assistance in 1960, and a border treaty in 1962. After joint demarcation of the border a protocol listing all 639 markers was signed in June 1964 by the foreign ministers of the two countries. The protocol also specified border maintenance measures and joint inspections every five years.

For a long period Sino-Mongolian relations were soured by the 'cultural revolution' in China and the Sino-Soviet dispute, during which Mao renewed his earlier proposals for the amalgamation of Mongolia with Inner Mongolia AR, and China published maps showing Mongolia as part of China. Chinese workers abandoned unfinished construction projects in Mongolia and returned to China, China's trade with Mongolia and the USSR plummeted, and military tension built up on the once again disputed borders following clashes over demarcation and incursions. It was not until the 1980s that relations with China began to return to normal.

In doing business with Mongolia China has a number of advantages over any other potential trading partner – short land routes, balance of mutual advantage, and familiarity with the market. As Mongolia's trade with Russia has fallen off, so its trade with China has grown. China also has an increased strategic interest in Mongolia, following the collapse of the USSR and the decline of Russian interest in Mongolia. At the same time there is evidence that the Chinese authorities are cracking down on Inner Mongolian dissidents and are suspicious of contacts between Mongols from the two countries.

Students from Inner Mongolia studying in Ulan Bator appealed to the UN in 1991 for help in obtaining the release of some Inner Mongols imprisoned by the Chinese authorities for political activities. Following PRC President Yang Shangkun's visit to Mongolia in the autumn of 1991, some of these students were withdrawn and sent home. Circulars issued by the Inner Mongolia AR Committee of the Communist Party of China (CPC) have warned repeatedly against 'incitement of splitting activities' (ethnic division) and threatened to punish people trying to 'destroy the unity of the motherland'.

In 1992 foreign journalists in China got to hear of a supposed 'movement against unification of the three Mongolias' in China and a leaked 'secret document' claiming that Mongolia and the Buryat Republic together with Inner Mongolia were part of China. The reports were denied by the Chinese authorities and the denials were reprinted in the Russian press. Mongolian Prime Minister Byambasuren, who had just returned from a visit to Peking, declared that China respected Mongolia's independence. The Mongolian Ministry of Foreign Relations stated in May 1992 that Mongolia had friendly ties with both Russia and China.

Nonetheless, another internal circular from the Inner Mongolia AR Committee of the CPC, dated February 1994, expressed similar concern about 'national independence' and the 'Union of the Three Mongolias'. Peking fears talk of the loss of Inner Mongolia to a united 'greater Mongolia' led by independent Mongolia because of the threat to China's unity. Mongolia fears absorption into a united 'greater Mongolia' led by China because of the threat to its independence. The Buryats have indicated that politically, they are sticking with Russia. Despite the resurgence of Mongol nationalism since 1990 and Ulan Bator's founding of international organisations for Mongol cultural development, the kind of Pan-Mongolism Japan backed in the 1930s is a lost cause.

Just as the Kyakhta/Altanbulag–Naushki/Suhbaatar node dominates Mongolia's northern border, the Zamyn-Uud/Ereen rail-road link is the only significant crossing point along the whole length of the Sino-Mongolian border. Much of the border, which is fenced, runs through uninhabited desert and semi-desert, except for the Hailar area to the east. The river Herlen (Kerulen) is unnavigable. In the west Mongolia is separated from Xinjiang by the Altai mountains and the Jungarian desert. There is a long-standing border crossing at Bulgan *sum* in Hovd province, giving access by international bus to Qinghe county and Urumqi, which is 580 km from Hovd town. Eight new border crossing points were agreed between Mongolia and the PRC in June 1991 and subsequently opened for local traffic according to an irregular schedule.

It seems that the once predominant northern outlet for Mongolian trade will give way to the 'southern gate'. Because of its dependence on the Trans-Siberian Railway in trading with third countries and the extra distance, time and cost entailed in shipping goods by this route, Mongolia has been seeking better access to the sea through China. On 26 August 1991 Mongolia and the PRC concluded an important agreement on Mongolian transit access to and from the sea. For the first time in an international agreement Mongolia is referred to as having 'special needs as a land-locked state' (in Mongolian, *dalayd gartsguy oron* – a country without an exit to the sea). The agreement detailed the rail and shipping facilities made available to Mongolia at Tianjin's Xingang international port and provided for use of the port by 'vessels flying the national flag of the land-locked state'.

A quarter of Mongolia's exports passed through Tianjin in 1991. The Joint Sea Freight Co., Tianjin, joined with the Mongolian Tuushin Co. and the Hongkong Hilco to form a company to operate a Mongolian flag-carrier with a Chinese crew. The company planned to handle 100,000 metric tons of exports a year. The transit agreement was followed up with a road freight agreement. However, China is said to be charging almost as much as Russia does for use of the Trans-Siberian route.

## Firm Borders for a Sea-going 'tiger'

Welcoming Chinese President Yang Shangkun's visit to Mongolia and the signing of the agreement on Mongolian access to the sea, the Society of Mongolian Sea-Lovers issued a statement expressing readiness to co-operate with Chinese organisations to promote implementation of the agreement. The society took out a large advertisement to publicise Mongolia's plight as a land-locked country and to draw attention to the proximity of Tianjin compared with the remoteness of Nakhodka, Leningrad and Odessa ports via the Trans-Siberian Railway.

Not long after the society published an 'appeal to all Mongol nationals' (abroad) from the Mongols 'who remained behind to keep watch over the hearth' for moral, material and financial support in gaining Mongolian access to the world's oceans, in provision of vessels, training of seamen and legal assistance. The appeal recalled that at one time, during the Mongol Empire, the Mongols had ventured into the oceans, but since then they had given up their seafaring ways, forgotten how to swim and grown afraid of the water.

Meanwhile, the Mongolian Social Democratic Party set up a Movement for the Integrity of the Sacred Border which published its own version of a border law in February 1991. It contained 55 articles on measures for border protection, defence of territorial integrity and operation of border crossing points.

Mongolia's 1992 Constitution has a special article devoted to the border:

> Article 4. (1) The integrity of Mongolia's territory and borders shall be inviolable. (2) Mongolia's borders shall be guaranteed by law. (3) Stationing of foreign forces on Mongolia's territory or their transit through its territory and across the state borders shall be prohibited unless provided for by law.

Soviet forces sent to Mongolia during the Sino-Soviet ideological and territorial dispute in the 1960s had totalled at its height over 100,000 men with tanks, APCs, artillery, missiles and aircraft. As Sino-Soviet relations improved after Mikhail Gorbachev's Vladivostok speech, Soviet units were gradually withdrawn from Mongolia and the last of the soldiers left in 1992.

The Mongolian Border Law, adopted in October 1993, says that the border may be crossed only at designated crossing points. Non-citizens are banned from the 30 km border zone, non-residents require a permit to visit it, and residents must have an official stamp in their 'citizen's passport'. The Border Troops (*khiliyn tsereg*) control all activity in the 5 km border strip. Local government organisations ensure that border regulations are observed and recruit border defence volunteers, who can check people's identity documents in the border zone and detain illegal border crossers.

In the past Mongolia has always been sensitive about any suggestion of disagreement with its neighbours about the borders or border territory. In March 1990, for example, the public relations department of the Mongolian Ministry of Foreign Affairs issued a statement:

> Our country has treaties and agreements with the USSR and PRC concerning the border and there is no question of any territorial conflict. The border is constantly checked in co-operation with the two countries.

Nonetheless, a brief history of the formation of Mongolia's borders, published in 1992, was unusual for its detailed listing of territory 'lost' by Mongolia as a result of border adjustments: the western part of Hovd province (Altai district) to Xinjiang in 1915; the Davst *uul* area of Uvs province to Tuva in 1932; 5,807 sq. km of northern Mongolia to the USSR in 1957; land east of the present border with China to Manchukuo in 1940; land between the new and 'historical' borders to China in 1962; and unspecified border areas to the USSR in 1975.

Even if there are no serious inter-state disagreements over Mongolia's borders – and that remains to be seen in the new situation, when there is no political need to conceal them – the international regulation of the existing borders will clearly continue.

In 1991 illegal crossings of the borders with Russia and China rose sharply, by 60 and 30 per cent respectively. Small-scale illegal crossing of the border has been a routine problem for Mongolia and its neighbours, which have regularly detained smugglers and poachers and also expelled visitors who fail to register, outstay their permits, or set up illegal businesses. In recent years cattle rustling has been particularly rife on the Mongolia–Tuva border, and several attempts have been made by the authorities on each side of the border to put a stop to it. The measures include increased patrolling by Mongolia's Border Troops.

Currently only one of the nine crossing points on the Mongolian–Chinese border is permanently open to all travellers. About half of the 40 crossing points on the Mongolian–Russian border are seasonal, many of the rest have no proper roads, and only one is permanently open to all travellers. Perhaps in celebration of the new freedom of movement, legal crossings of Mongolia's borders by people and vehicles in the first hundred days of 1992 were up by 100 and 150 per cent respectively on the year before. This rate of growth has now begun to fall off, with the imposition in 1995 of a visa regime to control the flow of travellers to and from Russia. As land-locked Mongolia gradually develops new transit links for freight as well as passengers, more crossing points will need to be expanded and operated on a permanent basis.

In 1990 Mongolia's first democratically elected government adopted a programme of privatisation and transition from the command economy to market relations, in the hope of eventually becoming another Asian 'tiger', like Hong Kong, Singapore, Taiwan, etc. However, the country was soon overwhelmed by problems arising from the backwardness of its industry, hard currency shortages and the collapse of the traditional trading partnership with Russia. To help Mongolia feed its people, resolve its immediate economic and financial difficulties and begin to rebuild its infrastructure, hundreds of millions of dollars' worth of aid in the form of grants and loans has been given by the IMF, World Bank, the ADB and UN agencies as well as individual governments, particularly Japan and the US. The annual donors' conferences are held in Tokyo.

If it is to overcome the disadvantages of land-lockedness and attract large-scale long-term investment to develop the new market economy and export trade, Mongolia needs to liberalise its laws and build up international confidence in its stability, flexibility, reliability and industriousness. It may then one day become a 'tiger', closer to the hub than to the rim of Asian development.

## SOURCES

Alatalu , T., 'Tuva – a state reawakens', *Soviet Studies* 44/5 (May 1992) pp.881–95.
An, Tai-Sung, *The Sino-Soviet territorial dispute* (Philadelphia: Westminster Press 1973).
Chimitdordzhiyev, Sh.B., *Rossiya i Mongoliya* (Moscow: Oriental Literature Publishers 1987).
Dolgikh, F.I. and Tserendorj, G. (eds) *Sovetsko-mongolskiye otnosheniya 1921–1974* (Moscow: International Relations Publishers 1979).
Golman, M.I. and Slesarchuk, G.I. (eds) *Sovetsko-mongolskiye otnosheniya 1921–1966* (Moscow: Nauka 1966).
Government of the People's Republic of China. *Agreement between the government of the MPR and the government of the PRC on the access to and from the sea and transit transport by Mongolia through China's territory* (in English) (Peking, 1991).
Higgins, A., 'Peking seeks to crush the embryo of a reborn Mongolia', *The Independent*, 11 June 1991.
Khokhlov, A.N., 'The Kyakhta trade and its effect on Russian and Chinese policy in the 18th and 19th centuries', in S.L. Tikhvinskiy (ed.), *Chapters from the history of Russo-Chinese relations in the 17th–19th centuries* (Moscow: Progress 1985).
Mongolian newspapers. *Ardyn Erh, Unen, Ug, Mongol Messenger* (various dates).
Sanders, A.J.K., 'Mongolia's new constitution: blueprint for democracy', *Asian Survey* XXXII/6 (June 1992) pp.506–20.
Sanders, A.J.K., *Mongolia: politics, economics and society* (London: Pinter 1987).
Sanders, A.J.K., 'The border dispute', in Father Ladany SJ (ed) *China News Analysis* (Hong Kong, China News Analysis 1975).
Sanders, A.J.K., *The People's Republic of Mongolia: A general reference guide* (London: OUP 1968).
Sanders, A.J.K., 'Mongolia', in *The Far East and Australasia* (London: Europa various years).
Sanders, A.J.K., 'Mongolia', in Robert Delfs, Michael Westlake (eds) *Asia Yearbook* (Hong

Kong: Far Eastern Economic Review, various years).

Sanders, A.J.K., 'Mongolia', in Alan J Day (ed) *The Annual Register* (Harlow: Longman, various years).

Translations on Communist China. *Sino-Mongolian border protocol* (Washington: JPRS 1971).

Stefashin, V.V., 'Variants for the development of the military-political situation in the Far East' (in Russian), in *Problemy Dalnego Vostoka* Nos.1, 2, 3 (Moscow: Institute of the Far East, USSR Academy of Sciences 1992).

Tang, Peter S.H., *Russian and Soviet policy in Manchuria and Outer Mongolia 1911–1931* (Durham NC: Duke University Press 1959).

Toka, S.K.(ed.), *Istoriya Tuvy* (Moscow: Nauka 1964).

Vedomosti Verkhovnogo Soveta SSSR. *Agreement on the Mongolian–Soviet border regime, co-operation and mutual aid on border issues 26 November 1980* (in Russian) (Moscow, 1981).

# Land-locked Laos: Dilemmas of Development at the Edge of the World

## JONATHAN RIGG

The Lao People's Democratic Republic (Lao PDR) receives little attention from the world's press, and equally little from academics. This is partly due to the long-standing difficulties of conducting field research in Laos and partly, no doubt, because of the country's low international profile. With a population of 4.6 million, a GDP of US$1.5 billion, total exports of just US$300 million, per capita income of US$335 – making it one of the poorest countries in the world – and in large part isolated from the world community from the final victory of the Pathet Lao in 1975 until the early 1990s, Laos has neither figured prominently in the world's economy, nor on the world's political stage (table 1). When the Lao PDR has received attention, it has invariably been through the lens of the Vietnam War which still casts a shadow over the countries of Indochina.

TABLE 1

LAOS: BASIC STATISTICS

| | |
|---|---|
| Land area | 236,800 sq. km |
| Population (1994) | 4.7 million |
| Population in urban areas (1994) | 21per cent |
| Life expectancy (1994) | 52 years |
| Infant mortality | 92/1,000 live births |
| GDP (1994) | US$1.534bn |
| GNP/capita (1994) | US$320 |
| GDP/capita (PPP$ 1991) | $1,760 |
| Economic growth | |
| 1984–1987 | 3.2per cent/year |
| 1987–1990 | 6.5per cent/year |
| 1990–1994 | 6.2per cent/year |
| Imports (1994) | US$564m |
| Exports (1994) | US$300m |

Note: some of the above statistics are prone to wide margins of error

*Sources*: World Bank (1996); UNDP (1995)

Among Laos' various claims to fame, is the fact that it is the only land-locked country in Southeast Asia (see map 1). Since 1975, when the Communist Pathet Lao achieved final and full control over the country, and the collapse of the former Soviet Union, Laos found itself a victim of the

MAP 1

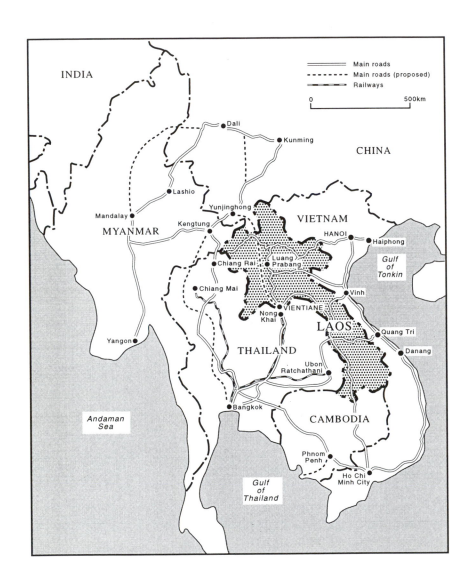

stand-off between East and West. The Cold War was reflected in a mirror image confrontation between the command economies of Indochina and the market economies of Asean.[1] Laos was caught within this maelstrom and suffered accordingly.

This short paper aims to do just two things. First, to look at the difficulties of overland transport in Laos; and second, to examine the extent to which the country's land-locked condition has accentuated these difficulties, focusing particularly on the period since 1975. However before beginning, it should be stressed that any work on Laos – and in this regard Laos mirrors the experience of many other Least Developed Countries – must contend with a general dearth of information, and an even greater shortage of accurate statistics. Indeed, one of the principal problems facing the United Nations Development Programme (UNDP) as it tries to co-ordinate aid to Laos is to know, even at an elemental level, the state of the economy and where the principal economic difficulties lie. An unpublished World Bank assessment of the country, for example, opens with the admission that the figures on which the report is based 'constitute educated guesses rather than confirmed facts', while the UNDP, in highlighting the country's principal development constraints highlights 'insufficient information on the country's key physical, social, economic and climatic variables...'[2] The lack of accurate information is partly due to a very real absence of data created by a combination of poverty, administrative weaknesses, the isolated and rugged nature of large areas of the country, and by the massive dislocations caused by an extended period of war and civil conflict. However, this is further compounded by the inaccuracy of the data that do exist. This partly reflects a lack of skilled personnel and funds to undertake data collection. But equally important has been the political imperative among government departments and individual bureaucrats – until very recently – of demonstrating progress in achieving targets. Sometimes, it seems, officials were reluctant to let 'reality' get in the way of this paramount objective.[3] It should be noted, however, that since the early 1990s, with encouragement from the UNDP, there has been some progress in improving the range and accuracy of statistics.[4] In 1995, for example, the National Statistical Centre (NSC) of the Committee for Planning and Co-operation in Vientiane published its first set of 'basic statistics'[5] and the country's first expenditure and consumption survey.[6] Even so, the NSC admits that many of the figures presented in the former document are based on data sets which are 'many years' old.[7]

This acute lack of information is becoming increasingly pertinent as Laos proceeds further down the road of economic reform. The so-called New Economic Mechanism (NEM) – in Lao, *chin thanakaan mai* ('new thinking') or *kanpatiphup setthakit* (the 'reform economy') – was introduced in the latter part of the 1980s. In essence the introduction of the NEM has involved a dramatic, and continuing, shift from a centrally controlled command economy to a market-oriented system. Most important, and most dramatic, has been the speed and intensity with which the NEM has been introduced since it was adopted by the Party Congress of 1986. Rather than the sometimes piecemeal approach adopted by many other reform-minded command economies during the same period, the government of the Lao PDR opted for a bold and rapid restructuring and reorientation of the economy (see table 2).

The Third Five-Year Plan (1991–1995) was drawn up reflecting the ethos of the NEM. It stressed indicative planning, the role of the market and the private sector in achieving development targets, and left the state to concentrate resources on upgrading and expanding the country's physical and social infrastructures. Central to the NEM is the appreciation that Laos must integrate more fully into the regional and global economies if it is to benefit – economically – from being located within one of the world's most dynamic regions. For much of the period since 1975, Laos has been an isolated backwater, and the rapid growth experienced by its neighbour across the Mekong River – Thailand – has scarcely impinged on the country. One key prerequisite of greater integration has already been addressed: political rapprochement with the West, Asean, and Thailand in particular. However, from an economic stand-point, an equally important element in the equation must be a significant improvement in Laos' access to neighbouring countries, and through them with the wider world. It is in this regard that the country's land-locked condition and extremely limited network of roads is particularly pertinent and which is discussed below.

## Laos: the Geographical, Human and Historical Contexts

The Lao PDR encompasses a land area of 235,690 square kilometres. Bordered by Vietnam, Cambodia, Thailand, China's Yunnan province, and Myanmar (formerly Burma), Laos is land-locked and has no easy access route to the sea (see map 1). Its southern portion is neatly delineated by the Mekong River to the west and by the mountains of the Annamite chain to the east. In the north, the country is almost entirely upland in character, with the exception of a ribbon of lowland extending along the valley of the Mekong River and its tributaries. It is here that Vientiane (Wiang Chan), the capital, is located as well as the former royal capital of Luang Prabang. About half of the land remains forested, and only about 2–4 per cent is said to be cultivated. Most of this agricultural land is found in the south of the country where forests are sparser and where expanses of lowland suited to cropping are more extensive.

TABLE 2

LAOS: LANDMARKS OF ECONOMIC REFORM, 1975–1994

**1975**  *Dec.*:   Full and final victory of the Communist Pathet Lao

**1982**  Reform first touted

**1985**  Pilot studies of financial autonomy in selected state-run industries

**1986**  Decentralisation of decision-making to the provinces including provincial tax administration; Freeing-up the market in rice and other samples
*Nov.*:   NEM endorsed by the Party Congress

**1987**  Restrictions on the cross-provincial movement of agricultural produce abolished; barriers to external trade reduced; provincial authorities charged with the responsibility of providing health and education services
*June*:   prices of most essentials market-determined

**1988**  Forced procurement of strategic goods at below market price abolished; reduction in public sector employment; tax reforms introduced; private sector involvement in sectors previously reserved as state monopolies permitted; introduction of new investment law
*March*:   prices of fuel, cement, machinery and vehicles freed; tax reforms enacted; state and commercial banking sectors separated; state enterprises made self-reliant and autonomous; explicit recognition of the rights of households and the private sector to use land and private property
*June*:   nation-wide elections held for 2,410 positions at the district level
*July*:   multiple exchange rate abolished; liberal foreign investment code introduced; payment of wages in kind abolished

**1989**  *June*:   second tax reform enacted
*Oct.*:   first joint venture bank with a foreign bank begins operation, the Joint Development Bank

**1990**  *March*:   privatisation ('disengagement') law introduced
*June*:   key economic laws covering contracts, property, banking and inheritance discussed by National Assembly
*July*:   State Bank (Central Bank) of the Lao PDR established and fiscal management of the economy formally handed over to the new bank

**1992**  Thai Military Bank begins operating a full branch in Vientiane
*Jan.*:   Commercial Bank and Financial Institutions Act introduced

**1993**  Accelerated privatisation programme announced
*Dec.*:   removal of last quantitative restrictions and licensing requirements for imports

**1994**  *March*:   new investment and labour laws passed in March by the National Assembly, to be enforced within 60 days. As an incentive to foreign investors, the investment law lowers some import taxes and the tax on net profit, streamlines the approval process and ends the foreign investment period limit of 15 years.

*Source*:  Jonathan Rigg, *Southeast Asia: The Human Landscape of Modernisation and Development* (London: Routledge, 1997).

The Lao economy is arguably the least developed in Southeast Asia. According to the 1996 *World Development Report*, and bearing in mind the data deficiencies noted above, life expectancy at birth is 52 years, 40 per cent of children under five are malnourished, 78 per cent of the labour force remains in agriculture, and only 28 per cent of the population have access to safe water.[8] The ethnically diverse population is officially divided, by ecological zone, into three groups: the wet rice-cultivating *Lao Loum* of the lowlands, who are numerically dominant, constituting over half of the total population; the *Lao Theung* or Midland Lao who occupy the mountain slopes and make up about a quarter of the population; and the *Lao Soung*, or Upland Lao, who live in the high mountains and practice shifting cultivation, and who represent less than a fifth of Laos' total population. In a number of respects this division of the country's population into three is unsatisfactory. The categories were invented by the Pathet Lao in an effort to forge a national identity and to make the point that all the people of Laos are 'Lao' and therefore Laotian. Ethnographically the groups make less sense and over-simplify Laos' ethnic jigsaw.[9]

It has often been stated that these three groups – divided by culture, economy and ecology – represent three separate Lao PDRs. Although slowly improving communications and the spread of the cash economy is beginning to break down these barriers, it is still true that over large areas social and economic intercourse between the three categories, and even between groups within each category, is limited. It is also true that the division does not just reflect differences of geography, economy and society, but also of political power and influence. The Lao government is dominated by Lao Loum and some commentators suggest that the Lao Soung and Lao Theung are regarded as primitive, even uncivilised, by their Buddhist, lowland-dwelling compatriots. Trankell, for example, writes that the upland groups '…are thought of [by those in government] as backward and less susceptible to socio-economic development…'[10] Stuart-Fox finds this perception reflected in a lack of convergence between Lao Loum and the other peoples that make up the country, and in an approach to development that sometimes discriminates against upland ('minority') groups:

> It is clearly essential for Laos today to reinforce steps already taken towards creating a national political culture…. Encouragement of Lao nationalism remains a priority, alone capable of countering Lao Loum exclusivism and nepotism. The contemporary historian can only be dismayed at signs since 1975 that the commitment of the party – in practice rather than theory – may be wavering. Schools and clinics in minority regions have been closed first when finance was short, and positive discrimination, despite some commendable attempts, has gone nowhere near far enough.[11]

Between 1863 and 1954, Laos was a colony of France and administered as part of French Indochina. During this period – technically-speaking – Laos was not land-locked; it only became so after independence. Although France did make some attempt to improve Laos' physical infrastructure – recognising efficient communications to be essential to economic progress – the challenge of the terrain proved too great. A road was built along the Mekong River from Pakse in the south to Luang Prabang in the north; a short, 5km-long railway was constructed to trans-ship goods being carried along the Mekong River to avoid the rapids at Khone in the south; and a limited telegraph network was provided. Roads were also built to promote the integration of Indochina as an integrated economic unit. Routes 7, 8 and 9 which all cross the Annamite chain to Vietnam's South China Sea coast were constructed, while route 13 which runs southwards into Cambodia (Phnom Penh) and from there to Saigon (Ho Chi Minh City) was built during World War II (see maps 1 and 2). However, plans to build a railway from Thakhek on the Mekong (opposite the Thai town of Nakhon Phanom) to Vietnam's South China Sea coast never materialised – only 18km of the projected 188km line was built.[12] These efforts on the part of the French were generally unsuccessful in realising any significant increase in the movement of goods between Laos and Vietnam and Cambodia. Routes 7, 8 and 9 were not all-weather roads and were impassable during the wet season. Hardstone writes:

> The east-west transit from the Vietnamese coast in Laos was, however, a totally unproductive venture from the stand-point of communications engineering and the lack of commercial traffic on even the routes which did exist served only to underline this fact.[13]

As Stuart-Fox points out, there are, very occasionally, advantages to being an isolated backwater. The French envisaged Laos as a resource-rich annex to Vietnam. Had the railway from Thakhek to Vietnam been built, and had the Second World War not intervened to interrupt these plans, then Laos 'might well have been effectively absorbed within a greater Vietnam'.[14] This notion of Laos being linked – and subservient – politically and economically with its more powerful neighbour to the east, has also been a feature of relations between the two countries since 1975. As is discussed below, road links between Laos and Vietnam have been markedly improved and there has also been some evidence of Vietnamese settlement in Laos (so-called Vietnamisation) as well as the secondment of Vietnamese military commanders and political cadres to the Lao army.[15] Reflecting these close links, and using characteristic hyperbole, while Lao officials have been reported as saying that the affection shared between themselves and the Vietnamese is 'deeper than the waters of the Mekong River',[16] the

MAP 2

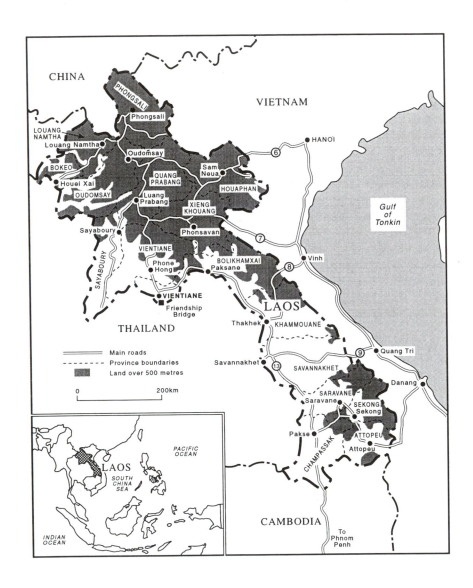

- Main roads
- - - - - Province boundaries
- Land over 500 metres

0      200km

Vietnamese in their turn have talked of a relationship that is 'closer than lips and teeth'.[17] Lao and Vietnamese officials have seen the relationship between their two countries as one of interdependence.[18] This view is founded partly on 'realities' of economy and geography, and partly on their shared revolutionary history. It is even said that Lao cadres are inculcated with the notion that solidarity between the three countries of Indochina is an immutable 'law of history'.[19]

In the case of Laos, it is important to stress that the country is by far the weakest state in mainland Southeast Asia. As land-lockedness necessarily involves maintaining close relations with neighbouring countries to guarantee access to the sea, geo-political issues take on heightened importance. Stuart-Fox offers the thought that the 'very cultural similarity between Thai and Lao has constituted a threat of national extinction for the Lao, for if 80 per cent of all ethnic Lao can be absorbed with the Thai state [in the North-eastern region of Thailand], why not the remainder?'.[20] In essence, Laos lacks the military and economic resources to guarantee its security and therefore has had to try to maintain friendly relations with neighbouring states – whatever the ideological differences and economic costs. It would not be going too far to say that Laos' successful economic development – in its own terms – is contingent upon maintaining improved relations with Bangkok and, to a lesser extent, Hanoi.

## Poor and Weak: Managing Land-locked Laos

Laos' land-locked condition has obstructed the country's integration into the regional and world economies. Physically, it has meant costly trans-shipment of goods through either Thailand or Vietnam; and politically it has meant that Laos has been dependent upon the goodwill of larger, and considerably more powerful, neighbours. But there are two – not mutually exclusive – facets to Laos' transport difficulties. On the one hand there is the question of the country's land-locked condition. But equally important are the difficulties of transportation within the country, irrespective of the additional difficulties that being land-locked bestows. The importance of these two linked impediments to Laos' development are highlighted in a 1989 UNDP report in which three out of six identified 'development constraints' highlight the twin issues of land-lockedness and insufficient physical infrastructure. The three are: 'economic and social fragmentation since many parts of the country are physically isolated...'; 'insufficient physical infrastructure'; and 'high transportation costs, particularly for exports, because of the country's land-locked position'.[21]

## The Environment of Transport and Communications in Laos

The Lao government considers the upgrading of transport and communications to be possibly its most important task. Through the period 1986–1990, government expenditure on transport averaged 40 per cent of total expenditure and up to 20 per cent of total investment has been allocated to road construction and improvement alone.[22] While in the 1991/92–1995/96 Public Investment Programme 40 per cent of total planned outlays were allocated to the transport sector – the highest for any sector.[23] Even so, the stock of roads is extremely limited: of 10,000km of roads, it is thought that only about 20 per cent are sealed and most of these are in chronically poor condition.[24] Even route 13, the national artery which runs from the old royal capital of Luang Prabang in the north, through Vientiane and from there south along the Mekong river to the Cambodian border, is only part made-up. This is despite the fact that it has been targeted for special attention by the government and international aid agencies.[25]

The problem facing the government as it attempts to upgrade Laos' road network has three facets. First, 80 per cent of the country is classified as mountainous, presenting a considerable engineering challenge. This, allied with a monsoon climate where torrential storms are a yearly occurrence, means that roads are difficult and expensive to build and need to be constantly monitored and repaired. A second facet is Laos' population density which, at 17 people/km$^2$ is one of the lowest in Asia. As a government report prepared for a meeting on Least Developed Countries in Geneva in 1989 stated, 'the cost per capita of providing the necessary infrastructure is in many cases prohibitive'.[26] In the 1993/94 budget, out of total state investment of 122 billion kip (US$168 million), just 57.6 billion kip (US$79 million) was allocated for 'communications, transportation, postal services and construction'.[27]

A third facet is the damage sustained during the war in Indochina. It has been estimated that 2.1 million tonnes of explosives were dropped on Laos in the clandestine American attempt to stifle the flow of arms along the Ho Chi Minh Trail from North Vietnam, through Laos, into South Vietnam (see map 1). The Lao PDR has the dubious honour of being, in per capita terms, the most heavily bombed country on earth – some 2 tonnes of ordnance per person.[28] This damage is still being repaired, some 20 years after the war in Indochina came to an end. Unexploded bombs, shells and mines mean that the legacy of the war does not just mean a continuing drain on economic resources, but also a threat to human life. In 1993 unexploded ordnance disturbed mostly by farmers as they cleared or prepared land for agriculture killed 100 people in Xieng Khouang province alone.[29]

Given the government's efforts to improve the country's road network, and the significant proportion of foreign development assistance which is devoted to infrastructural development, there is no doubt that overland communications are improving. The stretch of route 13 which links the capital, Vientiane and the old royal capital of Luang Prabang – a distance of some 225 km – was little more than a track over much of its length until 1996, when upgrading work was finally completed.[30] But even so severe deficiencies remain. Many roads are impassable after heavy rains, and even in the dry season and on main inter-provincial routes average speeds range between 30 and 50 km/hr (see table 3). Those who can afford it, when they travel between, say, Vientiane in the north and Pakse in the south, cross the Mekong to Thailand, use Thai buses and roads to follow the river south, and then nip back across to Laos. Even with a longer journey in terms of distance and two border crossings, it is still much faster – and considerably more comfortable.

The Mekong, one of the great rivers of Southeast Asia, is navigable for 1,150km (with another 875km being seasonally navigable) and might offer an alternative to road transportation in some areas. But as yet, river transport remains poorly developed. To try and rectify this situation, the Australian government allocated A$3.3 million to upgrade port facilities between 1986 and 1991, focusing upon Luang Prabang, Tha Deua, Khone and Houei Sai. Although there is little doubt that there is considerable potential to develop river transport still further, during the dry season low water levels would make the movement of large river boats hazardous. In addition, it seems that as road transport improves, so goods and passengers are switching from river to road. Passenger ferries between Vientiane and Thakhek, for example, are reported to be less frequent now that the road has been surfaced and new (and much faster) bus services introduced.

It virtually goes without saying that the Lao PDR's infrastructural deficiencies do not relate only to road and river transportation. There are also grave shortages of hospitals, schools, water facilities, power supplies, and telecommunications links – reflecting the country's status as one of the world's poorest countries. Many towns, even of provincial status, lack 24-hour electricity supplies and instead rely on generators for the evening hours. It could be argued that the difficulties of providing these other facilities is a product of poor transportation and the costs, in time and money, of gaining access to many areas. However, they are also part of the same condition.

**The Politics and Economics of Access to the Sea**

Laos' severe internal transport difficulties have been reinforced and accentuated by its land-locked condition. Although the latter cannot be

TABLE 3

TRANSPORT TIMES IN LAOS (MAY 1996)

| Route | Distance | Time | Average speed | Road conditions |
|---|---|---|---|---|
| *Roads north from Vientiane* | | | | |
| Vientiane to Van Vieng | 160km | 3 hrs | 53 km/hr | good, surfaced road |
| Van Vieng to Luang Prabang | | 13 hrs | – | upgrading completed end 1996 |
| *Roads south from Vientiane* | | | | |
| Vientiane to Pakxan | 155km | 2–3 hrs | 62 km/hr | good surfaced road with new bridges |
| Pakxan to Thakhek | 190 km | 5–6 hrs | 35 km/hr | undergoing upgrading, due for completion by 1997 |
| Thakhek to Savannakhet | 139 km | 3–4 hrs | 40 km/hr | good, surfaced road |
| Vientiane to Savannakhet | 484 km | 10–13 hrs | 44 km/hr | |
| Savennakhet to Vietnamese | 236 km | 5 hrs | 47 km/hr | rough road, partly sealed |
| Savannakhet to Pakse | 250 km | 6–8 hrs | 36 km/hr | poor road, unsurfaced but being upgraded slowly |
| Pakse to Saravan | 125 km | 3–4 hrs | 36 km/hr | new, surfaced road |
| Saravan to Sekong | 98 km | 4 hrs | 25 km/hr | dirt road undergoing improvement |
| Pakse to Don Khong | 130 km | 4–5 hrs | 29 km/hr | unsurfaced, laterite |

Note:   these are approximate bus/truck times for the dry season as of May 1996. During the wet season road travel except on newly sealed roads is considerably slower and some routes are impassable. Laos' roads are being gradually upgraded and this coupled with the arrival of new vehicles from Japan to replace ageing Soviet-era trucks and buses will increase average travel speeds.

*Source*: Jerndal and Rigg (forthcoming)[51]

divorced, in this instance, from the former it tends to be described in rather different terms and for this reason is often discussed as though it was separate and distinct. Deficiencies in internal transportation tend to be accounted for in terms of the physical challenge set by the terrain when placed against the financial resources available to the Lao government. The country's land-locked condition, meanwhile, is largely presented as being a geopolitical challenge. The shortcoming with such a division is that with regard to their economic and social impacts, the two issues are usually reduced to a simple question of ease of access. Whether that has its roots in terrain, geopolitics or economics, or a combination of factors, is – at the human level – by-the-by.

Nonetheless, the fragility of Laos' position as a poor and weak state in a fractious region was starkly exposed during the fifteen years between 1975 and 1989. In 1975, the Communist Pathet Lao achieved full and final victory over the Royal Lao Government (RLG). With the victories of Communist parties in Vietnam and Cambodia in the same year, Southeast Asia was riven into two competing blocs. Although scholars might not go so far as to call them client states, there is no doubt that while the market economies of Asean (at that time Indonesia, Malaysia, the Philippines, Singapore and Thailand) aligned themselves with the United States and more broadly with the West, the command economies of Indochina (Cambodia/Kampuchea, Laos and Vietnam) sought support and protection from the Soviet Union and the People's Republic of China.

This two-fold division was muddied somewhat with the Vietnamese defeat of Pol Pot's Khmers Rouges in Kampuchea/Cambodia in 1979. The Vietnamese installed a government led by Hun Sen in Phnom Penh, thus bringing Hanoi into conflict with Beijing. China lent its support to the Khmers Rouges while Asean and the West provided military and political assistance to two other rebel armies fighting the Hun Sen government in Phnom Penh. In 1982 these three groups banded together to form the Coalition Government of Democratic Kampuchea (CGDK) – which was subsequently recognised by the UN. This sequence of events placed the leadership in Laos in something of a quandary. Until the Vietnamese invasion of Cambodia, it had been possible to maintain cordial relations with both Hanoi and Beijing. But with Vietnam's invasion of Cambodia in 1979 and then, in the same year, China's military incursion into Vietnam, the leadership in Vientiane were forced to come off the fence. Even then, though, it was with extreme reluctance illustrating Vientiane's desire to avoid antagonising any of its more powerful neighbours – especially at a time when relations with Thailand were at such a low ebb (see below). Given the close revolutionary and personal links between the Lao People's Revolutionary Party and the Vietnamese Communist Party, it was almost inevitable that Vientiane should criticise the Chinese as 'international reactionaries', rather than the Vietnamese. Even so, it seems that the Lao leadership also sent messages to Beijing indicating their difficulties in this regard. Stuart-Fox believes that the fact that the Chinese media was notably less savage in its denunciations of Vientiane than it was of Moscow and Hanoi, indicated that Beijing accepted that Vientiane found itself in an almost impossible situation.[31] Nonetheless, relations between Vientiane and Beijing remained antagonistic, if not overtly hostile, until the mid-1980s.

In the case of Lao-Thai relations, however, Vientiane could do nothing to prevent their marked deterioration. This highlighted Laos' dependence on Thailand as a transit corridor and, at a more general level, provides a forceful case study of the particular difficulties that land-locked states encounter when they face the enmity of their neighbours.

Laos' most logical conduit to the coast is through Thailand. Despite improvements to highway 9 linking Savannakhet and Danang via Hué, highway 6 from Luang Prabang to Hanoi, highway 7 from Luang Prabang to Vinh, highway 8 from Thakhek to Vinh, and highway 13 from Luang Prabang to Ho Chi Minh City (Saigon) via Vientiane and Phnom Penh, Laos' geographical position means that transport through Thailand would, all things being equal, remain considerably cheaper and faster.[32] For the two decades following independence in 1954 relations between Thailand and Laos were generally cordial. With the completion of a railway line from Bangkok to the Thai town of Nong Khai on the Mekong River and close to Vientiane in 1955/56, so Laos became increasingly dependent on trade routes through Thailand. Just prior to the final victory of the Communist Pathet Lao over the RLG in 1975, over 80 per cent of official trade passed through Thailand. As Hardstone observed in a paper published in 1978, Thailand at that time 'held the key to the effective operation of the Lao import/export economy'.[33]

Not surprisingly therefore, during the period of confrontation in Southeast Asia between the countries of Asean and Indochina, spanning the years 1975–1989, Thailand consistently used the border as a political tool and as an economic weapon (see table 4). This has effectively taken five forms: outright border closure; limiting the number of border posts; restricting trade in 'strategic goods'; subjecting goods for sale in Thailand to stiff tariffs; and imposing various Non Tariff Barriers (NTBs). Lee Yong Leng wrote at the time that, Laos 'is a good example of a land-locked state at an ideological boundary suffering from the enmity of its neighbour'.[34] Although there have been a series of Lao-Thai transit agreements, these have not set a framework for easy trans-shipment of goods. For example, Glassner writes of the 1959 and 1978 treaties:

> The 1978 treaty…does not provide for simplification of customs formalities or harmonisation of documentation; it does not even have a protocol or memorandum which spell out procedures designed to reduce costs and avoid delays of traffic in transit. Both treaties [the 1959 and 1978], moreover, are at sharp variance with current international forwarding and transport practices in force for land-locked and transit countries. Instead, they establish a very restrictive transit regime in which Lao goods must be handled by Thai-designated agencies while providing no guarantees for timely

deliveries... Rather than expediting the growingly essential Lao export promotion and diversification, they are inhibited by requirements concerning origin, marking, valuation and sanitation.[35]

TABLE 4
THAILAND–LAOS TRADE RESTRICTIONS 1975–1994

| | |
|---|---|
| 1975 (–1989) | Ban or restriction on the export of 'strategic' goods |
| 1976–1977 | Border closed |
| 1979 | Improved relations under Thai Prime Minister General Kriangsak |
| June–Aug. 1980 | Border closed |
| Aug. 1980–Jan. 1981 | Two border posts opened |
| Jan.–Feb. 1981 | Border closed |
| 1987–1988 | Border war at Ban Rom Klao between Laos and Thailand |
| 1989 | Ban on the export of strategic goods lifted |
| 1990 | First bridge across the Mekong agreed |
| November 1991 | Foundation stone laid of the Friendship Bridge |
| April 1994 | Friendship Bridge officially opened |

*Source*: Jonathan Rigg, 'Managing dependency in a reforming economy: the LAO PDR', *Contemporary Southeast Asia* 17/2 (1995) p.159.

During the 14 years between 1975 and 1989, the border between Thailand and Laos was closed on at least four occasions, usually following border 'incidents' which have ranged from firing on river craft, to shelling, to a serious border war in 1987–88 over a series of contested villages at Ban Rom Klao. These border closures have tended to last relatively short periods – a month or so. The Thai government also periodically reduced the number of border posts. Indeed, one of its first actions when the Pathet Lao gained control of the country in 1975 was to close two of the five border posts (by far the most important are the posts at Tha Deua near Vientiane and at Keng Kabao, near Savannakhet; see map 1). The Thais, rather disingenuously, claimed at the time that the purpose of such closures was to control smuggling.

More important than these border closures was the ban or restriction (requiring an export license) on the export of 'strategic goods' which was in place throughout the period from 1975 to 1989. At its peak, the number of strategic goods numbered 363 products, including bicycles, needles and medicines.[37] For a two-month period between September and November 1977 oil exports to Laos were banned (prompted by the suspected presence of Mig-21s in Laos), virtually bringing the Lao economy to a standstill. In addition, agricultural products for sale in Thailand were subjected to tariffs of 30 per cent (e.g. rice) to 60 per cent (e.g. tea, meat). Finally, and perhaps most importantly, goods for transit through Thailand had to be transported by the infamous Thai Express Transport Association. It has been estimated that this monopoly carrier pushed transport costs up by 40–50 per cent through gross inefficiency and corruption, while failing to provide a timely service even for perishable goods.

There can be little doubt that in the past Thailand has used the border as an economic and political weapon. The difficulty in assessing the effect of Thailand's partial blockade was that during this period a large proportion of trade was smuggled across the 1,700km-long frontier between the two countries. Kroef estimates that smuggled goods probably accounted for between one half and two-thirds of total trade during this period.[37] In the main, the trade consisted of timber, precious stones, rice, coffee, forest products – even livestock – in exchange for consumer goods. But it should be emphasised that the high incidence of smuggling was not due just to successive Thai governments' imposition of trade barriers; it was also a function of the existence of Lao government monopolies in, for example, timber and coffee. Traders in Laos and Thailand were forced to resort to smuggling in order to circumvent Lao government controls on certain categories of good – an activity which the Thai authorities at least were only too ready to ignore.[38] Thus, although the Thais have officially closed the border on four occasions between 1975 and 1989, and restricted trade throughout that period, in each case the action has only partially affected the level of trade. The permeability of the Lao–Thai frontier means that the majority of trade lies beyond the control of either government.[39]

Notwithstanding the permeability of the Lao–Thai border, the actions of successive Thai governments to restrict the flow of trade whether partially or totally, did concentrate the minds of Lao government officials. Their principal response was to improve the French-built roads running east over the Annamite chain to the coast of Vietnam in an effort to re-direct trade and so reduce Laos' dependence on Thailand. With Vietnamese and Soviet assistance, highway 9 from Savannakhet to Danang, a Vietnamese port on the South China Sea, was upgraded and the work finally completed in 1989. Other roads running eastwards into Vietnam were also improved during the same period. These efforts did have results: whereas before 1975, 80 per cent of the Lao PDR's official trade (excluding hydropower exports) passed through or into Thailand, this quickly fell to 20 per cent following the victory of the Pathet Lao in 1975.[40] But despite some success in re-orienting trade, it should be emphasised that this does not negate the fact that Thailand remains Laos' logical conduit to the sea, and the construction programme improving links through Vietnam has not changed this position. It was Thailand's actions in restricting trade, and Laos' economic and political identification with Vietnam, the Soviet Union and the Eastern Bloc which forced the change in the pattern of trade. As political conditions changed from the late 1980s so the 'natural' pattern of trade and commerce quickly reasserted itself. The speed and extent to which the geopolitical landscape has altered in mainland Southeast Asia is hard to over-emphasise. In a paper published in 1988, for example, Zasloff found he was able to write that:

> Vietnamese leaders seem confident that history is with them. The refurbished road system, the new flow of commerce in Vietnam's direction, the emerging institutions of Indochina, the technical and political training of young Laotians will combine to give Vietnam an increasing role in shaping the destiny of Laos.[41]

Relations between the Lao PDR and Thailand have seen a marked improvement since 1989. The number of 'strategic' goods for which trans-shipment rights through Thailand were restricted fell from a peak of 363 (in force, roughly, 1975–1988) to 31 in 1988, the ban being finally lifted in November 1989.[42] The transport monopoly has also been abolished. To mark this new environment of goodwill, in March 1990 Thai Crown Princess Mahachakri Sirindhorn visited Laos for eight days, the first such visit since 1975. In November 1991 the foundation stone was laid for the first bridge across the lower reaches of the Mekong, linking the Thai town of Tha Deua, near Nong Khai, with Vientiane. The bridge was officially opened in April 1994 and is known, perhaps more with hope for the future than an appreciation of the past, as the Mittaphaap or 'Friendship Bridge'. There are now plans to extend the railway line from Bangkok across the Mekong all the way to Vientiane, adding a direct rail link to the new road link. During the construction phase of the Mittaphaab Bridge, in February 1992, a Treaty of Friendship and Co-operation was signed in Bangkok between Laos and Thailand. Other signs of the rapprochement between Laos and Thailand, and the concomitant increase in economic relations, include plans for several other bridges across the Mekong, each of which will tie the country more tightly into the Thai economic sphere of influence. Agreement has been reached to build a bridge between Savannakhet and Mukdahan, and two more bridges between Thakhek and Nakhon Phanom, and Chiang Khong and Ban Houei Xai are also under discussion.

## Shifting Grounds: Laos' Search for Security

The last two decades have starkly illustrated to the leaders of Laos the fragility of their country's position. Although new politicians, less imbued with the ideological certainties and the memories of the past, are beginning to take up senior posts in the Lao People's Revolutionary Party (LPRP), they still hold the view that Laos must maintain 'balance' in its foreign relations.[43] The rapprochement between Vientiane and Bangkok has not just improved transport links between the two countries. It has also, as former Thai Prime Minister Chatichai Choonhaven famously put it in 1988, stimulated the transformation of Indochina 'from a battlefield into a market place'.[44] Vientiane's immediate response to this Thai desire to exploit the natural wealth of Laos (as well as Vietnam and Cambodia) was reflected in a broadcast by state-run Radio Vientiane in July 1989: 'Having failed to destroy our country through their military might [referring to the Ban Rom Klao border conflict between Laos and Thailand of 1987–88], the enemy has now employed a new strategy in attacking us through the so-called attempt to turn the Indochinese battlefield into a marketplace.'[45]

Yet, despite the sentiments expressed in this broadcast, political rapprochement between Laos and Thailand, coupled with the adoption of the market orientated New Economic Policy or *Chin Thanakaan Mai* in 1986 and the promulgation of a new and more welcoming Foreign Investment Law in July 1988, has led to a surge of Thai business interest in Laos. It has been estimated that Thai investment over the period since the investment code was adopted in 1988, and 1994 amounted to two-thirds of total investment – some US$256 million.[46] The next largest investor was the United States with US$85 million. Like the French during the colonial era, it seems that Thai businessmen and politicians are coming to view Laos as a resource rich 'annex' to their own country, one whose exploitation is complementary to Thailand's development. The poor reputation that Thai businessmen have in Laos (and in Vietnam, Cambodia and Myanmar for that matter) is largely because of the perceived rapaciousness of their business practices and the cultural superiority which informs many of their views of Laos and its people.[47]

## A Golden Land

The most obvious sign that the government of Laos is trying to follow a policy of 'balance' in its relations with its neighbours is its support for developments which will tie it in more firmly into the wider region. The linking of Laos, Cambodia, Vietnam, Thailand, Myanmar and China's Yunnan province, with Laos as the 'keystone' of this so-called 'Golden Quadrangle' or 'Economic Rectangle', is an attempt to minimise the dependency that is part and parcel of being a poor, largely powerless, and land-locked state (see map 2).[48] At the same time, the Lao leadership are hoping that by integrating more fully into the regional economy, their country will be in a better position to benefit from the economic growth and prosperity of countries and regions like Thailand and southern China. In an interview in 1995, Laos' former Deputy Prime Minister Khamphoui Keoboualapha remarked that: 'We want to become the link between Vietnam, China, Thailand, Burma and Cambodia'.[49]

The end of the Cold War and improving relations between all the countries of mainland Southeast Asia have created a new niche for Laos. Lying as it does at the core of the region, it would seem to be well placed to exploit a role as a cross-roads state in one of the fastest growing economic areas of the world. Some analysts have also argued that Laos' geographical resources make it complementary to the other economies of the region. Rich in land and natural resources, but lacking technological skills and financial muscle, it could become a key node in mainland Southeast Asia's development.[50] This is certainly the view of the Asian Development Bank, which has been at the forefront of promoting what has been termed the Greater Mekong Sub-region, or GMS, comprising Laos, Cambodia, Vietnam, Thailand, Myanmar (Burma) and the Chinese province of Yunnan (see map 1). The rationale for the GMS, according to the ADB, rests on co-operative ventures in trade, investment, finance, technology, infrastructure, natural and human resource development, and in environmental protection.[51] As Pante has rather optimistically stated:

> While in the past, the Mekong River divided the six countries of the GMS on its banks, and no bridge joined its shores, today the river promises to bring the countries together. As the only country that shares borders with the subregion, Lao PDR could be considered the heart of the Mekong as it sits on the middle reaches of the river. As such, Lao PDR plays a crucial role in the success of co-operative efforts in the sub-region.[52]

The notion of the GMS and Laos' role within that formulation has interesting implications for the assumed link between land-lockedness and national development. For while during the period 1975–1989 being land-locked was seen as a hindrance to development, it is now being presented as the key to the country's modernisation. 'The GMS has, in short, become the vehicle by which land-lockedness can be transformed from a national liability into a national asset'.[54] The attraction for the government in Vientiane of becoming the 'keystone' of mainland Southeast Asia is that it will reduce the country's dependence on any single neighbour. It will spread the risks of dependence between five countries and will, the leadership seems to hope, ensure that Laos' vitality and independence will be in the interests of all the other members of the GMS. The Lao government's strategy as it attempts to reinvigorate the economy is informed by historical precedent – largely unobscured by ideology – and seems to be one driven by the simple, pragmatic desire to spread the risks of land-lockedness by developing and sustaining good relations with its neighbours.

## ACKNOWLEDGEMENTS

This paper is based upon an initial visit to Laos in 1991 sponsored by the Committee for Social Sciences of the Lao PDR and generously supported by the British Academy. I am grateful to both institutions for their support.

## NOTES

1. The countries of Indochina are Vietnam, Laos and Cambodia. Asean or the Association of Southeast Asian Nations includes Brunei, Indonesia, Malaysia, the Philippines, Singapore and Thailand; in July 1995 Vietnam became the seventh member of the Association and the first Communist signatory of the Bangkok Declaration. Laos and Cambodia have both already signed the Treaty of Amity and Co-operation and, along with Myanmor (Burma), are scheduled to become full Asean members in 1997. Should Cambodia, Laos and Myanmar become members, then Southeast Asia will be united as both a political and geographical region for the first time in history.
2. UNDP, *Development Co-operation: Lao People's Democratic Republic* (Vientiane, Laos: UNPD 1990) p.9.
3. See Joseph J. Zasloff, 'Political constraints on development in Laos' in Joseph J. Zasloff and Leonard Unger (eds) *Laos: Beyond the Revolution* (Basingstoke: Macmillan 1991) pp.27–9.
4. P. Handley, 'Making connections' in *Far Eastern Economic Review* 156/44 (4 November 1993) p.29.
5. NSC (1995a) *Expenditure and Consumption Survey and Social Indicator Survey* (1992–1993), Committee for Planning and Cooperation, National Statistical Centre: Vientiane, Laos.
6. NSC (1995b) *Basic Statistics about the Socio-economic Development in the Lao PDR, 1975–1995*, Committee for Planning and Cooperation, National Statistical Centre: Vientiane, Laos.
7. NSC, 1995 p.2.
8. World Bank, *World Development Report 1996: from Plan to Market* (New York: OUP 1996).
9. Jan Ovesen, *Anthropological Reconnaissance in Central Laos: a Survey of Communities in a Hydropower Project Area*, Uppsala Research Reports in Cultural Anthropology No. 13 (Uppsala: Uppsala University 1993) pp.31–2 and I-B Trankell, *On the Road in Laos: an Anthropological Study of Road Construction and Rural Communities*, Uppsala Research Reports in Cultural Anthropology, No. 12 (Uppsala: Uppsala University 1993) pp.12-15.
10. Trankell, p.14.
11. Martin Stuart-Fox, 'On the writing of Leo history: Continuities and discontinuities', in Journal of Southeast Asian Studies 24/1 (1992) p.116.
12. Martin I. Glassner, *Transit Problems of Three Asian Land-locked Countries: Afghanistan, Nepal and Laos*, Occasional papers in Contemporary Asian Studies no. 4 (University of Maryland, School of Law) pp.40–1.
13. Peter C.N. Hardstone, 'Laos: the transportation problems of an Indochinese land-locked state' in *Philippines Geographical Journal* 22/3 (1978) p.155.
14. Martin Stuart-Fox, *Laos: Politics, Economics and Society* (London: Pinter 1986) p.14.
15. Ibid., pp.171–83. And William S. Turley, 'Vietnam's strategy for Indochina and security in Southeast Asia' in Young Whan Kihl and Lawrence E. Grinter (eds) *Security, Strategy and Policy Responses in the Pacific Rim* (Boulder, Colorado: Lynne Rienner Publishers 1989) p.178.
16. A river which is, in fact, quite shallow over much of its course.
17. Stuart-Fox (1986), p.180.
18. The famous Vietnamese general Vo Nguyen Giap talked of Indochina as a '...strategic unit, a single theatre of operations' quoted in Gareth Porter, 'Vietnamese policy and the Indochina crisis' in David W.P. Elliott (ed.) *The Third Indochina Conflict* (Boulder, Colorado: Westview Press 1981) p.88.
19. Stuart-Fox (1990), p.282. See also Joseph J. Zasloff, 'Vietnam and Laos: master and

apprentice' in Joseph J. Zasloff (ed.) *Postwar Indochina: Old Enemies and New Allies* (Washington D.C.: Foreign Services Institute, US Department of State 1988) pp.37–62.

20. Stuart-Fox (1990), p.282.
21. UNDP (1990), p.9.
22. Joseph J. Zasloff and MacAlister Brown, 'Laos 1990: socialism postponed but leadership intact' in *Southeast Asian Affairs* 1991 (Singapore: Institute of Southeast Asian Studies 1991) p.149. The 1989 UNDP report stated that over 30 per cent of all aid from donors in the convertible currency area was allocated to the transport sector (UNDP 1990) p.18.
23. Preben Nielsen, 'Transportation network: current status and future plans', in Chi Do Pham (ed.) *Economic Development in Lao PDR: Horizon 2000* (Vientiane: Government of the Lao PDR 1994) p.184.
24. 'An Asian snail', *The Economist* (5 November 1994) p.74–80.
25. This was dramatically underscored in 1977/88 – though the road has improved considerably since then – when the rice harvest in the north failed, and rice surpluses from the south had to be trans-shipped through Thailand such was the state of this north–south highway. Lao PDR, *Report on the Economic and Social Situation, Development Strategy, and Assistance Needs of the Lao PDR*, volume 1 (Geneva: Lao PDR 1989).
26. Lao PDR (1989), p.49.
27. Arthur J. Dommen, *Laos: Keystone of Indochina* (Boulder, Colorado: Westview 1985) p.168.
28. G. Evans, 'Deadly debris' in *Far Eastern Economic Review* 157/38 (22 September 1994) pp.58–9.
29. Ibid.
30. Though this stretch of road has been much improved it is plagued by attacks by armed Hmong. The government portrays the perpetrators as criminal bandits while the Hmong, the remnants of the army that fought for the Americans and the Royal Lao Government against the Communist Pathet Lao, would prefer the label freedom fighters. Given that the motivation for the attacks seems to be to extract money and valuables from those who brave this upland road, the former characterization would seem to be closer to the truth. Bertil Linter, 'Road of death: Hmong tribesmen are killing travellers to the north', *Far Eastern Economic Review* 159/48 (28 November 1996) pp.32–6.
31. Martin Stuart-Fox, *Buddhist Kingdom, Marxist State: the Making of Modern Laos* (Bangkok: White Lotus 1996) pp.147–57.
32. This network of highways linking Laos with seaports on Vietnam's South China Sea coast was originally conceived, and partially built, by the French in their attempt to build an integrated Indochinese 'federation'.
33. Hardstone, p.157.
34. Lee Yong Leng, *Southeast Asia and the Law of the Sea* (Singapore: Singapore University Press 1980) p.47.
35. Glassner, p.37.
36. Martin Stuart-Fox, *Laos: Politics, Economics and Society* (London: Pinter 1986).
37. Justus M. van der Kroef, 'Laos and Thailand: the balancing of conflict and accommodation', p. 278 in Martin Stuart-Fox (ed.) *Contemporary Laos: Studies in the Politics and Society of the Lao People's Democratic Republic* (St. Lucia: University of Queensland Press 1986) pp.274–90.
38. There is considerable evidence to indicate that Thai army and political interests (both local and national) were involved in this illegal trade. Kroef wrote at the time that: 'No Thai government is likely to risk the outburst of public wrath and the even greater upsurge of black marketeering and smuggling that tighter controls over cross-border trade would bring' (1986) p.278.
39. On the subject of border permeability, it is also worth noting that between 1975 and 1989, 350,000 Lao refugees crossed the frontier into Thailand, representing about 10 per cent of the Lao population.
40. Lao PDR, p.48.
41. Zasloff (1988), p.58.
42. Zasloff and Brown, p.154.
43. In November 1992 President Kaysone Phomvihane died. He had been chairman of the LPRP

since the mid-1950s, led the Prathet Lao in their war against the Royalists, and was a comrade of Ho Chi Minh. A little over two years later, in January 1995, the so-called Red Prince, Souphanouvong died – one of the last links with the pre-1975 revolutionary period.

44. Taking war with words a step further, a senior Thai diplomat, Suvidhya Simaskul, was quoted as saying that 'We have passed the stage of turning battlefields into markets; now the market itself has become the battlefield'. See Michael Vatikiotis, 'Trading on culture: Thailand takes a new tack with its neighbours', *Far Eastern Economic Review* 158/13 (30 March 1995) p.28.

45. Rodney Tasker, 'New war of words', *Far Eastern Economic Review* 145/30 (27 July 1989) pp.25–6.

46. Gordon Fairclough, 'Different drummer: Thai firms follow profits, not policy', *Far Eastern Economic Review* 158/13 (30 March 1995) p.30, and 'Laos attracts labour-intensive industry', *Inside Indochina* 50/87 (28 March 1995) p.3.

47. Vatikiot is 1995: pp.28–29.

48. See Handley 1993, Dommen 1985, Bertil Lintner, 'Ties that bind', *Far Eastern Economic Review* 158/6 (9 February 1995a) pp.18–19 and Bertil Lintner, 'Open for business', *Far Eastern Economic Review* 158/6 (9 February 1995b) pp.22–3.

49. Lintner (1995a), p.19.

50. Martin Stuart-Fox, 'Laos at the Crossroads', *Indochina Issues* (Washington D.C.: Indochina Project March 1991) and Lintner 1995b.

51. Filiologo Pante Jr. 'Lao PDR and the Mekong Sub-Regional Development Project', in: Chi Do Pham (ed.) *Economic Development in Lao PDR*, (Vientiane: Horizon 2000 1994) pp.262–77 and Randi Jerndal and Jonathan Rigg, 'From buffer state to crossroads state: spaces of human activity and integration in the Lao PDR' in: Grant Evans (ed.) *Laos: Culture and Society* (Chiang Mai, Thailand: Silkworm Books forthcoming).

52. Pante, pp.276–7.

53. Jerndal and Rigg.

# Transit Arrangements between Nepal and India: A Study in International Law

## SURYA P. SUBEDI

### Introduction

Nursing a long-time grievance that Nepal has observed 'neither the letter nor the spirit' of the 1950 treaty with India which was meant to guide the relationship between the two countries, India has decided to look afresh at the ties with its strategically placed neighbour in the north-east.[1]

This is how the 'cold war'[2] began between Nepal (virtually an India-locked, land-locked country) and India in the latter part of 1988. It culminated in March 1989 not only in the closure of all but two of the 21 trade routes, but also in the closure of 13 of the 15 transit routes through India used by Nepal for her international trade under the 1978 transit treaty with India.[3] It should be noted here that March 1989 was the time when the term of Nepal's 1978 trade and transit treaties with India expired[4] and the Indian government refused to negotiate a new transit treaty or to sign the new trade treaty initialled a few months before but awaiting formal signing by the ministers of the two countries.[5]

Among the principal reasons advanced by India for its refusal were: the non-withdrawal by Nepal of additional tariffs imposed on Indian goods; the import of certain weapons by Nepal from China in June 1988; the alleged mistreatment by Nepal of Indians living in Nepal; the introduction of a work permit scheme for Indians seeking employment in Nepal; and the alleged lack of Nepal's whole-hearted co-operation in controlling the unauthorised trade between the two countries.[6] From the perspective of New Delhi, most of these actions by Kathmandu amounted to 'blatant violation' of the Peace and Friendship Treaty concluded between the two countries in 1950 from which flowed special terms in the areas of trade, economy, education and culture. That is why India wanted to discuss the whole gamut of its relations with Nepal and to negotiate a *single* comprehensive treaty dealing with both trade and transit matters since they were, in India's view, interrelated.

For its part, Nepal denied all allegations made by India and claimed that India had violated international law by imposing an 'economic blockade'[7] upon Nepal and by restricting the latter's freedom of transit and the right of free access to and from the sea. Nepal asserted that since her right of free access to and from the sea and freedom of transit was guaranteed by international law, India was obliged to negotiate a separate treaty on transit, without making Nepal's right of transit conditional upon its granting concessions to Indian nationals and business or upon other bilateral matters of trade and purchase of weapons, etc.

This row continued for over a year and ended only when a change in government in Nepal took place. The new regime was headed by a leader of a political party, Nepali Congress, which critics often characterise as a party favoured by New Delhi. The whole political system (under which all political parties were banned) that had prevailed in Nepal for over 30 years was overthrown by a popular movement, a movement partly sparked by the scarcity of essential commodities created by the Indo-Nepal stalemate and partly encouraged and assisted by India.[8] The new interim government was quick to improve Nepal's relations with India. At the conclusion of the new Nepalese Prime Minister's visit to India in June 1990, a joint communiqué was signed under which India agreed to restore the *status quo ante* to April 1987 in matters of trade and transit.[9]

This meant that India would reinstate the 15 transit routes for Nepal's transit trade, through India, with third countries. This was after Nepal and India had agreed, *inter alia,* fully to respect each other's security interests; this was understood by many to mean that Nepal would not buy any weapons from China without consulting India and would not have any defence dealings with China to the detriment of India. Nepal had also agreed to restore tariff preferences to Indian goods, to remove Indian nationals from the ambit of the work permit scheme and to grant a number of other concessions to Indian nationals. This understanding led to the conclusion in December 1991 of two separate treaties on trade and transit for the period of five and seven years respectively.

Thus, an unhappy chapter in the relationship between India and Nepal was, on the surface, closed with the conclusion of these two treaties. But this conclusion does not seem to have laid to rest many important legal questions raised during the crisis between 1988 and 1990. Past experience shows that whenever the term of the transit treaty expired, Nepal had to brace itself for the attitude of the Government in New Delhi; without securing a favourable trade treaty India did not let the transit arrangements operate smoothly. Most importantly, India raised the issue of the violation of the 1950 Peace and Friendship Treaty by Nepal as this treaty deals with a number of bilateral issues but is ambiguous in many points leaving enough room for different interpretations to serve different purposes.[10] As Nepal insists that this is now an outmoded treaty, derogations from its provisions are bound to occur.[11]

Since the trade and transit treaties have been concluded, one has to ask is Nepal's transit right conditional upon the observance of the 'letter and spirit' of the 1950 treaty or upon Nepal's agreeing to a trade treaty favourable to India? Does international law oblige India to negotiate and conclude a new transit treaty with Nepal upon the expiry of the old one? Is Nepal entitled under international law to only one transit route through India as interpreted by the latter? Is the right of free access of land-locked countries established in general international law? If so, does this right operate even in the absence of a transit treaty with the transit State? If not, is this right conditional upon the conclusion of a transit treaty? Before examining these questions it seems necessary to examine briefly the nature of the Indo-Nepal relationship and its impact on Nepal's transit arrangements with India.

### The Nature of the Indo-Nepal Relationship

Describing the nature of the Indo-Nepal relationship, a former foreign minister of Nepal rightly states that, 'There are few countries in the world whose histories, cultures and traditions have been so closely interlinked for such a long time.'[12] Nepal shares a 500-mile border with India and the border remains open. Although Nepal borders on China to the north, it is extremely hard for Nepal to gain access to the Chinese market and to the sea via Chinese territories as Nepal lies on the southern slopes of the Himalayas. Nepal is surrounded by India from all other sides, i.e. the east, west and south. Although Nepal has trade relationships with nearly 70 States, the bulk of its trade is either with India or through India. The nearest sea port to Nepal is 1,127 km away in Calcutta, India. Nepal could potentially use some of Bangladesh's ports, but Indian territory separates Nepal from Bangladesh. This makes Nepal virtually dependent on India for her access to the sea and international market. In other words, geography dictates the Nepal-India relationship.[13]

Wedged between two colossal powers with two different social and political systems, Nepal has since its unification tried to maintain a stance of political neutrality. An unbalanced foreign policy could at any time endanger Nepal's sovereignty. But in the aftermath of World War II, many changes took place in this region of Asia. India gained independence in 1947. Many small entities agreed to join the Union of India while a few others were annexed by force. The Communists came into power in China in 1949. With a view to preventing the communist influence spilling over into the neighbouring Himalayan kingdoms, the newly independent India wished to strengthen the 'Himalayan frontier policy' of British India under which the Himalayas were regarded as its ultimate frontier, its proper line of defence. For this, India concluded unbalanced treaties of peace and friendship with her three small neighbouring kingdoms – Nepal, Bhutan and Sikkim – in order to bring them within her sphere of influence. The Peace and Friendship Treaty concluded with Nepal in 1950 was accompanied by a letter attached to the treaty and exchanged between the two countries (hereafter the letters of exchange) on the day the treaty was concluded; this letter was kept secret and not attached to the treaty when the treaty was registered with the secretary-general of the United Nations.

(1)   Each country agree 'to give to the nationals of the other, in its territory, national treatment with regard to participation in industrial and economic development of such territory and to the grant of concessions and contracts to such development.' (Article VI of the treaty)

(2)   The two Governments agree 'to grant, on a reciprocal basis, to the nationals of one country in the territories of the other the same privileges in the matter of residence, ownership of property, participation in trade and commerce, movement and other privileges of a similar nature.' (Article VII of the treaty)

(3)   'Any arms, ammunition or warlike material and equipment necessary for the security of Nepal that the Government of Nepal may import through the territory of India shall be so imported with the assistance and agreement of the Government of India...' (paragraph 2 of the letters of exchange)[14]

In view of these provisions, India describes its relationship with Nepal as a 'special relationship'. Although none of the provisions of the 1950 treaty imply in any way that India has a right to oversee Nepal's foreign affairs, New Delhi uses this treaty to ensure that Nepal does not compromise India's security concerns in its relations with China.

Although, on the surface, Nepal's dispute with India seemed to be concerned with relatively straightforward trade and transit issues (especially Nepal's demand for two separate treaties on trade and transit and India's insistence on the conclusion of a single comprehensive treaty dealing with all matters of mutual trade and transit), one of the real problems was rooted in the import of certain weapons by Nepal from China in June 1988. In New Delhi's view, Nepal had a duty to consult India before purchasing such weapons from China – a country with whom India had a tenuous relationship. Although that purchase was small and consisted mainly of anti-aircraft guns, which would in no way pose any threat to India – a country trying to be a regional superpower, India took this matter very seriously. An Indian diplomat was reported as saying that 'First it's a handful of rusty guns, then it's the training team, then it's nuclear weapons'.[15]

The above-cited provision of the 1950 treaty makes it clear that the government of Nepal would have to seek India's agreement to import weapons only when importing *through* Indian territories but not when Nepal is importing weapons from China or through Chinese territories. Whether the decision of the government of Nepal to procure certain weapons from China was a prudent course of action or not is a different matter and beyond the scope of this article. So far as the treaty relationship is concerned Nepal is under no obligation to refrain from procuring weapons from States other than India or to consult it before procuring weapons from other countries. However, the security issue was not the only reason for India's refusal to conclude a transit treaty with Nepal; there was also an economic reason. Nepal is a market on the doorstep for India and New Delhi seems very aware of the fact that the midget cannot defy the mammoth. Thus, when Nepal, in keeping with its policy of lessening its dependence on a single country, India, and of diversifying its trade, introduced a new tariff system in 1987 India reacted with indignation. There followed other issues, e.g. the introduction of a work permit scheme for Indians and the mistreatment of Indian nationals living in Nepal.

Although it is clear from the provisions of the 1950 Treaty of Peace and Friendship that the granting of national treatment in certain matters (i.e. in matters of residence, ownership of property, participation in trade and commerce, movement and other privileges of a similar nature) by one contracting party to the nationals of the other does not imply national treatment in employment too, India asserted that Nepal's introduction of a work permit scheme for Indian nationals was against the 1950 treaty. Of course, a large number of Nepalese work in India without being required to obtain a work permit and vice versa. But that does not mean that this matter falls under the ambit of the 1950 treaty; neither government is under a treaty obligation to accord national treatment in matters of employment opportunities to the nationals of the other. Nevertheless, under Indian pressure Nepal had to remove Indian nationals from the ambit of its work permit scheme.

There is yet another dimension to this problem. Numerous rivers originate in the Himalayas and flow through Nepal to India and ultimately to the Bay of Bengal; they could provide a great deal of hydro-electric power, a cheap and durable form of energy, much needed by both States. It is estimated that Nepalese rivers could generate up to 83,000 megawatts of hydro-electric power,[16] which is more than the combined total hydro-electric power currently produced by USA, Canada and Mexico. For instance, a single hydro-electric power project, the Karnali Project, would have an installed capacity of 10,800

MW, the second largest in the world.[17] India has developed considerable interest in these projects.[18] As Clad writes, India views 'foreign investment in Nepal with suspicion, fearing that Nepal will become a back door for multinationals to India's domestic economy.'[19] Obviously, New Delhi would like to see Kathmandu acting in a way which would also benefit India if any gigantic projects like Karnali were to be implemented. Here too India could argue that under the 1950 treaty Nepal is obliged to lend its ears to Indian concerns[20] and unless Nepal acts according to Indian wishes, India might create problems of one type or another.

Thus, from an Indian viewpoint the 1950 treaty provides grounds for putting pressure on Nepal on virtually all matters affecting India. However, this is not how the Nepalese view the treaty; for them it is outmoded and rendered inoperative by non-observance of its key provisions by both States in the last 40 years. In a press statement in May 1989 the Chief Spokesman of the government of Nepal stated that Nepal was willing to review the 1950 treaty 'with a view to making it in tune with time'. The Spokesman maintained that 'the treaty was concluded by India with the last Rana Prime Minister [who headed an oligarchical rule and was overthrown by a popular movement soon after the treaty was concluded] four decades ago in a different political, economic and social setting.'[21]

### The Indo-Nepal Problem from a Legal Perspective

Principal international instruments concerning land-locked States are: the Barcelona Convention and Statute on Freedom of Transit of 1921;[22] the High Seas Convention (HSC) of 1958;[23] the Convention on Transit Trade of Land-locked Countries of 1965[24] and the Convention on the Law of the Sea (LOSC) of 1982 (which has yet to enter into force).[25] Both Nepal and India are party to the Barcelona Convention and Statute. Nepal is party also to the 1958 High Seas Convention and the 1965 Convention on land-locked States, but India is not party to these Conventions. Although both countries are signatory to the 1982 Convention, neither has ratified it. Thus, so far as the governance of India–Nepal bilateral transit relations by multilateral treaties is concerned, only the Barcelona Convention and Statute seems relevant. This does not explicitly provide a right of free access for land-locked States but provides freedom of transit. While Article 1 of the Statute defines the term 'traffic in transit', Article 2 lays down the principle that free transit should be facilitated by the States concerned. It reads as follows:

> Subject to the provisions of this Statute, the measures taken by the
> Contracting States for regulating and forwarding traffic across

territory under their sovereignty or authority shall facilitate free transit by rail or waterway on routes in use convenient for international transit.

Since both countries are signatory to the 1982 Convention, which, *inter alia*, guarantees the right of free access for land-locked States,[26] it could be argued that the signatories are obliged, under Article 18 of the 1969 Vienna Convention on the Law of Treaties, to which both Nepal and India are party, 'to refrain from acts which would defeat the object and purpose' of the Convention.[27] Moreover, in view of the mandatory character of Article 125 (1) of the LOSC and the approval of this provision by consensus during the UNCLOS III the right of free access as embodied in the 1982 Convention could now be regarded as part of customary international law.[28]

A substantial weight of authority supports the view that the right of free access to and from the sea of land-locked States and the principle of freedom of transit are now a part of customary international law, binding on all States.[29] This was the view advanced by several land-locked States, including Nepal,[30] during UNCLOS III. Writers also support this view: Fawcett writes that 'a duty to accord freedom of transit on reasonable conditions to another is now a customary rule.'[31] According to Lauterpacht the right of transit exists in international law, provided that the State claiming the right is able to justify it by reference to considerations of necessity or convenience and the exercise of the right does not cause harm or prejudice to the transit State.[32] He goes on to state that 'When circumstances warranting a claim to transit exist, the legal right to freedom of transit then arises. It exists independently of treaty.'[33]

The question as to whether the right of free transit is established in general international law has attracted considerable academic debate and the surveying of all arguments advanced for and against it is beyond the scope of this paper. So far as our discussion is concerned, India implicitly acknowledged during the recent crisis that the absence of an agreement did not excuse it from the obligation to provide access. Although Mr Narasimha Rao, the then Indian Minister of External Affairs, speaking in the lower house of the Indian parliament on 26 April 1989 stated that since India was party neither to the 1965 Convention on land-locked States nor to the 1982 Convention on the Law of the Sea, 'in matters of transit, India has, strictly speaking, no obligation towards Nepal', he, nevertheless, acknowledged during the same speech that 'In the field of transit, *a land-locked country has a* **right** only to one transit route to the sea under International Law' (emphasis added).[34] This was evidenced by the fact that even in the absence of a transit treaty India allowed, albeit under very restrictive conditions and only through two of the 15 transit routes that were in use prior to the expiry of the old treaty, Nepalese exports and imports to and from third countries. As Nepal had launched a publicity campaign to gain support and sympathy from the outside world in its trouble with India, Indian officials were making strenuous efforts to convey the message that India did not intend to deny Nepal its right of transit even in the absence of a transit treaty.[35] But what India was saying was that because of its 'special relationship' with Nepal it had been very 'generous' to its neighbour in extending transit facilities and now, since Nepal was intent on changing this special relationship, in the view of New Delhi, Nepal was merely another neighbour like Bangladesh and Pakistan, and, thus, not worthy of 'generous' treatment by India.

As quoted earlier, according to Indian officials, India was required by international law to provide only one transit route and not 15 routes as enjoyed by Nepal under the 1978 transit treaty.[36] This assertion of India, however, has no legal basis. No international legal rule states that only one route is enough. Although Vasciannie[37] writes that 'In strict terms, only one transit route is necessary for a given land-locked State to reach the sea, and from this it may possibly be argued that additional routes are granted to the land-locked State for reasons other than those relating to its special geographical location', he fails to provide any clue as to how he arrived at this conclusion. He seems to have left out of account the significance of not only Article V of the 1947 GATT (Article V of the GATT rules provides that the right of transit must be allowed 'via the route<u>s</u> most convenient for international transit')[38] and Article 2 of the Barcelona Statute on Freedom of Transit (free transit shall be facilitated by States concerned 'on route<u>s</u> in *use* convenient for international transit').[39] Also other relevant doctrines of international law such as the doctrine of prescription, according to Lauterpacht, 'may be of relevance in determining whether a State is entitled to the continued enjoyment of a means of transit of which the transit State seeks to deprive it either by outright prohibition or by the modification of the conditions of transit in a manner so unreasonable or onerous as to be tantamount to prohibition.'[40]

Nepal, for its part, argued that given its shape (Nepal is a narrow strip across the northern frontier of India with a 500-mile border with India), geography (the terrain is mostly mountainous with several ranges running at different elevations from east to west and north to south), and the state of economic development (a large part of the country is still remote and not connected by modern means of transport to the capital and other industrial cities), Nepal needs several transit routes for its trade and communications. It is worth noting here that there remain some areas which cannot be reached by rail or road from other parts of the country without going via India. Nepal thus suffers from two geographical handicaps – one is land-lockedness and the other its mountainous nature without a proper network of modern transportation and communications. Because of this situation, there seems a clear need for several outlets not only for exports and imports, but also for the livelihood of some of the population. Although in ordinary circumstances a need might not justify a legal right, such a geographical need of a land-locked country justifies a legal right because the very source of the right of land-locked States is their special geographical condition. Since 15 transit routes were in *use* under the 1978 transit treaty, India seems obliged under the Barcelona Statute to grant Nepal all 15 routes even in the absence of a transit treaty. The words 'routes in use convenient for international transit' were inserted in Article 2 of the Barcelona Statute with a view to laying down that the right of free transit may not be exercised except over routes in existence. Hence, India is not obliged to construct new routes for Nepal but is obliged to allow Nepal's traffic in transit through all routes in existence.

On the basis of the provisions of Article 2 of the Barcelona Statute on Freedom of Transit and the other principles of international law and provisions of international instruments described above it could be argued that Nepal's claim to several outlets is justified under international law. HSC Article 3(2) requires the transit State to take into account the 'special conditions' of the land-locked State in concluding transit agreements to give effect to the transit right of that State. It appears that if Nepal is able to justify its demand for several routes of transit by reference to considerations of necessity or convenience, India would be obliged to agree to these routes.

Both HSC Articles 3 and LOSC 125 require the transit States to conclude appropriate agreements with land-locked States to give effect to the rights and freedoms enshrined therein. However, one could argue that although Article 125 (1) provides for the right of free access for land-locked States, it does not provide independent measures for the implementation of this right as it is tied to freedom of transit. In other words, there is a right of free access for land-locked States but the exercise of this right will be governed by the rules of freedom of transit. Therefore, what seems more important here is the nature and scope of the institution of freedom of transit rather than the right of free access. Paragraph 2 of Article 125 makes this point clearer: the bilateral, subregional or regional agreements envisaged under this paragraph are for determining the terms and modalities *for exercising freedom of transit* but not for exercising the right of free access to and from the sea.

Nevertheless, since the legal effect of the notion of 'freedom of transit' can be equated to that of a 'right' of transit, the use of the term 'freedom of transit' in the second sentence of paragraph 1 and in paragraph 2 should not be regarded as undermining the legal position of the land-locked States.

This is because the notion of freedom of transit also implies that the transit State concerned cannot interfere with lawful transit. Since the transit State has a legal duty under the institution of freedom of transit to allow lawful passage to land-locked States, the use of the term 'freedom' is, as Vasciannie writes, 'sufficient to ensure that the latter will have an enforceable claim in instances where their access to the sea is barred.'[41] Therefore, 'In practical terms, this is equivalent to the result which would have been reached if free transit had been described as a 'right' in Part X.'[42]

Hence, it could be contended that the transit State has a duty to negotiate and conclude a transit treaty with its land-locked neighbour. Although this argument may sound quite absurd in view of the rule that States, as sovereigns, are free to enter or not to enter into such treaties as they wish. Yet, as Lauterpacht argues, 'practice and precedent have acknowledged that in a number of respects the freedom of a State *not* to conclude a treaty is not absolute. The *pactum de contrahendo* is a notion familiar to international lawyers as a binding arrangement between States on points to be incorporated in a future treaty.'[43]

LOSC Article 125(2) requires the conclusion of an agreement between the transit State and land-locked States concerned. After agreeing the major principle in paragraph 1, the provision of paragraph 2, which contains subordinate procedural arrangements for the realisation of the foregoing provision, may have been left open in the understanding that it will be properly implemented in each and every situation according to the principle of *pacta sunt servanda*. Since the terms and modalities differ according to the location and situation of a land-locked State, it is not possible to incorporate all of these practical issues in an 'umbrella' convention such as the LOSC. Nevertheless, the words in paragraph 2 'shall be agreed' are of great significance. The transit State can neither simply delay the negotiations nor impose difficult conditions. The effective exercise of freedom of transit under this Convention depends upon the conclusion of appropriate agreements between the land-locked State and transit State concerned providing for the terms and modalities for such exercise. Therefore, it can plausibly be argued that since Article 125(2) is a *pactum de contrahendo*, the transit State concerned would be legally obliged to reach an agreement with the land-locked State.

However, a transit State could argue that this provision only requires it to negotiate and not necessarily to agree to an agreement if it is not satisfactory to it. Since Article 125 (2) does not envisage the possibility of the transit and the land-locked State failing to reach an agreement, it does not provide any alternative. A problem of this character does not fall under the competence of any tribunals established by the Convention. Therefore, the refusal by a transit State to conclude an agreement could cause a serious problem for the land-locked State concerned. This is what actually happened between Nepal and India in 1989 and Nepal had no alternative but to change its policy and concede to the conditions put forward by India. Nevertheless, when a land-locked State's demands are based on past practice or multilateral treaties the transit State concerned seems obliged to conclude a transit treaty. That appears to be precisely the case between Nepal and India. The latter had concluded a separate transit treaty with the former in 1978 providing for 15 transit routes for Nepal.[44]

Whether the past practice of these two countries amounts to a local custom[45] and whether Nepal is entitled under the concept of local custom to the same facilities as those enjoyed in the past may be a matter for argument, but what is clear is that if Nepal is asking for no more than what it enjoyed in the past under the old treaty, India seems bound not only to enter into negotiations in good faith with Nepal but also to conclude an agreement.[46] Thapa, a former Law Secretary in Nepal, maintains that the 1978 Transit Treaty 'had codified customary practices existing between the two countries from time immemorial.'[47] While examining the nature of Indo-Nepal trade and transit relations in the aftermath of the 1970/71 crisis between these countries, Sarup concluded that India was 'under a legal obligation to facilitate and conclude' a transit treaty with Nepal.'[48]

One of the highly publicised issues in the 1989/90 crisis with India was that Nepal wanted to conclude a separate treaty on transit with India, whereas India wished to conclude a single treaty dealing with all matters of bilateral trade and transit. Strictly speaking, India does not seem obliged to conclude a separate treaty dealing only with transit, provided that it, accords Nepal all the transit facilities that this country is entitled to under international law and bilateral practice. But it is quite logical to argue that while trade is a periodic arrangement, transit is a necessary permanent condition for international trade for land-locked States and should be treated as such under a separate treaty.[49] Then one might ask, should the transit treaty be of permanent character? The answer can be both yes and no.

Yes, in the sense that since the freedom of transit is recognised in international law, that freedom should be incorporated in a permanent treaty whereby a change of mind of the transit State or the change of government in the transit State would not affect the transit facilities of the land-locked country. Since land-lockedness is a permanent condition a treaty dealing with this condition should also be of permanent character. But no, in the sense that neither the population nor the economic activities of the land-locked States are static, and their requirements as to transit facilities tend to expand. The legal provisions have to keep pace with the changes in technology and science. From a purely legal point of view too, a permanent transit treaty is not necessary if we accept that freedom of transit is established in international law. A freedom already firmly established does not need new documents to establish it. As we stated earlier, since India recognises Nepal's right of free access and freedom of transit under international law, there is no need to seek India's commitment through a permanent transit treaty.

Although it may be helpful to insert a clause on freedom of transit in a bilateral treaty of permanent character spelling out the basic nature of the overall relationship between the two countries, a transit treaty that also deals with the terms and modalities of transit cannot be of permanent character. Alternatively, the transit right may be incorporated in a permanent transit treaty, provided that the treaty contains only the basic principles of transit and the details on the terms and modalities of the exercise of this right are incorporated in the protocols attached to it which could be reviewed periodically without affecting the main treaty.

## Nepal's Transit Arrangements with India

### Background

The Treaty of Transit signed on 6 December 1991 is the second transit treaty concluded by Nepal with India. The 1978 transit treaty was the first treaty between these two countries solely concerned with transit. Prior to that, transit matters used to be incorporated in single treaties dealing with both trade and transit. After India gained independence, a Treaty of Trade and Commerce was concluded by Nepal with India in 1950. Under this treaty India recognised in favour of Nepal 'full and unrestricted right of *commercial transit*'.[50] Although this right was restricted to commercial transit, the facilities provided for such transit were generally favourable to Nepal. The Trade and Transit Treaty of 1960[51] between the two countries replaced the 1950 Treaty of Trade and Commerce. Although the 1960 treaty also granted Nepal fairly liberal transit facilities, it made Nepal's transit right reciprocal[52] and no reference was made to its land-locked character.

When this treaty expired on 31 October 1970 Nepal wished to conclude two treaties, one governing transit right and the other dealing with bilateral trade. This was after the adoption of the 1965 New York Convention on trade and transit of Land-Locked States, which recognises transit as a right of land-locked States in its Preamble.[53] But India wanted both these subjects to be dealt with within one single treaty, maintaining that both were interrelated. As the differences could not be sorted out, Nepal proposed that the *status quo* of the expired treaty be maintained for another year to enable both sides to hold more talks towards concluding a new treaty. India declined this plea too and, according to Nepalese officials, India resorted to pressure tactics by imposing restrictions on the export–import trade with

Nepal and stopped the supply of even essential commodities to her. This action of India's was characterised in Nepal as 'economic blockade'.[54]

The political background leading up to this crisis seems to be Nepal's unilateral denunciation in 1969 of a secret arms agreement signed in 1965 with India and Nepal's assertion that the 1950 Treaty of Peace and Friendship had fallen into disuse since India had not consulted Nepal either at the time of the 1962 Sino-Indian armed conflict or during the 1965 Indo-Pakistan war. Nepal had also demanded the immediate withdrawal of the Indian military personnel deployed along Nepal's border with China as well as the Indian Military Liaison Group, who entered Nepal supposedly under the 1950 Peace and Friendship Treaty. Although this uneasy chapter in Indo-Nepal relations ended in the conclusion of a mutual trade and transit treaty on 13 August 1971, Nepal emerged as a clear loser since there was neither a separate treaty on transit nor a recognition by India of Nepal's demand for an overland transit route to Bangladesh (formerly East Pakistan). Nepal lost in other fronts too. For instance, the term 'freedom of transit' was given a narrower meaning than under the previous treaty. India would have the right to take all indispensable measures to ensure that the freedom of transit, accorded by it on its territory, did not in any way infringe on its legitimate interests of any kind.[55] According to a former foreign minister of Nepal, India, under this treaty, could legally stop transit to Nepal if in its opinion Nepal was importing more than its requirement or exporting more than its available surplus because the freedom of transit was restricted to 'goods required by each contracting party and goods available for export from that party'.[56]

After the expiry of the 1971 treaty of trade and transit, India and Nepal concluded on 17 March 1978 two separate treaties, one governing transit facilities and the other governing trade. This time Nepal had some reasons to celebrate the conclusion of the treaties. First, Nepal had secured a separate treaty on transit – its long standing demand. Second, the new transit treaty recognised that 'Nepal as a land-locked country needs access to and from the sea to promote its international trade'.[57] Third, India agreed to provide Nepal necessary overland transit facilities through Indian territory (known as the Radhikapur route) to Bangladesh. Fourth, while the trade treaty was concluded for five years, the transit treaty was for seven years. This was done with the understanding that both treaties would not expire at the same time and separate negotiations could be conducted for separate treaties. It was hoped that this arrangement would make future negotiations easier and matters of bilateral trade would not creep in during negotiations for a transit treaty.

Nevertheless, India was able to tailor things[58] in such a way that not only both trade and transit treaties but also the agreements relating to petroleum products and some other essential commodities expired in March 1989.[59] For some weeks chaos reigned in Nepal; the Government claimed that no goods were entering Nepal from India;[60] all exports and imports were suspended; long queues for essential commodities, including cooking fuel, sugar, salt, and other petroleum products, in cities like Kathmandu brought life virtually to a standstill. Although India stated that two transit routes would be kept open for Nepal's international trade in keeping with international law even in the absence of a transit treaty, owing to administrative confusion and chaos in the aftermath of the expiry of the trade and transit treaties, Nepal's international trade to and from the Indian port of Calcutta was hampered and essential commodities had to be flown in from other countries. Most industries were shut down due to the lack of raw materials and oil. Nepal's GDP, which was growing at 5.7 per cent annually before the crisis was reported to have contracted by 2 per cent in the financial year ending July 1990.

These activities of India were described by Nepal as economic blockade, allegations denied by India.[61] However, after some weeks, Nepal's transit trade began to flow through the two transit points designated unilaterally for Nepal by India. This no-treaty regime continued for over a year and ended when both sides decided to revert to the *status quo ante* under a joint communiqué issued at the conclusion of the new Nepalese Prime Minister's visit to India in June 1990, and this unpleasant chapter was finally closed on 6 December 1991 when the two parties signed two new treaties, one on trade and the other on transit.

*Principal Provisions of the New Transit Treaty*[62]

It should be stated at the outset that the new transit treaty repeats, with minor alterations, the provisions of the 1978 transit treaty.[63] The Preamble to the treaty recognises that 'Nepal as a land-locked country needs access to and from the sea to promote its international trade'. But this recognition is diluted by the inclusion of the principle of reciprocity in the treaty. Moreover, the treaty fails to specify that as a land-locked country Nepal has the right of free access to and from the sea or needs access to and from the sea in order to enjoy the freedom of the high seas. Under Article I the Contracting Parties agreed that:

> The Contracting Parties shall accord to 'traffic in transit' freedom of transit across their respective territories through routes mutually agreed upon. No distinction shall be made which is based on flag of vessels, the places of origin, departure, entry, exit, destination, ownership of goods or vessels.

This article makes the transit right of Nepal subject to reciprocity, which is not consistent with the very concept of a right of free access of land-locked States. According to Article 125 of the LOSC, the right of free access to and from the sea is not subject to reciprocity; this right is unilaterally and solely available to land-locked States.

Article III defines the term 'traffic in transit', but the definition is narrower even than that provided for in the Barcelona Statute on Freedom of Transit, let alone the LOSC. Among other things the definition excludes persons, accompanied baggage, and most importantly, the means of transport. Article IV exempts traffic in transit 'from customs duties or other charges except reasonable charges for transportation and such other charges as are commensurate with the costs of services rendered in respect of such transit.' Article VII accords, subject to Indian laws and regulations, only to *merchant ships* sailing under the flag of Nepal treatment no less favourable than that accorded to ships of any other foreign country. Although Nepal does not have at present any warship, this article should have extended this facility to all ships flying the flag of Nepal since Nepal may in the future need warships to protect its commerce and fishing vessels to fish in the high seas and the Indian and, arguably, the Bangladesh's EEZ under Article 69 of the LOSC when it enters into force.[64]

Articles II, VIII and IX of the Transit Treaty impose several types of limitations on the freedom of transit accorded to traffic in transit. While the limitations of Articles VIII and IX seem justifiable as being broadly in line with international practice, the limitations imposed under Article II raise some questions. This article reads as follows:

(a) Each Contracting Party shall have the right to take all indispensable measures to ensure that such freedom, accorded by it on its territory does not in any way infringe its legitimate interests of any kind.

(b) Nothing in this treaty shall prevent either Contracting Party from taking any measures which may be necessary for the protection of its essential security interests.

The vague words 'all indispensable measures' and 'legitimate interests of any kind' might allow an obdurate government, and especially during friction between two countries, to impose unnecessary limitations on Nepal's right transit rights: they should be more specific on 'measures'.[65] In the absence of any indication of what may be regarded as 'indispensable measures'[66] and 'legitimate interests', India may consider itself free to impose any restrictions deemed 'necessary'[67] by it to protect its 'legitimate interests'. In fact, the limitation imposed under Article II (b) suffices to encompass the main purpose of limitations. The limitation imposed under Article II (a) is arbitrary, undesirable and ambiguous. Since the restrictions imposed under Articles VIII and IX of the Transit Treaty are designed to protect those interests of India which could appropriately be called 'legitimate interests', it is not clear what other interests are intended to be protected under Article II (a).[68]

Details of port facilities and transit routes are incorporated in a Protocol to the Treaty of Transit and exports and imports procedures applicable to Nepal's traffic in transit are outlined in a Memorandum attached to the treaty. The Protocol designates 15 routes for Nepal's traffic in transit. It allows Nepal to use both rail and road facilities of India for her convenience. But in contrast to the 1978 treaty, the 1991 treaty does not provide Nepal any facilities in Haldia. The 1978 treaty had stated that India would arrange with the Trustees for the Port of Calcutta to make suitable land in Haldia available for the construction of facilities for the storage of Nepalese cargo.

## Evaluation of the New Transit Treaty

On the surface Nepal seems to have achieved a satisfactory transit treaty with India since the latter conceded to the Nepalese demand for a separate treaty on transit and for 15 transit routes, in contrast to the stance taken by New Delhi during the Indo-Nepal stalemate that under international law Nepal was entitled to only one transit route. India agreed to continue to provide overland transit facilities through Radhikapur for Nepal's trade with or via Bangladesh. This could well be hailed as a success. But the fact remains that the whole exercise on the right of land-locked States during UNCLOS III and the incorporation in the resulting 1982 Law of the Sea Convention of the right of free access of land-locked States does not seem to have influenced the latest transit treaty. Nor, apparently, has account been taken of other provisions of the LOSC on land-locked States. For instance, the Transit Treaty disregards not only Article 125(1), but also Article 126 of the LOSC. Nepal has secured neither simplified exports and imports procedures[69] nor India's recognition of Nepal's 'right' of free access to and from the sea. No new facility has been added and no new concession secured. Rather, Nepal appears to have lost the facilities available to it in Haldia under the 1978 treaty. Most striking of all is the incorporation of the principle of reciprocity in the treaty. The elimination of the requirement of reciprocity in Part X of the LOSC represented a major breakthrough for the land-locked States. But if a bilateral transit treaty concluded nearly ten years after the conclusion of the LOSC still embodies the principle of reciprocity it could be regarded, from international legal point of view, as disastrous.[70]

At first glance, Kathmandu's granting of reciprocal transit facilities to India does not sound disastrous so long as India is interested merely in securing general transit facilities in the event of need. In fact, India too is entitled to certain transit facilities under the general principle of the freedom of transit.[71] But the reality is that Nepal's exercise of the right of free access to and from the sea should not be made dependent on Nepal's granting of similar facilities to India which is not land-locked. It is hardly justifiable to ask Nepal to offer similar facilities in return for something that is available to Nepal by virtue of its land-lockedness. As the 1991 treaty is intended to provide transit facilities to Nepal for her access to the sea, the reciprocity requirement seems, in practical terms, meaningless, since land-locked Nepal, by definition, lacks the means to reciprocate.[72] In fact India's transit trade through Nepal is nil; it does not actually need to use Nepalese territories for its international trade. India seems to have employed this reciprocity clause merely as political leverage. Moreover, the requirement of reciprocity incorporated in Article 1 of the Transit Treaty is in conflict with India's own admission in the Preamble to the treaty that 'Nepal as a land-locked country needs access to and from the sea to promote its international trade'.

So far as the Indo-Nepal relationship is concerned, the concept of reciprocity raises numerous issues. As stated earlier, India wishes to tie the transit right of Nepal to other issues like bilateral trade, treatment of Indians living in Nepal, India's strategic interests. This is because Nepal and India have a very complex bilateral relationship governed by a number of treaties some of which are quite ambiguous and outmoded.

Nevertheless, the new transit treaty represents some success for Nepal in the sense that India, a regional superpower and a conservative transit State, agreed after all this legal wrangling to conclude a separate treaty on transit and conceded to the Nepalese demand to have 15 transit routes reinstated by the new treaty. The separation of transit matters from other bilateral issues is vital to Nepal and the new transit treaty has achieved this objective. From this Nepal can hope that India will not try again in the future to put pressure on Nepal by mingling her transit facilities with other bilateral matters. In that case Nepal's right of access will have been strengthened as a legal right rather than as facilities dependent on the transit State's goodwill.

ACKNOWLEDGEMENT

I would like to express my sincere thanks to Dr Christine Gray, Fellow of St.Hilda's College, Oxford for her very useful comments on an earlier draft of this article.

NOTES

1. *The Times of India*, 7 October 1988, p.1.
2. See 'Nepal offers to end cold war with India', *The Times* (London: 24 May 1989); 'Nepal counts the cost of defying Indian crocodile', *The Financial Times* (London: 24 October

1989); 'India leans on a neighbour', *Time* (17 April 1989) p.9; 'Nepal counts the cost of independence', *The Independent* (London: 10 April 1989); Colin Smith, 'Nepal suffers to fend off the New Raj', *The Observer* (London: 16 July 1989).

3. Nepal claimed that all transit routes were closed for some time in the beginning of the crisis. But this assertion conflicts with the stance maintained by India that it had always kept open two transit routes for Nepal's exports and imports from third countries. Nevertheless, under one pretext or another (e.g. administrative complications, etc.) all transit routes seem to have been closed for some time in the beginning of the crisis.

4. The 1978 trade treaty was concluded for five years and renewable for a further five-year period, while the transit treaty was for seven years and renewable for a further seven-year period. Both treaties had expired before March 1989. But they were constantly but only temporarily renewed by mutual agreement until this date. In the beginning of March Nepal learned from India that she was no longer prepared to renew, even temporarily, the trade and transit treaties. Nepalese officials maintained this came to them as a shock as they had not expected such an abrupt end of the trade and transit relationship between the two countries.

5. The reason given by India for refusing to sign the trade treaty was that Nepal had not kept its promise to scrap the additional tariffs levied on Indian goods soon after the negotiations for the trade treaty were completed but before the final signing took place. But Nepal's interpretation was that it had agreed to scrap the additional tariffs levied on Indian goods once the trade treaty was finally and formally concluded and since India had notified Nepal of its intention not to sign the already initialled trade treaty there was no question of Nepal not keeping its promise. See for two conflicting views of the two countries. *The Times of India* (7 April 1989) p.7.

6. The then Prime Minister of India, Rajiv Gandhi, stated on 16 April 1989 that India had taken a strong position with Nepal because apart from a series of other things 'two or three recent happenings upset' India. He went on to state that the two most upsetting things were the question of work permits for Indians and certain new taxes imposed on Indian goods. Although these two things were not in clear contravention of any bilateral treaty in force, Mr Gandhi claimed that these things were 'totally against the spirit' of India's relations and the treaty India had with Nepal. *The Times of India* (17 April 1989) p.1. It is worth noting that even in his view Nepal had not violated any *treaty provisions* but the *spirit* of bilateral relations and other bilateral treaties – a difficult thing to ascertain.

7. See Brian James, 'Nepalese united in adversity as Indian blockade bites', *The Times* (London: 30 June 1989); *Le Monde* (Paris), as cited in *The Rising Nepal*, (10 July 1989) p.3; *The Nation* (Pakistan: 26 April 1989) in ibid.

8. See S.D. Muni, 'India factor in Nepal's elections', *The Times of India* (6 May 1991) p.6 and ibid. 'Koirala's visit marks a new beginning', (3 December 1991) p.8.

9. 'India agrees to lift trade blockade from Nepal', *The Daily Telegraph* (London: 9 June 1990) p.11. Full text of the Nepal–India Joint Communiqué is reproduced in *The Rising Nepal* (12 June 1990) p.3.

10. See text of the treaty A.S. Bhasin, *Documents on Nepal's Relations with India and China 1949–66* (Bombay: Academic Books 1970) p.32. See for a letter attached to the treaty R. Shaha, *Nepali Politics: Retrospect and Prospect* (Delhi: Oxford University Press 1978) p.252.

11. See the views expressed by an Indian external affairs official in *Time* (17 April 1989) p.9. The official accused Nepal of not respecting the 'special relationship': 'Nepal carried its game of brinkmanship too far – and for too long.' But a Nepalese official stated that 'India is challenging our independence and sovereignty'. See also 'Up to Kathmandu', *The Times of India* (8 May 1989) p.6 and ibid. 'Kathmandu's Complaint' (12 August 1989) p.6.

12. R. Shaha, 'Himalayan impasse: need for new perspectives', *The Times of India* (7 June 1989) p.4.

13. See K. Natwar Singh, 'An agenda for talks with Mr Bhattarai', *The Times of India* (7 June 1990) p.8.

14. See supra note 10.

15. See Colin Smith 'Nepal suffers to fend off the New Raj' in *The Observer* (London: 16 July 1989): report on India's efforts to Bhutanise a neighbour.

16. 'Only 0.64 per cent of that potential is now harnessed. Foreign consultants say 25,000 MW are easily exploitable if and when India and Nepal reach some agreement on pricing.' *Far Eastern Economic Review* (8 March 1990) p.26.

17. *The Foreign Affairs Record,* 37/3 (March 1991) p.35, Ministry of Foreign Affairs, Government of India.

18. See for recent developments in this matter an understanding agreed between India and Nepal, *Nepal Gazette,* Part IV, 41/36 (1992) pp.7–10.

19. James Clad, 'GDP set to slump in wake of transit dispute: gasping for breath', *Far Eastern Economic Review* (8 March 1990) pp.26–25.

20. See paragraph (4) of the letter exchanged between Nepal and India with the 1950 treaty.

21. *India and Nepal: Facts and Chronology of the Problem* (HMG/Nepal: Department of Printing and Publications 1989) p.78. Arguments have also been put forward to assert that the treaty has fallen into disuse. Examples cited are India's failure to consult with Nepal before going to war with China in 1962 and with Pakistan in 1965 and 1971, India's expulsion of Nepalese living in Assam and Meghalaya, and introduction of a permit system for Nepalese to enter Sikkim and certain other parts of India. See the then Nepalese Prime Minister, K.N. Bista's interview in *The Rising Nepal* (25 June 1969).

22.. 7 *League of Nations Treaty Series,* Nos. 1–3 pp.11ff.

23. 450 *United Nations Treaty Series* pp.11–113.

24. 597 *United Nations Treaty Series* pp.42–63.

25. UN Doc. A/CONF.62/122, 7 October 1982.

26. Article 125 (1) of the 1982 Convention on the Law of the Sea.

27. The Vienna Convention entered into force on 27 January 1980. See text of the Convention UKTS No. 58 (1980), Cmnd.7964; 8 ILM 679 (1969).

28. Cf. the Preamble to the HSC which states that its provisions are 'generally declaratory of established principles of international law' and its Article 3.

29. See generally, United Nations, UNCLOS I, *Official Records,* I, UN DOC. A/CONF.13/29 and Add. 1, 311ff; M.I. Glassner, *Access to the Sea for Developing Land-Locked States* (1970); V.C. Govindraj, 'Land-locked States and their right of access to the sea', *Indian Journal of International Law* (1974) p.190; A.M. Sinjela, *Land-Locked States and the UNCLOS Regime* (1983).

30. UNCLOS III, *Official Records,* 2 p.238. See also Czechoslovakia, in the Sea-bed Committee, A/AC. 138/SC. II/SR. p.56.

31. J.Fawcett, 'Trade and finance in international law', *Hague Recueil Des Cours,* 1 (1968) pp.215–310, at p.267.

32. E. Lauterpacht, 'Freedom of transit in international law', *The Grotius Society Transactions, 1958 & 1959* pp.313–56, at p.332. See generally Reid, *International Servitude in Law and Practice* (1932) P.168; Caflisch, 'Land-locked States and their access to and from the sea', *British Yearbook of International Law* (1978) PP.71–100. Vasciannie, *Land-Locked and Geographically Disadvantaged States in the International Law of the Sea* (Oxford: Clarendon Press 1990) chapter 8.

33. Lauterpacht, p.349.

34. *Foreign Affairs Record,* 35/5 (New Delhi: May 1989) pp.131–3. Here it should be noted that at the UNCLOS III, proposals were put forward by the Group of Land-locked and Geographically Disadvantaged States maintaining that the absence of a bilateral transit treaty could not be invoked by transit States to deny the right of free access for land-locked States. Proposals dated 28 April 1976 (in R. Platzoder *Third United Nations Conference on the Law of the Sea: Documents* 4 [Oceana Publications 1984] p.332) and ibid. (28 June 1977), **381** at p.387. As none of these proposals was incorporated in the LOSC, India could have argued that it is not obliged to grant transit facilities to Nepal in the absence of a transit treaty with India. But India did not adopt this approach. This may be due to India's conviction that transit is a right of a land-locked Nepal as well as the principle, as Freid writes, that 'international law does not permit, except for reasons recognised by it, to harm or, in the extreme case, as it were, to blockade another country by cutting off its transit trade.' John H.E. Fried, 'The 1965 Convention on Transit Trade of Land-Locked States', *Indian Journal of International Law* 6 (1966) pp.9–30 at p.16.

35. See *The Times of India* (17 April 1989). A similar problem had occurred in 1970 after the expiry of the 1960 trade and transit treaty with India. At that time too India had unilaterally issued a notification providing for continued trade between the two countries. Notification No.192-ITC(PN) p.70 of 31 December 1970, *The Gazette*, Govt. of India, New Delhi. See in A. Sarup, 'Transit trade of land-locked Nepal', *International and Comparative Law Quarterly* 21(1972) pp.287–306 at p.294.

36. See *supra* note 34. See also Dilip Mukerjee, 'Himalayan stalemate: Indian stake in Nepali goodwill', *The Times of India* (4 April 1989) p.4; 'India rejects Nepal plea on treaties', ibid. (27 March 1989) p.1.

37. Vasciannie, p.193.

38. 55 *United Nations Treaty Series* 187; 210 (1950).

39. Supra note 22.

40. Lauterpacht, p.333.

41. Vasciannie, p.190.

42. Ibid.

43. Lauterpacht, p.347.

44. See also Article 43 of the Vienna Convention on the Law of Treaties of 1969 (both India and Nepal are party to it). It states that the invalidity, termination or denunciation of a treaty does not 'impair the duty of any State to fulfil any obligation embodied in the treaty to which it would be subject under international law independently of the treaty.' 8 *International Legal Materials* 679 (1969); *United Kingdom Treaty Series* No. 58 (1980).

45. See the *Case Concerning Right of Passage Over Indian Territory* (Merits) I.C.J. Reports, (1960), p.6. At p. 39 the Judgement stated that 'the Court sees no reason why long continued practice between two States accepted by them as regulating their relations should not form the basis of mutual rights and obligations between the two States.' The Court then decided that Portugal enjoyed a right of transit for private persons, civil officials, and goods between two of its territories enclaved within India and the coastal district of Daman by virtue of a local custom to this effect.

46. See the judgement of the International Court of Justice in the *North Sea Continental Shelf Cases* I.C.J. Reports (1969) p.47 for the Court's opinion on the nature of obligations of States to enter into negotiations with a view to arriving at an agreement.

47. Dhruba B.S. Thapa, 'India-Nepal relations, perspectives on present problem: a legal approach', paper presented at a seminar on 'Transit' organised by the Nepal University Teachers Association, Kathmandu, May 1989, p.2. Making a statement on the topic of public importance at a meeting of National Assembly (Rastriya Panchayat) the then Nepalese Foreign Minister also asserted that the 15 transit points designated by the 1978 treaty were customary transit points. See *Nepal and India: Facts and Chronology of the Problem* (HMG/Nepal: Department of Printing and Publications 1989) pp.88–9.

48. Sarup, p.302.

49. See for a similar argument by the then Nepalese Foreign Minister, Mr Upadhyay, in 'Nepal suffers but is standing firm', *The Independent* (London: 11 April 1989).

50. Article I of the treaty. See Bhasin, p.124.

51. Ibid., p.125.

52. Article VII of the 1960 trade and transit treaty provides that 'Goods intended for import into or export from the territories of either Contracting Party from or to a third country shall be accorded freedom of transit through the territories of the other party.' Bhasin, p.127.

53. Principle I of the Preamble to the Convention.

54. Editorial in *The Rising Nepal*, (6 January 1971).

55. Article VIII of the Treaty of Trade and Transit of 1971. See for text of the treaty (1971) 257 *Indian Trade Journal* 2132 (380.5 GOV) p.B-890–9.

56. Shaha, p.132.

57. Preamble to the treaty of transit. See for text of the treaty Surya P. Subedi, *Land-Locked Nepal and International Law* (Kathmandu: 1989) pp.85–112.

58. See Thapa, *supra* note. 47 and 'India rejects Nepal plea on treaties', *The Times of India* (27 March 1989) p.1.

59. Until this date the trade and transit treaties were being renewed for differing periods after they had expired.

60. 'No goods from India enter Nepal for 15th day' was a front page headline in the government owned national daily English newspaper *The Rising Nepal* (4 April 1989); Tony Allen-Mills, 'Nepal suffers but is standing firm', *The Independent* (London: 11 April 1989) and the editorial of the same date: 'Coming of age in India'.

61. The Nepalese ambassador to India said in a press conference in New Delhi on 7 April 1989 that since India was not allowing even essential commodities to enter Nepal this action of India was economic blockade. But an Indian external affairs ministry spokesman stated on the same date that 'An economic blockade of Nepal is the furthest from our intentions'. The spokesman claimed that two transit points were kept open for Nepal's trade. *The Times of India* (7 April 1989) p.7.

62. See for text of the *Treaty of Transit, Treaty of Trade and Agreement of Co-operation to Control Unauthorised Trade between His Majesty's Government of Nepal and the Government of India* (Kathmandu, Nepal: Nepal Transit and Warehousing Company Limited 1991).

63. See for an assessment of the 1978 Transit Treaty, Subedi, Ch.3.

64. See Surya P. Subedi, 'The marine fishery rights of land-locked States with particular reference to the EEZ' *International Journal of Estuarine and Coastal Law* 2/4 (1987) pp.227–39.

65. For instance, under Article XXI(b) of the GATT the 'essential security interests' which may be protected, must be of very specific character: they must either be '(i) relating to *fissionable* materials...' or '(ii) to the traffic in *arms*, ammunition and implements of war and to such traffic in other goods...as is supplying the *military* establishment;' or '(iii) taken in time of war or other emergency in *international* relations'. Cited in John H.E. Fried, 'The 1965 Convention on Transit Trade of Land-Locked States', *Indian Journal of International Law* 6 (1966) pp.9–30, at p.26. As Fried writes, it is hard to conceive how it could become 'necessary' for 'essential' security reasons to suspend any of the basic rules of transit. A clause like this does not give a carte blanche to disregard the essentials of the right of transit. Ibid., pp.26–7.

66. It should, however, be noted that the term 'indispensable measures' used in the Transit Treaty is much more restrictive than the word 'necessary measures' used in Article 125 (3) of the LOSC. Therefore, it can be regarded as a positive thing from the perspective of Nepal.

67. However, as Caflisch writes, 'the reference to 'necessary' measures suggests, *a contrario*, that the transit State has no power to take measures which are objectively unnecessary.' Caflisch, p.96.

68. Article 11 of the 1965 Convention on Transit Trade of Land-Locked States.

69. See for a discussion on cumbersome customs and transit procedure, Subedi, Ch.3. Pilferage of Nepalese goods on Indian railways increases Nepalese export costs. According to a survey transit costs consume 8 per cent of Nepal's GDP. See *Far Eastern Economic Review* (8 March 1990) p.24.

70. Among other deficiencies of the 1991 transit treaty is the absence of a dispute resolution provision. Since the transit dispute has often soured the entire Indo-Nepal relationship it was high time to provide for a dispute resolution mechanism in the treaty. Since both Nepal and India are party to the Barcelona Convention and the Statute on Freedom of Transit, any dispute arising from matters covered by the Statute could be taken for adjudication before the International Court of Justice (ICJ) in accordance with Article 13 of the Statute, which provides that disputes relating to the interpretation or application of the Statute could be brought before the former Permanent Court of International Justice (PCIJ), and Article 37 of the Statute of the International Court of Justice, to which both Nepal and India are party and which states that whenever a treaty or convention in force provides for reference of a matter to the PCIJ, the matter shall, as between the parties to the present Statute, be referred to the ICJ. However, there are many matters in the transit treaty which are not covered by the Barcelona Convention and the Statute and for such matters no international tribunal has jurisdiction, unless both States, by special agreement, consent to take the case to an international tribunal or to the ICJ.

71. Article 2 of the Barcelona Statute on Freedom of Transit provides a general freedom of transit for all States party to it. But this general freedom of transit is limited to transit by rail or waterway.

72. Caflisch, writes that 'The natural and ordinary meaning of the term "reciprocity" in matters of transit would seem to be that if a coastal transit State gives a land-locked country *access to and from the sea* by granting it rights of transit, that country has to concede the *same right* to the coastal transit State. This is absurd, for by definition a land-locked State lacks a sea-coast and hence is incapable of giving anyone access to the sea.' Caflisch, p.89.

# Resolving the Problems of Land-lockedness

## MARTIN IRA GLASSNER

The professional literature on land-locked states has increased substantially in the past two decades. There is now a considerable body of writings by people in many countries around the world reporting on, inquiring into or carefully analysing most aspects of land-lockedness from various disciplinal and national viewpoints. In addition, there is a roughly equally large body of material related to land-lockedness produced by the United Nations and its organs and affiliates; by other intergovernmental organisations, including many regional and subregional groups; and by private consultants and consulting firms, chiefly in the fields of economics and engineering.[1]

Regrettably, however, there is very little interaction between the two groups. Academics, journalists and other writers seldom utilise the materials produced by those doing the daily, pragmatic, unglamorous work of actually trying to reduce the difficulties inherent in a country's lack of sovereignty over a seacoast. The only exception is work on treaties, their background and ancillary documents, agreed on by states and by such organisations as the League of Nations and the United Nations. Similarly, those producing international legal instruments and those working 'on the ground' on transport and related matters are seldom even aware of the theoretical work being done in academia or the actual unfolding of events relating to land-lockedness in places and professions beyond their own limited kens. The purpose of this paper is to marry the two: to provide a bit of theoretical and background material on the problems of land-lockedness, but to stress what is actually being done and what further can be done to resolve or at least mitigate these problems. It draws on both the professional literature and reports from the field, but largely on my own experience.

I first encountered the issue of land-lockedness in 1962–63, when I was serving as American Vice Consul in Antofagasta, Chile and reporting to Washington on Bolivian complaints about alleged deficiencies in the transit of Bolivian imports and exports across Chilean territory and through Chilean ports. When I returned to academia in 1964, I wrote my master's thesis on Bolivia's access to the sea, using materials collected in the field, in Bolivia and Chile, as well as the very sparse literature available at the time. Perceiving a significant issue in international relations that had been largely neglected, I went on to write my doctoral dissertation, later published verbatim, on access to the sea for developing land-locked states, using Bolivia, Afghanistan and Uganda as case studies.

Since then I have produced many papers and articles on the subject, but perhaps more importantly, have actually worked in the field at various levels. I was adviser to His Majesty's Government of Nepal, for example, in 1976 and 1989, helping them prepare to negotiate transit treaties with India, and served as representative of the International Law Association and adviser to the delegation of Nepal at most sessions of the Third United Nations Conference on the Law of the Sea (UNCLOS III, 1973–1982). I evaluated, on behalf of the United Nations Development Programme (UNDP), transit transport projects in Asia (1979) and Africa (1984 and 1990), actually travelling through the fifteen countries involved, both coastal and land-locked, interviewing officials, shippers, truckers and others, inspecting facilities and collecting relevant maps and documents. I served as a member of the *ad hoc* group of experts assembled in Geneva in 1984 by the United Nations Conference on Trade and Development (UNCTAD) to prepare formal recommendations for the improvement of transit transport; and, with the aid of research grants, did field work in Bolivia and all of its neighbours in 1983 and 1985, visiting government offices, railway stations, customs posts, sea and river ports, and libraries, everywhere interviewing people and collecting documents and maps.

It is this experience, even more than the professional literature, that informs my presentation here. It is this experience also that convinces me that what is needed now is not more theorising or philosophising about land-lockedness, but practical ideas for resolving real, specific problems at every level from international law to the smallest customs office.

## The Problems of Land-lockedness

The problems generated by lack of a seacoast, particularly for poor countries, fall into two broad categories: access to and from the sea; that is, transit across the territory of one or more neighbouring states for an interior state's third-country imports and exports (those bound to or from countries other than immediate neighbours); and uses of the sea, chiefly mining, fishing and transport. Of the two, the less important historically and at present is the latter, the uses of the sea.

The United Nations Convention on the Law of the Sea (LOSC), produced in 1982 by UNCLOS III, has proven to be so generally acceptable as expressive of both settled and emerging international law that numerous states are already implementing large portions of it and harmonising their domestic legislation with many of its provisions. Thus, such principles as non-discrimination against ships flying the flags of land-locked states, first codified by the League of Nations, remain in force. Since land-locked countries lack sovereignty over seaports and their approaches, however, application of these principles often must be negotiated with port states. More important in the present context, however, is the extension of national (coastal state) jurisdiction far out to sea.

The 1982 Law of the Sea Convention provides for various degrees of coastal state jurisdiction over internal waters, a territorial sea of up to twelve nautical miles seaward of its natural or straight baseline, a zone contiguous to the territorial sea of up to an additional twelve nautical miles in breadth, an exclusive economic zone (EEZ) of up to 188 nautical miles from outer limit of the territorial sea (or 200 nm from the baseline), the continental shelf (defined as being the entire submerged continental margin beyond the territorial sea, plus a bit more for good measure) and assorted other zones of less consequence for land-locked states. This means that under the provisions of the LOSC, a land-locked state no longer has a right to utilise the resources of the sea, the continental shelf, the seabed and the subsoil thereof within 200 miles of the coast. Generally speaking, it may not drill into or erect structures on the shelf, conduct scientific research, dump wastes or engage in any other activity in the EEZ without the express consent of the coastal state, and it has only a greatly restricted right to a small portion of the living resources of the EEZ (chiefly finfish and shellfish, but also including such things as corals, sponges and seaweeds).

In practice, these provisions have not caused any real hardship for any land-locked country and are not likely to for a while. Those that wish to engage in such activities now or in the near future and have the wherewithal to do so are located primarily in Europe and have sufficient economic and political strength to be able to bargain with coastal states for favourable terms. The developing land-locked states of Africa, Asia and South America, however, face far more difficult obstacles in deriving benefits from the resources of the sea. The picture is a bit different, however, with maritime transport.

Several European land-locked countries – notably Switzerland but also Czechoslovakia and Hungary – have long operated high-seas merchant fleets that fluctuate in size and profitability but may be considered legitimate economic enterprises having, at least in the case of Switzerland, the added value of providing some measure of security in times of severe political stress in the region. Paraguay is the only *developing* land-locked country that has consistently operated not only a variety of river craft carrying its transit trade but also a number of seagoing merchant vessels, with a modest navy to patrol parts of their routes. Others, however, have made at least a gesture toward creating or operating national shipping lines, among them Nepal, Uganda, Swaziland and Mali. Of them, the only one currently in regular operation is Linabol, a Bolivian company operating one ship between North and South America, apparently at a reasonable profit. A detailed study of the maritime activities of land-locked developing countries has never been done and could be most useful.

In most respects the situation in respect of land-locked states in Europe and elsewhere is similar to that of their coastal neighbours. In fact, the interior districts of a number of countries, such as Brazil, Zaire, Myanmar and Mozambique, suffer from the same geographic handicaps as land-locked states. So do some states, such as Iraq, Jordan and Zaire, that have very short and nearly useless coastlines. The distinction, however, the single factor that distinguishes any land-locked country, regardless of political, geographic or economic circumstances, from any coastal country is that it must cross an international boundary en route to or from the sea. All of the problems of land-lockedness, then, from unwarranted delays in transit to exclusion from offshore petroleum deposits, are inherently political. It follows that ultimately they can only be solved politically. Meanwhile, much can be done – and is being done – to resolve these problems, of which those related to access to and from the sea are by far the most important.

### Five Approaches to Transit Problems

For many centuries land-locked territories suffered from numerous obstructions, restrictions, tolls and heavy transit fees on goods and persons moving to and from the sea, in addition to the inherent problems of distance, inhospitable terrain and primitive transport. This was not always a handicap, for indeed isolation from the sea often provided protection from all manner of hazards from hurricanes to seaborne invasions. Generally, however, the lack of seaports, incomparable 'windows on the world', meant isolation from the flows and eddies of international intercourse that fertilise and stimulate both human minds and whole societies. As industrialisation accelerated, so did commerce and it became evident that a free flow of trade was of benefit to land-locked and coastal peoples alike. Gradually through the nineteenth century tolls and restrictions on transit were eliminated, including those applying to coastal states.

The League of Nations sponsored a series of conferences during the 1920s which produced both bilateral and multilateral treaties designed to facilitate free transit. This process continued after the Second World War both within and outside the framework of the United Nations, culminating in the 1965 United Nations Convention on Transit Trade of Land-locked States. Still the only multilateral instrument dealing exclusively with the subject, it never attained sufficient status to create norms binding on non-parties, and few coastal states ever became parties. It has in effect been superseded by the 1982 Law of the Sea Convention.

Part X of this convention is titled Right of Access of Land-locked States to and from the Sea and Freedom of Transit. Note that coastal states are still not willing to concede a *right* of transit across their territories for land-locked countries, only a right of access which they could hardly deny in view of all that has happened in the past century and of the present state of international political and economic relations. Of course, this right is meaningless, it cannot be implemented, without transit, but transit must be negotiated on a bilateral or regional basis and then administered effectively by all parties if coastal state sovereignty is to be accommodated. Nevertheless, since land-locked countries and legal theorists largely abandoned claims of 'natural' rights of transit and such notions as free transit deriving directly from the traditional freedom of the high seas, and began stressing the importance of a free flow of world trade as an instrument of economic development – of transit as a necessity, not a right – transit has, in fact, generally faced fewer legal and political obstacles than it has for centuries.

Part X of the LOSC, however, is still far from perfect from the standpoint of the interior states. Its defects have been amply demonstrated by the deliberate interference by transit states with the transit traffic of Uganda, Nepal and Afghanistan, among others. Nevertheless, the time does not appear ripe – and probably will not be for decades – for the establishment of a *right* of transit through international law. International law has, however, created a datum plane, a set of minimum standards that can be used as guidelines by parties negotiating transit regions. However defective it may be, it is still indispensable and must be clearly understood by anyone concerned with the problems of land-lockedness.

A second approach to these problems is to encourage overall economic development. This, of course, if properly managed, brings many benefits to a poor country, of which improved transit may not be the most important. Economic development invariably requires improved transport. Whatever its other purposes or benefits, improved transport within a country does facilitate its foreign trade, both with its immediate neighbours and with third parties. Development also frequently involves new products, new suppliers and consumers outside the country, large shipments of aid goods of all kinds, and in general a larger volume of international trade. This, of course, does at times add to the woes of an overburdened transport system in a transit state and disputes over priorities in use of available facilities, but it also has the salutary effect of providing greater revenue for the transit state for the servicing of increased traffic in transit, thus strengthening the bargaining power of the enclave state.

Third, land-locked states are becoming more skilled at negotiating transit agreements, often with the aid of UNCTAD or other outside agencies. They are able, for example, to swap surplus water for improved transit, provide troops to guard transport routes and facilities in a transit state, provide transit for the third-party trade of transit states, and otherwise strike deals without insisting on legal 'rights'. Gradually, much too gradually, the transit arrangements between some countries and within some regions are becoming better known to those elsewhere and provide useful ideas for improving transit locally. Again, the United Nations is the principal, though still inefficient, intermediary for the exchange of this type of information.

Land-locked countries are also encouraging, even participating in and generally benefiting from, the improvement of transport facilities and transit procedures in their transit countries, at the border, at transhipment points, along the transit routes and in the sea and river ports. At the same time, they are trying to develop new transit routes, sometimes through other countries, so they would be able to shift their transit traffic from traditional routes to new ones in case of interruptions or higher costs. New routes can also service sections of a land-locked country hitherto isolated and economically backward. The availability of alternative routes, of course, also enhances their bargaining power, an advantage not available to such countries as Nepal and Lesotho, which are effectively confined to using a single state for transit. A corollary to this is the increased use of air transport to overfly a transit state. Because of economic, meteorological, political and security considerations, however, air transport can only be a supplement to and not a substitute for overland transport.

Fifth, land-locked countries are participating actively in regional and sub-regional organisations. Such participation has many purposes, advantages and costs, and improved transit may not be very important in some cases. In others, however, such as the Andean Group, the Plata Basin and the Southern African Development Community (SADC) it is a high priority activity. By pooling their resources, the members of such organisations can share the costs, risks and benefits, presumably for the benefit of all. Regionalism, however, is seldom easy and not always successful. Witness the failure of the Latin American Free Trade Area, the Asia and Pacific Council and, saddest of all, the East African Community. Nevertheless, most land-locked countries have derived some transit benefits from regional organisations as part of overall efforts to strengthen links and improve the flow of goods, people and ideas among the members.

## Transit Agreements

All of the elements of transit arrangements between land-locked and transit states, it seems to me, fall naturally into three categories: principles, facilities and procedures. These are commonly formalised in written agreements, sometimes in a package of two or three documents of different types. Principles, for example, may be outlined in a basic treaty, the facilities (routes, carriers, ports, etc.) to be used for transit listed in some detail in a protocol to the treaty, and the procedures to be used in clearing goods through customs at ports and borders (and perhaps transhipment points) spelled out in a memorandum or similar document, often with samples of the relevant forms and documents annexed. Sometimes all of these elements are placed in a single document, and there are still cases in which transit is covered quite sketchily within a standard trade or friendship treaty. The type of agreement chosen depends on many intangible factors: the degree of importance of transit to the parties, the state of relations between them, the complexity of the transit arrangements, tradition and so on. All forms of agreement are equally binding in international law and the chief difference is probably in the degree of ease of amendment.

An important aspect of any transit agreement is its duration. Ideally, such an agreement should have no expiry date, since land-lockedness may be assumed to be a permanent condition and the need for transit equally permanent.[2] If an open-ended agreement is not possible, then the longer its duration the better for the enclave state. In its (or their) provisions for administration (which may be considered a fourth category of elements in a transit system), there is generally a procedure for routine adjustments in the arrangements to accommodate changing circumstances, and for resolving disputes over the interpretation or application of the agreements. This is commonly done by establishing a joint committee to oversee the transit arrangements, which typically is composed of deputy ministers or senior civil servants responsible for trade and/or transport. Sometimes there are provisions for formally amending one or more of the documents before the expiry date; in other cases, they are amended informally by the joint committee or similar body and the amendments ratified by a simple exchange of notes or memoranda of understanding.

The principles enunciated in the basic document are frequently similar to those found in Part X of the United Nations Convention on the Law of the Sea. This should not be surprising, for Part X (indeed, the Convention as a whole), for all its deficiencies, represents the best compromise that could have been worked out at this stage of history between land-locked and transit states, and may be considered to represent a consensus of the international community. Some of the more important of these principles are:

1. Traffic in transit shall not be subject to any customs duties, taxes or other charges except charges levied for specific services rendered in connection with such traffic. (Article 127[1])

2. For the convenience of traffic in transit, free zones or other customs facilities may be provided at the ports of entry and exit in the transit states, by agreement between those states and the land-locked states. (Article 128)

3. Transit states shall take all appropriate measures to avoid delays or other difficulties of a technical nature in traffic in transit. (Article 130[1])

4. Transit states, in the exercise of their full sovereignty over their territory, shall have the right to take all measures necessary to ensure that the rights and facilities provided for in this part for land-locked states shall in no way infringe their legitimate interests. (Article 125[3])

The last cited provision, of course, is the great escape clause for transit states. If used only sparingly and in *extremis,* it should not prove troublesome; if misused, however, it can nullify even existing transit agreements and wreak great hardship in a mediterranean (middle of the land) state. Fortunately, such actions have been uncommon in the recent past, but this is no guarantee that they will be so in the future.

As for facilities and procedures, it is difficult to generalise about them because local conditions vary so greatly around the world and the application of transit principles must respond to these varied conditions. This is the pragmatic reason for the provision in the LOSC that 'the terms and modalities for exercising freedom of transit shall be agreed between the land-locked states and transit states concerned through bilateral, subregional or regional agreements' (Art. 125[2]). Although there has been a long-running ideological debate over this provision between the land-locked and transit states, some version of it really is necessary if practical solutions are to be found to the myriad real transit problems that still plague international commerce.

Various agencies of the United Nations system have provided technical assistance to developing land-locked countries in all three areas. UNCTAD, for example, has provided experts to Malawi and the BLS countries (Botswana, Lesotho and Swaziland) and myself to Nepal to help these countries prepare to negotiate transit agreements. Overwhelmingly, however, technical assistance has been in the areas of facilities and procedures. Small amounts of money have been allocated in the past to a few countries (mostly in Asia) for trucks, barges, warehouses and other facilities, but most assistance has been and continues to be in the form of information, advice, collection and analysis of statistics, research and studies, liaison, seminars and workshops, training and other services. The range of such services is too great to describe here. A reasonably clear picture, however, may be obtained from the titles of the documents listed in my bibliography that have been produced by UNCTAD; the regional commissions for Africa (ECA), Asia and the Pacific (ESCAP) and Latin America and the Caribbean (CEPAL); and several specialised agencies. The Organisation of American States, The Club du Sahel, SADC, the World Customs Organisation in Brussels and other intergovernmental organisations also provide technical assistance in transit matters, as do the aid programs of individual countries, some of which also provide material assistance to transit transport.

UNCTAD currently operates important, long-range projects that provide technical assistance to transit in West-central, East-central and Southern Africa, and formerly operated such projects for the five land-locked countries of Asia, all funded by UNDP, with some help from other donors. Most of their studies and reports are listed in my bibliography; they constitute by far the best source of factual, current information on the day-to-day problems and progress of transit in these countries and subregions. Any serious researcher in this area would find ample reward in these documents for the effort necessary to obtain access to them, since most of them are restricted.

## Potential Models for Transit Agreements

I have already mentioned that the land-locked countries of Europe have few serious problems with transit, and that most of them, in fact, also provide transit routes and facilities for other countries, both coastal and land-locked. One of the major reasons for this has been the TIR Convention, done at Geneva on 15 January 1959.[3] This little – appreciated agreement has facilitated the flow of truck traffic through most of Western Europe. It has been so successful that efforts are under way to introduce a modified version of it in South America, and certainly its basic concepts and adaptations of its detailed provisions would be applicable elsewhere. Two more recent agreements in *developing* regions are scarcely known outside their regions and have not yet been analysed or even reported in the professional literature. Though not yet as important as the TIR Convention, they certainly deserve more attention than they have received so far and more than I can devote to them here.

First is the *Sistema Integrado de Tránsito (SIT)*, the Integrated Transit System, developed by CEPAL in 1975 to expedite the flow of Bolivian imports through the port of Arica, Chile. It has since been applied to the larger Chilean port of Antofagasta, and negotiations have long been under way for its introduction into the Peruvian ports of Ilo and Matarani and into Buenos Aires, Argentina. Regrettably, the most recent analysis of this system is available only in Spanish, covers only Arica and is already quite old.[4] This detailed evaluation of the system after its first twelve years of operation indicates that it is functioning reasonably well and has proven adaptable to highway as well as railway transport up to Bolivia, but is in need of modernisation to accommodate the enormous increase in container use and integration into the rapidly developing global system of multimodal transport. Meanwhile, it has been successful in reducing the paperwork and is simplifying the procedures necessary to move goods in transit rapidly and safely. It is likely that important elements of this system can be adapted for use in Africa and Asia, and it should be better known there.

Much newer, more complex and larger in scope is the Northern Corridor Transit Agreement, signed in 1985 by Burundi, Kenya, Rwanda and Uganda and acceded to by Zaire in 1987. Most of the technical work on this agreement was done over a number of years by UNCTAD. In general, it follows the format described earlier: the agreement itself, which contains principles, nine protocols that detail the transit facilities and procedures, an annex that establishes a Northern Corridor Transit Transport Co-ordination Authority which has much greater responsibilities than the typical bilateral transit committee, and a number of ancillary documents, all forming a single package which may be amended or supplemented as necessary. Since it is newer and takes into account a greater variety of circumstances than the SIT, it is probably an even better model for countries in other sub-regions, particularly in Africa.

There is as yet nothing comparable to either of these agreements in Asia. Afghanistan, Bhutan, Laos, Mongolia and Nepal differ from one another in almost every conceivable way (except that Bhutan and Nepal differ from one another less than the others); none is contiguous with any of the others; they all depend for their transit on giant countries generally larger than any transit states to be found in South America or Africa (except for Brazil and South Africa); and they have little tradition of co-operation with one another and only a little more with their transit states. It is likely, notwithstanding the apparent success of ASEAN (the Association of Southeast Asian Nations) and SAARC (the South Asian Association for Regional Co-operation), that nothing as comprehensive as the Northern Corridor Transit Agreement will emerge in Asia for decades. Nevertheless, there is much in this agreement that could be adapted to the Asian situation.

## Conclusion

In the past two years the number of land-locked states in the world has increased by a third and may well increase still further by the end of the century. I am unaware of any transit problems experienced to date by any of the nine land-locked states that emerged from the dissolution of the Soviet

Union, or by Macedonia. The imminent independence of Slovakia and the possible further fragmentation of Yugoslavia and the former Soviet Union will probably not generate such problems immediately. Each, however, is a candidate for transit problems with unfriendly or uncooperative neighbours and none has been or will be born with automatic access to the resources of any EEZ, including that of Russia. The rights and claims of land-locked states, therefore, are likely to become more, not less, prominent as we approach the end of the twentieth century (which indeed, may already have ended except on the calendar). The problems of land-lockedness are unlikely to go away very soon.

Clearly, the only way to solve these problems definitively is to eliminate the boundaries between the land-locked and transit states.[5] That is, political integration between them would instantly convert the land-locked states into simply interior districts of coastal states. Since that is seldom accomplished, however, since all states are reluctant to surrender their sovereignty land (indeed the trend seems to be in quite the opposite direction), we may eliminate this solution for the present. The next best, then, is economic integration. This is only slightly less difficult to achieve, but even in the early stages it can result in reduction of formalities at the borders and perhaps in the ports. Regional co-operation, as in SADC, SAARC and ECOWAS (the Economic Community of West African States), can achieve results in respect of transit and utilisation of the sea similar to those of integration without the costs and risks invariably attached thereto. Again, there is a dearth of serious research on the subject of regional transit arrangements, and there is almost nothing in print about the practical aspects of land-locked countries' use of the sea.

I conclude this very sketchy presentation with a plea to geographers to get involved in the problems of land-lockedness, to study existing principles, facilities and procedures for access to the sea and uses of the sea by the increasing number of land-locked states in the world. Surely they have as much to contribute to the solution of the problem as the lawyers and economists who have long dominated the field. And they may have very much more to gain as well, if my own experience is any guide.

## NOTES

1. The world's only comprehensive bibliography on the subject is my own *Bibliography on Land-locked States*, Fourth Revised and Enlarged Edition (Dordrecht: Martinus Nijhoff 1995). It lists over 3,000 items of all kinds, including unpublished items, in all disciplines, in 23 languages. Nearly all items listed (except restricted documents and studies) are available on request from me.
2. Only one land-locked country – Ethiopia – has acquired a seacoast since World War II, and it has rejoined the ranks of the land-locked since Eritrea's secession.

3.  TIR – Transports International Routiers: Customs Convention on the International Transport of Goods Under Cover of TIR Carnets.
4.  CEPAL document LC/L.436, 7 December 1987. Sistema Integrado de Tránsito para Mercaderías Bolivianas Transbordadas a Través del Puerto de Arica: Evaluación a los 12 Años de Funcionamiento.
5.  In a moment of levity, I explained to my Nepalese colleagues in 1976 that the solution to their transit problems was really quite simple; all they had to do was to annex West Bengal. They appreciated this suggestion, but upon reflection concluded that, however attractive the proposal might be, it seemed to present rather more difficulties than peacefully negotiating a transit agreement with India.

# Conclusions

## DICK HODDER

There is as yet very little general or theoretical writing on land-locked states: the variety and apparent uniqueness of each case seems to inhibit any general analysis of the land-locked state phenomenon, or what may perhaps be termed land-lockedness. Only in the case of Africa has there as yet been any attempt at regional or continental analysis and that was over twenty years ago. For the most part the material, though increasingly voluminous, is scattered widely and mainly involves descriptive and analytical studies of individual land-locked states. The present volume adds significantly to this literature with a number of important new case studies, including a study of five new land-locked states in Central Asia, and attempts to make a wider analysis of the problems generated by land-lockedness for the land-locked states of Africa and Asia. This decade has witnessed a surge in the number of land-locked states in the world – now well over forty – and it seems reasonable to suggest that it is an appropriate time for more general and theoretical writing and research to be directed at the phenomenon of land-lockedness.

Before identifying the main issues which seem to arise from a reading of this volume it seems important to make two general points about the land-locked states of Africa and Asia.

First, the definition of land-lockedness is of course self-evident, but requires some further elucidation. Land-locked states have no coastline open to the oceans and no sovereignty over any route of access to the sea or any right of access to the sea over any particular route. This renders them dependent on another state or other states for access to the sea – a condition which interferes fundamentally with their ability to participate freely in international trade. Land-lockedness can also be a changing or dynamic condition, as is illustrated by the case of Ethiopia. Ethiopia won sovereignty over Eritrea as a means of gaining access to the sea because of Ethiopia's perceived strategic importance: it therefore received the self-interested strong backing of the United States and enjoyed high political and diplomatic standing within Africa during the early days of African independence. But with the end of the Cold War Ethiopia again became land-locked, not just because of unquenchable Eritrean nationalism, but also because in the wider world geo-political context it lost much of its strategic significance and had filtered away much of its diplomatic strength.

It should be emphasised that there are different degrees of land-lockedness and, indeed, that some coastal states may feel themselves to be land-locked in some important respects. Zaire is an obvious case, for although as the colonial Congo Free State it was given a land corridor of access to the sea, it feels itself to be land-locked today as much as many land-locked countries. In some cases, too, part of a state is effectively land-locked – the Shaba (Katanga) province of Zaire, the Casamance region of southern Senegal and the Caprivi strip of Namibia are cases in point. Even coastal states may depend on seaports other than their own. In other cases, transit trade is necessary because of inadequate facilities for specialised goods within a coastal state.

Secondly, land-locked states have been created in two main ways. Many have colonial or imperial origins. Indeed, almost all the land-locked states of Africa and Asia are the product of the break-up of empires: the overseas empires of Belgium, Britain and France in the case of Africa, the French and British empires in Asia, and the contiguous empire of the former Soviet Union.

This creation of land-locked states though the break-up of empires may also in some cases be seen primarily as secessionism expressed as a fierce nationalism, usually combined with a complex amalgam of ethnic, linguistic or religious sentiments and a determination to achieve national independence from the state in which it was formerly embedded and incorporated. Rather than reacting against distant overseas colonial or imperial powers, these states express local nationalistic aims. Such secessionist movements largely explain the recent emergence of new land-locked states in the former Soviet Union and in the former Yugoslavia.

## Problems of Land-locked States

The land-locked states of Africa and Asia may be characterised by their dependency, which is in reality a double dependency. They are dependent in the sense that they rely on other states for access to the sea, but they are also dependent in the sense that all poor states are dependent. The land-locked states of Africa are poor, as is easily demonstrated by GNP per capita statistics, and all are effectively third-world countries. Their double dependency, arising from poverty and lack of independent access to the sea, sets African and Asian land-locked states at a serious disadvantage which contrasts strongly with the condition of land-locked states in Europe on the one hand and the seaboard states of Africa and Asia on the other. The extreme poverty of most land-locked states in Africa and Asia is largely, though not entirely, due to their land-lockedness. Poverty adds to the effects of land-lockedness; and land-lockedness reinforces poverty. Theirs is a pernicious vicious circle of poverty and lack of independent access to the sea.

It is immediately apparent from any reading of the chapters in this book that most of the problems faced by land-locked states in Africa and Asia derive from their dependency. As a matter of fact these states have often been denied access to the sea by particular routes and occasionally denied access to the sea via any route at all. For many political, military and economic reasons, routes have been closed deliberately to deny access to the sea to land-locked states in Africa and Asia. Access routes to the sea have also been denied to land-locked states by border closures incidental to the relationship between land-locked states and access states. Unrest or war within the access state, often quite unrelated to the land-locked state, may lead to such border closures which, even though not intended to harm the land-locked state, have a deleterious effect on them. The access dependency of the land-locked states of Africa and Asia is a frequently demonstrated occurrence. It is therefore a very harsh reality and not just a theoretical concept.

The political and economic costs of land-lockedness are many and obvious. The colonial or imperial origin of most of the land-locked states of Africa and Asia has imposed a burden on these states. The established former imperial routes of access were not always the shortest or the most convenient for the newly independent land-locked states in Africa and Asia, and in the case of the former Soviet Union gave access to the heart of empire rather than to the sea and the outside world; but at least they were safe routes which were not subject to arbitrary closure for political reasons. The withdrawal of the over-arching protective umbrellas of empire has often encouraged or forced newly independent land-locked states to seek alternative routes of access to the sea for three main reasons: to assert independence from the former empire; to avoid post-imperial political pressures, which might make expedient, or necessary, the need for an alternative route; and to gain the advantages of routes shorter than those bequeathed to them by their former colonial power.

These alternatives to the former imperial routes of access, developed for whatever reason, have been costly to create or improve and have placed severe burdens on what are often among the poorest states in the world. Moreover, land-locked states may not only have no sovereignty over or even right of passage over a route of access to the sea: they also have no means of controlling the quality of transport or security of movement over any access route, including investment in seaport facilities, road surface, width and route configuration, or rail maintenance and day-to-day operation.

Then there are other problems arising from a land-locked state having a different imperial inheritance from the access seaboard state. Differences in currency, banking and customs procedures are important to international trade and transit. Overall lie the differences in language, both local and former imperial, the latter usually retained officially and often used exclusively as the language of commerce.

The economic priorities of access states may differ significantly from those of land-locked states with regard to the access route to the sea on which the land-locked state depends. This is likely to be particularly acute in third-world countries where resources are scarce and even basic infrastructure limited. The access state may well have a completely different set of priorities, perhaps involving other projects in distant parts of the country, in the allocation of meagre resources.

Land-locked states rich in mineral wealth which rely on transport links with the coast to get their metals, ores, oil and coal to the world markets are peculiarly disadvantaged by their remoteness. The length, vulnerability and their lack of control over their routes of access to the sea are critical to their economic well-being or even survival. The access routes are the essential arteries of the life-blood of the raw material exports on which their economies depend.

It is difficult to separate out factors which stem directly from land-lockedness from other issues affecting poverty. Resource endowment, economic and social infrastructure levels as well as bad government, including ideological inflexibility, maladministration or corruption play their part, as they do in all third world countries. But land-lockedness in itself does contribute significantly to poverty and low economic performance. It is an additional burden borne by the poorest, and the linkage between land-lockedness and third world poverty must be acknowledged.

In addition, there are undoubtedly severe political costs for land-locked countries in their dependence on other states for physical access to the sea. As the previous chapter argues, all problems faced by land-locked states are fundamentally political in nature. Examples of the political problems posed by transit state governments are to be found in every chapter of this book, and this points to the immense practical significance of international law in protecting land-locked states against arbitrary or exploitative treatment by coastal transit states. Nevertheless, the political legacies bequeathed by their former colonial powers still present some land-locked states with intractable problems.

## Solutions

One way of tackling the various problems of land-locked states is to create *ad hoc* bilateral agreements between a land-locked state and its transit coastal neighbour or, where alternative routes of access exist, neighbours. In a few cases, such as Rwanda and Burundi, it may be necessary also to establish such agreements with other land-locked states through which access routes to the sea actually run.

Such bilateral agreements are directed primarily at securing the use of land transport facilities for the land-locked state. The problems of land-locked states arise basically from the need for free and secure access to the high seas across territory over which the land-locked state has no sovereignty. The legal position on this point is highly complex and by no means generally agreed. There is a clear division of opinion between those who argue that right of free access to the sea for all is supportable in international law, and those who argue that such right must be achieved by negotiation between the parties concerned. At the practical level, clearly, this division is largely between land-locked countries, which claim access to the sea as a right in international law, and many coastal states which insist that this right is of a contractual nature and is therefore revocable. A great deal has been written on the practical problems such a conflict of opinion raises – notably the problem of outlets to the sea for land-locked states through neighbouring transit states.

This issue relates very closely to the creation of land corridors of access. When Africa was partitioned the European powers perceived the need for land corridors of access of undisputed sovereignty. It was the division of colonial empires into separate units which in independence created the African land-locked states problem of today. The awareness of the need for corridors of access was carried over from the colonial period in the case of Ethiopia which was given sovereignty over Eritrea at the same time as other colonies were attaining their independence.

Similar considerations apply to air transport. While international law relating to air transport requires that overflying rights be obtained before the air space of another country may be entered, such a form of transport is of particular value to land-locked states. This is especially so where distances are great, population densities are low, and where the costs of good rail and road works and their maintenance are a major burden. Air transport has the great advantage of requiring very much lower capital outlays in this respect. Especially if the goods to be carried are of high value in relation to bulk, then air transport may well have an important role to play. Air transport is not necessarily a luxury and the development of air transport can have profound effects on the economic and psychological isolation of land-locked states.

A second means of ameliorating the ill-effects of land-lockedness is to reduce a country's dependence on external trade – in other words to restructure the internal economy of a land-locked state so that it faces its geographical realities, strives to become more self-sufficient, and so less dependent on transit states for access to the sea. This rather theoretical solution, however, is unlikely to be acceptable to most land-locked countries, compounding as it does the economic, political and psychological isolation land-lockedness already imposes and appearing to acknowledge the second-class status of land-locked states.

A third solutions is, in the opinion of most writers, the most attractive. That is to overcome the problem of land-lockedness by establishing reciprocal economic institutions, sometimes backed by multinational treaties, on the basis of international regions or groupings of states of one kind or another. However, the difficulty in practice of this course of action is that it does not necessarily avoid the political problems already referred to, though the wider spirit of economic and political co-operation engendered might contribute to creating the right context in which the specific problems of access to the sea by land-locked states could be addressed.

Yet experience suggests that the above 'solutions' are largely unrealistic or at best only long-term. In the face of fierce and increasing nationalism all solutions will in the end depend on the goodwill between neighbouring states. An immediate aim for all international agencies must be to foster such goodwill and co-operation. Meanwhile the only immediately practical solution is for each land-locked state to face the stark realities of its own particular geography and location and to act accordingly. As Seretse Khama put it for Botswana long ago: 'We decided never to ignore the harsh realities of our situation as an integral part of Southern Africa. We cannot pick up our vast country and replace it on some more comfortable portion of the map.'[1]

This perhaps sums it all up.

In many ways the land-locked state issue is simply one expression of the problem of international boundaries. This is an important point, for it can be argued – and this seems to be supported by many of the essays in this book – that land-lockedness, like a boundary, only becomes a problem when conflict between states has already been engendered by some other cause. As Hermans has put it:

> The hypothesis…is that the problems confronting landlocked states, like those of island states, stem not so much from the fact of their geographical situation as from the character of the environment which surrounds them – whether it is hostile or friendly, whether it encourages isolation or contact, whether it creates opportunities for internal development or drains domestic sources.[2]

The analogy Hermans draws between land-locked states and island states is an interesting one, emphasising as it does not so much the isolation that comes from lack of access to the sea as the isolation that comes from the unsatisfactory relationship a state has with its neighbours. The land-locked issue then becomes not only, as argued above, a question of relativity of power: it also mirrors the statement made by Ancel about boundaries – that there are no problems of boundaries; there are only problems between states.

After all, Switzerland demonstrates that a state need not necessarily or permanently be disadvantaged by its land-locked nature. A land-locked state can have strategic importance and may possess an important function as a buffer state, though, as in the case of Afghanistan, a buffer state can act negatively as a zone which increases rather than decreases its isolation. The relativity of power relationship is by no means simple or one-sided. The relationship between a large and/or economically powerful land-locked country and a relatively smaller and weaker neighbouring access country on the coast, admittedly rare in Africa and Asia, is very different from that which exists between a land-locked state and its equally or more powerful transit state. In analysing the consequences for a land-locked country it is crucial to bear in mind the dynamic relativity of power between it and its transit state or states. Important, too, is whether competing interests between neighbouring states within a land-locked state can result in inhibiting or encouraging investment and development in that state, as has been demonstrated for Mongolia.

In discussing land-locked states there is always the danger of emphasising exclusively the negative effects of being land-locked. But it may well be that the problems of land-locked states arise not so much from their geographical position away from any coastline as from the relations that exist between a land-locked state and its neighbour. It cannot be emphasised enough that a land-locked state can perhaps in the long term best deal with its problems by practising good relations with its neighbours. This demands an acceptance of its geographical realities and a determination to demonstrate that a land-locked country can prosper as a viable autonomous state.

## NOTES

1.  Seretse Khama, H.C.L. Hermans, 'Botswana's Options for Independent Existence', in Z. Cervenka, *Land-locked Countries of Africa* (Uppsala 1973) p.211.
2.  Ibid., p.197.

# Biographical Notes

**Ali Djimba** is the manager of TRANSPORT-CONSULT in Niamey, Niger. He has a MSc in Ports and Shipping Administration from the World Maritime University in Sweden. Mr. Djimba has been working on transportation problems related to the land-locked countries of West Africa for over 15 years.

**Martin Glassner** is Professor Emeritus of Geography at Southern Connecticut State University. He has advised the Government of Nepal on negotiating transit treaties with India (1976 and 1989) and has been a consultant for the United Nations Development Programme in South and Southeast Asia (1979) and Southern Africa (1984 and 1990). He is author of *Neptune's Domain: a Political Geography of the Sea* (Boston: Unwin Hyman, 1990) and *Political Geography* (New York: John Wiley & Sons, 1993).

**Ieuan Griffiths** is Professor Emeritus of Geography at the School of African and Asian Studies, University of Sussex. He is author of *The African Inheritance* (London: Routledge, 1995) and *An Atlas of African Affairs* (London: Methuen 1984).

**Dick Hodder** is Professor Emeritus of Geography at the School of Oriental and African Studies (SOAS), University of London. He has also taught at universities in Singapore, Ibadan, Nigeria and Queen Mary College, University of London. He is author of *Economic Development in the Tropics* (London: Methuen, 1980); *Economic Geography* (with Roger Lee) (London: Methuen, 1974) and editor of *Africa in Transition: Geographical Essays* (London: Barnes and Nobel, 1967).

**George Joffé** is Deputy Director at the Royal Institute of International Affairs. Before joining Chatham House, he was the Deputy Director of the Geopolitics and International Boundaries Research Centre, SOAS and an independent consultant on North Africa and the Middle East. Mr Joffé is co-author (with Keith McLachlan) of *The Gulf War: A Survey of Political Issues and Economic Consequences* (London: Economist Intelligence Unit, 1984); co-editor (with C.R. Pennell) of *Tribe and State: Essays in Honour of David Montgomery Hart* (Menas Press, Wesbech, 1991) and editor of *North Africa: nation, state and region* (London; Routledge, 1993).

**Sarah Lloyd** writes on oil and natural resource related-issues for the Cancasus, Central Asia and Middle East regions. She has worked as an independent consultant on regional issues and was a research associate at the Geopolitics and International Boundaries Research Centre, SOAS. Her publications include: "Pipelines to Prosperity?", in *The International Spectator* (Rome: Istituto Affari Internazionali, January 1997), and "Economic Development and Underdevelopment of Central Asia", in *Politica Internazionale* (Rome: IPALMO, Oct.–Dec. 1993).

**Keith McLachlan** is Professor Emeritus of Geography at SOAS and former Director of the Geopolitics and International Boundaries Research Centre, SOAS. He is author of *The Neglected Garden: the Politics and Ecology of Agriculture in Iran* (London: IB Tauris, 1988) and co-author (with George Joffé) of *Iran and Iraq: the Next Five Years* (London: Economist Intelligence Unit, 1987) and (with Richard Schofield) of *A Bibliography of the Iran-Iraq Borderland* (Wisbech: Menas Press, 1987.

**Wuhib Muluneh** recently undertook doctoral research in Geography at SOAS. He is a translator of Amharic and Urdu for the Foreign and Commonwealth Office, London. He has worked for the Border Research Department at the Ethiopian Ministry of Foreign Affairs and was the First Counsellor at the Ethiopian Embassy in London. Mr. Muluneh was also a member of the Ethiopian Government's Boundary Commission.

**Jonathan Rigg** is Reader in Geography at the University of Durham. He has published widely on the Southeast Asian region and worked in Thailand, Indonesia and Laos. His more recent publications include *Southeast Asia: a Region in Transition* (London: Routledge, 1994), an edited volume, *Counting the Costs: Economic Growth and Environmental Change in Thailand* (Institute of Southeast Asian Studies, 1995) and *Southeast Asia: the Human Landscape of Modernisation and Development* (London: Routledge, 1997). Other papers on Laos include: "Plenty in the context of scarcity: forest management in Laos" (with Randi Jerndal) in Raymond Bryant and Mike Parnwell (eds.) *Environmental Change in South East Asia: Rendering the Human Impact Sustainable,* (London: Routledge, 1996).

**Alan Sanders** is Lecturer in Mongolian Studies at SOAS. Prior to this appointment in 1991, he was an editor of the BBC Summary of World Broadcasts and specialised in Sino-Soviet border affairs. He speaks Mongolian and Russian. Over the past 30 years he has written numerous articles about Mongolia for reference works and journals. He is author of

*The Historical Dictionary of Mongolia* (Lanham, Md: Scarecrow, 1996); *Mongolian Phrasebook* (with J. Bat-Ireedui) (Hawthorn Lonely Planet, 1995); *Mongolia: Politics, Economics and Society* (London: Pinter, 1987); and *The PR of Mongolia: A General Reference Guide* (Oxford: Oxford University Press, 1968).

**Surya Subedi** is a lecturer in law at the University of Hull. Previously he was a lecturer in international law and development at the Institutue of Social Studies in The Hague. He has worked as a Legal Officer in the International Law and Treaty Division of the Napelese Ministry of Law and as an Assistant Public Prosector at the Attorney General's office in Nepal. He is author of *Land-locked Nepal and International Law* (Kathmandu: Kokila Gautam, 1989) and *Nepalese Administration Law* (Kathmandu: Ratna Book Store, 1985). Mr. Subedi has also written numerous articles including: "Transit rights of Nepal: Just and undeniable", *The Rising Nepal* (Kathmandu: April 17, 1989) and "The marine fishery rights of land-locked States with particular reference to the EEZ", *International Journal of Estuarine and Coastal Law* (London: 1987).

# Index

Abacha, Ibrahim 35
Abakan 144
Abbay 58
ADB 151
Abidjan 13, 47, 50
Adamec, L.W. 90, 91
Addis Ababa 23, 58, 62
Addis Ababa-Asmara axis 63, 75, 80
Adowa, Battle of 75
Afghanistan 2, 6–7, 82–96, 99, 101, 102,
   105, 106, 119, 120, 123, 124, 198, 201,
   206, 215
   1973 coup 87, 94
   borders 84, 86, 87 see also Durand Line
Africa 1, 3, 8, 199, 205, 206, 207, 209, 210,
   211, 213, 214, 215
   Central 29, 30, 32
   East 3, 13, 21, 22
      British territories in, 3
      German 14, 73
   French, Equatorial 1, 28, 30
      North 30
      West 1, 13, 29
   scramble for, 58, 70, 74, 75
   West 3, 29, 34, 41, 44, 45, 54
African Development Report 60
African National Congress (ANC) 20, 79
Afrique Equatoriale Française (AEF) 13, 74
Afrique Occidentale Française (AOF) 13
Aga 137
Agades 17, 18, 45, 50
Agip 115
Akhal Tekke 102
Albert, Lake 6, 74
Alexandroupoulis 116
Algeria 36, 44, 78
Algiers 50
all-Amhara Peoples Organisation (AAPO) 59
Almaty 124, 144
Altai mountains 97, 134, 148
Altai Republic 137, 138, 142
Altanbulag 143, 144, 148 see also
   Maimachen
Amarsanaa 139
America, North 200
   South 199, 200, 205, 206
Amin, Idi 21, 77–78
Amu Darya 84, 86, 88 see also Oxus
Amur river 138
Andhijan 102
Andorra 2

Angara river 136
Anglo-Boer war 16, 74
Anglo-French convention 31
Anglo-French Exchange of Notes (1931) 31
Anglo-French Spheres of Influence
   Agreement 30, 31
Anglo-German Agreement (1890) 73
Angola 15, 20, 22, 70, 71
Annamite mountains 156, 159, 168
Antofagasta 197, 205
Arabian Sea 82, 85
Arabs 4, 28, 29
Ardabil 123
Argentina 118, 205
Argun 138
Arkangel 123
Arlit 50
Arica 205
Armenia 2
   Turkish 106
Ashkabad 105
Ashkabad-Kuchan road 102, 123
Asia 199, 206, 209, 210, 211, 215
   Central 1, 3, 7, 8, 89, 90, 93, 94, 97–129,
      209 see also Kazakhstan;
      Kyrgyzstan;
      Tajikistan; Turkmenistan; Uzbekistan
   Minor 105, 106
   Southeast 119, 158, 161, 163, 165, 166,
      169, 171
   Southwest 7
Asian Development Bank 171
Asia and Pacific Council (APC) 202
Asiasat 143
Asmara 62, 63, 76
Assab 5, 18, 60, 62, 63, 76
Association of Southeast Asian Nations
   (ASEAN) 155, 156, 165, 166, 206
Astara 123
Astrabad 105
Atlantic Ocean 4, 71, 78
Atyrau 112
Australia 163
Austria 2, 45
Avarzad (Mongolian Foreign Minister) 142
Awash River 58
Awlad Sulayman 28
Azadshahr 123
Azerbaijan 2, 3, 105, 115, 120
Azerbaijan International Operating Company
   (AIOC) 116

Baganuur 145
Baguirmi 29
Baikal, Lake 136, 140
Bajgiran 123
Balkh 99
Baluchestan 82, 119
Bamako 13
Ban Houei Xai 169
Ban Rom Klao border conflict 167, 170
Banda, President 77
Bandar Abbas 8, 105, 121, 123
Bandar-e Anzali 118
Bandar Khomeini 114
Bandar Janoubi 114
Bandar Nowshahr 114
Bandar-e Turkoman 123, 124
Bangladesh 177, 182, 187, 189, 190
Bangui 13, 18
Barberton 16
Barcelona Convention on Freedom of Transit 9, 180, 182, 183, 189
Barcelona Declaration (1920) 46
Basutoland see Lesotho
Batoum 106
Batumi 116
Bayan-Olgiy 137
Bayangolin 137
Bayantumen 143, 144
al-Bayda 29
Bazargan 123
Bechar 78
Bechuanaland 73 see also Botswana
Beijing 134, 140, 144, 145, 147
Beira 15, 19, 20, 74, 77, 78
   corridor 78, 80
Beit Bridge 16
Belarus 2, 126
Belgium 6, 14, 42, 72, 74, 125, 210
Bengal, Bay of 179
Benin 5, 42, 44, 47, 53
Benin-Niger corridor 47
Benin-Niger Agreement (1975) 47
Beri 28, 29, 33
Berlin Africa Conference (1884) 1, 42, 70, 71
BET (Borkou-Ennedi-Tibesti) 30, 32, 33, 34, 35 see also individual regions
Bhutan 2, 178, 206
Bideyat 28
Bilgrami, A.H. 90
Bilma oasis 28
Bishkek 124
Biysk 140, 144
Black Sea 6, 7, 80, 114, 115, 116
Bobo Dioulasso 13
Boers 74, 76, 77, 79, 80

Bolivia 2, 197, 198, 200, 205, 206
Bombay 123
Bor-Ondor 145
Borkou 28, 35 see also BET
Bornu 29
Bortala 137
Borzya 144
Bosnia & Herzegovina 2
Bosporus 115, 116, 127
Botswana 2, 16, 17, 21, 22, 27, 73, 74, 204, 214
Botte de Diolo 72
Boudouma 45
Bourgas 116
Brazza, De 72
Brazil 200, 206
Brazzaville 13, 17, 18
Bridas 118
Britain 6, 7, 16, 18, 19, 31, 42, 58, 71, 73, 74, 75, 76, 77, 82 ,86, 89–94, 97, 102, 105, 106, 107, 125, 146, 210
British Gas 115
British Indian army 92
British South Africa Company 15
British-Russian agreements 89, 90, 91, 92, 102, 127
Brown & Root 116
Brunei 123
Buddhists 158
Budun 143
Buenos Aires 205
Buir, Lake 134
Bujnurd 106
Bukhara 99, 101, 102, 104, 105, 106
Bulgan sum 148
Bulgaria 115, 125
Burkina Faso 2, 13, 17, 18, 21, 22, 44, 47, 49, 52
Burma see Myanmar
Burundi 2, 3, 14, 17, 18, 22, 206, 213
Buryat Republic 134, 137, 138, 145, 147, 148
Buryats 137, 139
Bushire 105
Byambasuren, Prime Minister 147

Cabinda 71, 73
Cairo Declaration (1964) 3, 27
Calcutta 177, 188, 190
Cambodia 156, 159, 162, 165, 170, 171
Cameroon 18, 21, 22, 23, 29, 31, 33, 37 see also Kamerun
Canada 179
Canton 85
Cape, the 6, 15
   Colony 74, 77

Caprivi strip 5, 73, 79, 210 *see also* Zipfel
Casamanace 210
Caspian sea 7, 97, 105, 114, 116, 118, 123,
   124, 136
   basin 7
   states 8
Caspian Pipeline Consortium (CPC) 115, 116
Caucasia 1
Caucasus 97, 102, 106, 116, 118, 119
Central Treaty Organisation (CENTO) 86, 120
Central African Republic (CAR) 2, 13, 17,
   21, 30, 37
CEPAL 205
Cervenka, Zdenek 67
Ceyhan 116
Chad 2, 3, 4, 13, 17, 18, 21, 22, 23, 25–38, 44
   Aozou strip 3, 4, 27, 32, 35, 36, 37 *see*
   *also* Libya-Chad dispute
   borders 30, 31–32, 35, 36
   civil war 4, 35–36, 37, 38
   French in 29, 30
   Muslim Sultanates 29, 33, 34
Chah Bahar 8, 84
Chahar 138
Chaman 86, 87
Charlemagne 89
Celeken 114
Chechnya 116
Cherikar 86
Chevron 97, 114, 115 *see also* Tengizchevroil
Chiang Khong 169
Chicualacuala *see* Railway, Malvernia
Chile 197, 205
Chiloango River 71
Chimkent 101, 112
China 7, 8, 9, 19, 82, 85, 113, 118, 121, 124,
   125, 126, 134, 137, 138–140, 141, 145,
   146–149, 150, 156, 165, 170, 171, 175,
   176, 177, 178, 179, 187
Chinde 15
Chingunjav 139
Chirag 116
Chita 137, 138
Chobe River 73 *see also* Cuando River;
   Linyanti River
Choybalsan *see* Bayantumen
Christianity 58, 137
Chuluunhoroot *see* Ereentsav
Chuya *trakt* 144
Clad, J. 180
Club du Sahel 206
cold war 9, 93, 155, 171, 209
COMESA (Common Market of Eastern,
   Central and South Africa) 67
Community of Independent States (CIS) 82,
   85

Conakry 13
Congo 5, 13, 70–73, 74, 79
   Belgian 14 *see also* Congo Free State
Congo Free State 71, 210
Congo River 6, 18, 70, 71–73, 74 *see also*
   Kinshasa-Matadi corridor
Conoco 118
Convention on Transit Trade of Land-Locked
   States (1965) 46, 180, 181, 186, 200
Convention on the Law of the Sea (1982) 9,
   10, 180, 181, 183, 184, 189, 190, 198,
   199, 201, 20 *see also* UNCLOS III
Copperbelt 15, 18, 19, 20
corridors *see* land corridors
Cotonou 44, 45, 47, 49, 50, 51, 53
Cotonou-Niger corridor 51, 52, 53
COTTONTCHAD 33
COTTONFRAN 32
Crimean war 89
Cuando River 73 *see also* Chobe River;
   Linyanti River
Customs Co-operation Council 205
Cuba 125
Cubango River 73
Curzon, Lord 92
Customs Union 77
Cyrenaica 29
Czech Republic 2
Czechoslovakia 125, 199

Daghestan 116
Dahomey *see* Benin
Dakar 13, 17
Damghan 123
Danang 166
Dar es Salaam 18, 19, 20
Darfur 28, 33, 36, 37, 38
Darhan (Mongolia) 143
Datong 134
Davst *uul* 141, 142, 150
Daza 35, 36
Dazaga 28
Debre Margos 59
Deby, Ibrahim 36, 37, 38
Delta Oil 119
Dendi 45
Derde 33, 35
Dergie 58
Diffa 45, 50
Diolo *see Botte de Diolo*
Diredawa 59
Djamous, Hassan 36
Djcheina 28
Djellaba 28
Djibouti 5, 18, 56, 58, 60, 61, 63, 65, 66, 67,
   76, 80

Don Khong 164
Dorbod see Heilongjiang
Doshi 86
Dosso 45
Douala 18
Druzhba 113, 121
Dungans 140
Dupree, Louis 92
Durand Line 85, 86, 92
Durban 76, 80

East African Economic Community (EAEC)
   67, 202
East London (South Africa) 20
East Siberian River Shipping Line 143
East Turkestan 137, 139 see also Xinjiang
East Turkestan Republic see Xinjiang Uighur
   Autonomous Region
ECA 205
Economic Co-operation Organisation (ECO)
   120, 121
Economic Community of West African States
   (ECOWAS) 53, 67, 207
Edward, Lake 6, 74
Egypt 29, 36, 37, 56, 102, 104, 107
Economist Intelligence Unit (EIU) 60, 61,
   62, 63
Elizabethville see Lubumbashi
Ennedi 4, 28 see also BET
Ente Nazionale Idrocarburi (ENI) 118
Erdenet 143, 145
Ereen 134, 145, 146
Ereentsav 144
Erenhot see Ereen
Erhlien see Ereen
Eritrea 1, 5, 6, 12, 14, 56, 58, 60, 61, 62, 66,
   67, 75–76, 80, 209, 213
ESCAP 205
Ethiopia 2, 5, 6, 12, 14, 18, 21, 22, 23,
   56–68, 75–76, 80, 209, 213
Ethiopia, Eritrea and Djibouti Economic Co-
   operation Body (EEDEC) 67
Ethiopian Highway Authority 63
Ethiopian Peoples Revolutionary Democratic
   Front (EPRDF) 59
Europe 22, 41, 42, 62, 105, 114, 116, 118,
   124, 199, 205, 213
   Eastern 58, 136, 145
European Union 66, 116
Evenkis 139
Ezenwe, Uka 40

Forces Armées du Nord (FAN) 35
Forces Armées Tchadiennes (FAT) 35
Fawcett, J. 181
Faya Largeau 35

Ferghana valley 104
Fezzan 28, 29
Fort Lamy see N'djamena
Fort Salisbury see Harare
Fort Troitskiy see Troitskosavsk
Fotokol 23
Four Power Commission 75, 76
France 8, 32, 35, 36, 37, 42, 58, 65, 66, 71,
   74, 75, 80, 89, 159, 210
Franco-British agreement 31
Franco-German conventions 31, 74
Franco-Italian Agreement (1919) 4, 31, 32
Franco-Italian Exchange of Notes 31
Franco-Libyan Friendship Treaty (1955) 32
FRELIMO 19, 78
French Sudan see Mali
French Union 34
'Friendship Bridge' 167
FROLINAT 34, 35, 36, 37
Fulani 41
Fulbe 29
Fuxin and Harqin see Liaoning

Gambia 70
Gansu 138
Gardez 87
Ghana 18, 47
gas, natural 3, 114, 115, 118–119
Gaudan 123
Gazprom 115, 119
General Agreement on Tariffs and Trade
   (GATT) 182
Geneva 162
Genghis Khan 136, 137
Genoa Convention (1923) 46
Geok Tepe 102
Georgia 115, 116, 123, 127
Germany 32, 42, 62, 71, 73, 74, 77, 91, 93,
   102, 125
Ghaus, A.S. 91
Ghion Hotel explosion 59
Glassner, M.I. 1, 166
Giorgis, Gerbre Hiwet Tesfa 62
Gissar 99
Gobi desert 134
Gobi Altai mountains 134
Gomal river 87
Goshen 74
Gonder 59
Gorbachev, Mikhail 142, 149
Gorchakov, Prince 89, 127 see also British-
   Russian agreements
Gornyy Altai see Altai republic
Granville, Lord 89 see also British-Russian
   agreements
Great Horde 101

Greece 116, 125
Grozny 116
Guadeloupe 34
Guera 29, 36
Guinea 13
Guneshli oil fields 116
Guryev *see* Atyrau
GUNT 35
Gusinoozersk 145

Habre, Hissan 35, 36, 37, 38
Hadjeray 29, 36
Hague, The *see* International Court of Justice
Hailar 148
Haile Sellasee I, Emperor 58, 63, 75, 76
Haldia 190
Halh 139
Halhyn Gol, Battle of 138
Handgayt 144
Hanh 143
Hanoi 166
Hara *gol* 143
Harare 74
Hardstone, P.C.N. 159, 166
Hari Rud river 84
Hassaouna 28
Hatgal 142, 143
Hausa 41, 45
Heavenly Mountains *see* Tien Shan
Heilongjiang 137, 138
Helmand river 84
Henan and Haixi *see* Qinghai
Hentiy 134
Herat 86, 87, 89, 99, 106, 124
Herlen river 148
Hermans, H.C.L. 214
High Seas Convention (1958) 180, 183
Himalayas 177, 179
'Himalayas frontier policy' 177
Hindu Kush 82, 84, 86, 92
Ho Chi Minh City 159, 166
Ho Chi Minh Trail 162
Hoboksar 137
Hohhot 144
Hongkong 151
Hongkong Hilco 148
Horn of Africa 56, 61, 67, 76
Horn of Arica Free Trade Area (HAFTA) 60
Houei Sai 163
Houphouet-Boigny, Felix 34
Hovd 137, 140, 141, 142, 144, 148, 150
Hovsgol, Lake 136, 141, 142, 143
Hué 166
Huis *see* Dungans
Hun Sen 165
Hungary 2, 125, 199

Hyman, A. 91

ICNL 54
'ideal-typical sequences' model 42
Ilebo 15, 72
Ilo 205
India 7, 9–10, 82, 85, 86, 89, 92, 97, 101, 102, 104, 105, 106, 123, 175–191 *see also* Durand Line
Indian Ocean 7, 71, 77, 78, 94
Indian subcontinent 82, 90, 94
Indo-Pakistan war 187
Indochina 153, 155, 159, 161, 165, 166, 169, 170
Indonesia 123, 165
Ingettolgoy 143
Inner Mongolia *see* Mongolia
Integrated Transit System *see* Sistema Integrada de Tránsito
International Association of the Congo (IAC) 70–71, 72
International Court of Justice 4, 32, 36, 37
International Monetary Fund (IMF) 151
Iran 7, 8, 82, 84, 85, 86, 87, 90, 94, 99, 114, 115, 118, 119, 120, 121, 123, 124, 127
Iraq 1, 200
Irkutsk 137, 139, 140, 142, 143, 144
Isiolo 23
Islam 29, 56, 124
Islam Qaleh 86, 87
Islamic fundamentalism 111
Israel 78
Italian East African Empire 75
Italy 31, 32, 58, 62, 65, 75, 118, 125
  -Sanusi war 31
  Treaty of Peace with Ottoman empire 32
Ivory Coast 22, 47

Jandaq 123
Japan 62, 65, 118, 124, 138, 144, 146, 148, 151
Jarabub 29
Jilin 137, 138
Johanis, Emperor 58
Joint Sea Freight Company 148
Jolfa 121
Jonathan, Chief 20
Jordan 200
Jungaria 139
Jungarian basin 134
Jungarian desert 148

Kabul 84, 85, 86, 87, 89
Kabul river 84, 86
Kaduna 52
Kalahari Desert 6, 16, 73, 74

Kalgan 140
Kalmyk Republic see Khalmg Tangkhch
Kalmyks 137
Kamadja 4, 28
Kamerun 6, 74
Kampala 14
Kampuchea, Coalition Government of
    Democratic 165 see also Cambodia
Kandahar 124
Kanem 28, 29
KaNgwane 79
Kano 18, 52, 54
Kanuri 4, 28, 41, 45
Kara Kum desert 97
Karachaganak oil field 115
Karachi 124
Karakoram 124
Karnali Project 179–180
Kasai River 15, 72
Kashgar see Kashi
Kashi 124
Kashmir 102
Katanga 72, 210
Kathmandu 188, 190
Katun river 140
Kavir desert 123
Kawwar oasis 28
Kayes 13
Kazakhs 101, 137
Kazakhstan 2, 7, 97, 101, 108, 111–113, 114,
    121, 124, 125, 126, 137
Kazangula ferry 74
Keleft 88
Keng Kabao 167
Kenya 17, 18, 21, 22, 23, 58, 60, 206
Keoboualapha, Khamphoui 170
Kerman 121
Kerulen river see Herlen river
Khalmg Tangkhch 136, 137
Khama, Seretse 214
Khan, Amir Abdur Rahman 91
Khan, Daud 94
Khan dynasties 99
Kharg Island 114
Khiva 99, 101, 104, 105
Khmer Rouges 165
Khone 159, 163
Khorasan 99, 105
Khorezm 104
Khrushchev, N. 110
Khwaja Gogerdak 88
Kinshasa 15, 17, 79
Kinshasa-Matadi corridor 72, 73, 79 see also
    Congo river; Zaire river
Kisangani 14
Kisumu 14

Kobdo see Hovd
Koh Sefid 84
Koh-e Baba 84, 88
Kokand 99, 101, 138
Kopet Dagh 105
Korea, North 20
Korolev oil field 97
Kosh-Agash 142, 144
Kosi Bay 6, 77, 79, 80
Kouroussa 13
Krasnovodsk see Turkmenbashi
Kriangsak, General 167
Kroef, J. van der 168
Kruger, S.J.P. 77
Kufrah 28, 29
Kulyab 99
Kushka 86, 124
Kuwait 111
    invasion of 1
KwaZulu 79
Kyakhta 136, 138–140, 142, 145, 148
Kyakhta conference (1915) 141
Kyrgyzstan 2, 7, 108, 124, 126
Kyzl Kum desert 97
Kyzyl 141, 144

Lagos 18, 47, 49, 50, 51, 52, 53, 54
Lagos-Niger corridor 51, 52, 53
Lagos Accords 35, 3
Lake Chad 30, 31
Lamaism 137
Lamido-Dorayi, S. 54
land corridors 5–6, 15, 40, 69–80, 213 see
    also individual corridors
Lao Loum 158
Lao Theung 158
Lao Soung 158
Laos 2, 8–9, 153–174, 206
Laos-Thailand treaties 169
Larmag 114
Latin American Free Trade Area (LAFTA)
    202
Lauterpacht, E. 181, 182, 183
La'youn 78
League of Nations 14, 18, 73, 197, 199, 200
Lebombo mountains 77, 79
Lee Yong Leng 166
Lekhanya, Major-General Justin 20
Lenin, V.I. 107, 110
Leningrad 149 see also St Petersburg
Leopold II 71
Leopoldville 70, 71, 72 see also Kinshasa
Lesotho 2, 12, 16, 20–21, 22, 204
Lianyungang 124
Liaoning 137
Liberia 12

Libya 3, 4, 28, 29, 30, 31, 32, 33, 34, 35, 36, 37, 38, 44, 118
-Chad dispute 27, 32
Linabol 200
Liechtenstein 2
Linyanti River 73 see also Chobe River; Cuando River
Lisette, Gabriel 34
Little Horde 101
Living Buddha 140
Livingstone, David 73
Lobito 20
Lomakin, defeat of 102
Lomé 44, 47, 50, 51
Lomé-Niger corridor 51, 52, 53
Lourenco Marques 76, 77 see also Maputo
Luang Prabang 156, 159, 162, 163, 166
Lubumbashi 72
Lukoil 112, 115
Luxemburg 2

Macedonia 2, 207
Mafikeng see railway, Mafeking-Bulawayo
Mahamid 28
Mahaqi Strip 74
Mahgi strip 6
Maiduguri 18
Maimachen 139
Maiubeni 118
Makariyev 139
Makhachkala 116
Malawi 2, 6, 14, 22, 77, 204
Malawi, Lake 77
Malaysia 123, 165
Mali 2, 13, 17, 18, 19, 21, 22, 44, 200
Malloum, Felix 35
Maltham 23
Manchus 134, 138, 139, 140
Manchukuo 138, 144, 150
Mangalme 35
Mao 146, 147
Maputo 15, 17, 19, 76
Maradi 44, 45, 49, 50, 51, 52, 53
Marday 145
Marwa 84
Mashhad 123
Massawa 58, 62, 63
Matadi 14, 15, 18, 20, 70, 71, 72
Matarani 205
Matun 87
Mazandaran 123
Mazar-e Sharif 86, 88
Mbabane 17
Mecca 102, 124
Mediterranean 78, 115
Mekong River 8, 156, 159, 162, 163, 166,

167, 169, 171
Greater Mekong Sub-region 171
Menelik, Emperor 58, 65
Mengist Hallemarion, Col. 58, 63, 76
Merv 8, 90
Meshhed 8, 86, 101, 102, 105, 106
Mexico 179
Mfecane 16
Middle East 7
Middle Horde 101
Midland Lao see Lao Theung
Minusinsk 140
Mittaphaap see 'Friendship Bridge'
Mo'alleman 123
Mobil 118
Moldova 2
Molo 30
Molotov, Vyacheslav 142
Mombasa 17
Mondy 142, 143
Mongol Empire 149
Mongolian-Tuvan agreements 141, 142
Mongolia 2, 8, 134–152, 206, 215
Inner 147, 148
Mongolian Social Democratic Party 149
Mongolian People's Revolutionary Party 141
Mongolian Tuushin Company 148
Mongols 137, 138, 139, 140
Montego Bay Convention (1982) 47, 181
Moors 28
Morocco 36, 74, 78
Moscow 101, 144
Moubi 35
Moundang 29
Movement for the Integrity of the Sacred Border 149
Moyale 23
Mozambique 16, 20, 22, 77, 78, 80, 200
civil war 78
Portuguese 15
see also Nkomati Accord
Mozambique Channel 19
Mukdahan 169
Munaigaz 115
Murzuq 28
Muslims 102, 111, 140
Mussolini-Laval Agreement 32
Mutare 6, 19, 78
Myanmar 156, 170, 171, 200

Nairobi 23
Nakhodka 149
Nakhon Phanom 159, 169
Nalayh 144
Namibia 5, 73, 74, 210
Naser ed-Din 106

Natal 77
Natalia Republic 76
Naushki 145, 148
Ndebele rebellion 74
N'Jamena 18, 29, 34, 36
Neka 123
Nepal 2, 9–10, 175–191, 198, 200, 201, 204, 206
Nepalese treaties 175, 176, 177, 178, 179, 180, 187 see also Transit Treaties
Netherlands 125
New Economic Mechanism (NEM) 155–156, 157
Ngaoundere 23
Nguigmi 50
Ngwavuma 79
Niassa 77
Niassa corridor 6
Niamey 45, 47, 49, 50, 51
Nice 32
Niger 2, 4–5, 13, 17, 21, 31, 40–55
Niger River 4, 13
Nigeria 21, 22, 23, 31, 35, 37, 44, 45, 47, 49, 50, 54
Nigeria-Niger Agreement (1977) 49
Nigerian Corridor, 49
Nijni Novgorod 106, 139
Nile 13 see also Abbay
Ningxia Hui 138
Nkomati Accord 79
Nokki see Noqui
Nomonhan see Halhyn Gol, Battle of
Noqui 71
Nong Khai 169
North America Free Trade Agreement (NAFTA) 67
North West Frontier 93
Northern Corridor Transit Agreement 206
Northern Corridor Transit Transport Co-ordination Authority 206
Northern Rhodesia see Zambia
Norway 97, 140
Novorossiysk 114, 115, 116
Nyasaland see Malawi

Ob river 140
Obangui River 6, 74
Obangui-Chari see Central African Republic, Ochirbat, President 144
Odessa 149
Ogaden 27
oil 3, 7, 19, 61, 62, 65, 71, 111–113, 115–118, 119, 120, 121, 127, 145
Oirats 137, 139
Okavango River see Cubango River
Oman 115

Oman, Gulf of 84, 85, 114
Oman Oil Company 115
Opium War 140
Orange Free State 15
Organisation of African Unity (OAU) 12, 27, 35
Organisation of American States 205
Organisation Commune Benin Niger des Chemins de Fer (OCBM) 47
Organisation for Economic Cooperation and Development (OECD) 7
Orhon river 143
OROMO Liberation Front (OLF) 59
Oryx Energy Company 115
Ottoman empire 28, 29, 31, 32, 56
Ouaddai 29
Ouagadougou 13
Oueddei, Goukouni 35, 36
Outer Mongolia see Mongolia
Oxus river 84 see also Amu Darya

PAC-EEC Convention of Lome 47
Pact of Steel 32
Pakistan 82, 85, 86, 87, 92, 93, 94, 119, 120, 121, 123, 124, 182
Pakse 159, 163, 164
Pakxan 164
Pamir 84, 90, 97, 99
Pan-Mongolism 148
Pante, F. 171
Paraguay 2
Parakou 49, 52
Partem, M. 89
Party Progressiste Tchadien 34
Pathan 82
Pathet Lao 153, 157, 158, 165, 166, 167, 168
Pavlodar 112
Peking see Beijing
Penjdeh 90
Persia 89, 93, 99, 101, 102, 105, 106
Persian Gulf 6, 7, 82, 86, 87, 94, 114, 124
Peshawar 85, 86
Philippines 123, 165
Phnom Penh 159, 165, 166
Pointe Noire 13, 18
Pol Pot 165
Poland 125
POLISARIO 78
Pongola river 79
Port Florence see Kisumu
Port Francqui see Ilebo
Port Harcourt 18
Portugal 71, 72, 77
Poti 116
Prescott, J.R.V. 89
Pul-e Khumri 86

Pular 45
Punjab 102
Pushtun 93

Qadhadhfa 28
Qadhafi 36, 37
Qandahar 86, 87
Qian Gorlos *see* Jilin
Qing empire 137, 139, 140, 146
Qinghai 138
Qinghe county 148
Quchan 8, 123
Quetta 85, 124
Qunduz 84
Quchan 106

Rabih 29
Radhikapur 187, 190
Ragunzinskiy, Savva 139
Rana Prime Minister 180
railway
   Abidjan 18
   Abidjan-Ouagadougou 18–19
   in Afghanistan 85, 91
   in Africa 3 *see also* individual lines
   all-Congo route 20
   Bafq-Tehran-Tabriz line 121
   Bandar Abbas-Bafq 121
   Bandar Nowshahr- Bandar Janoubi 114
   Bangkok-Nong Khai 166
   Bangkok-Vientiane 169
   Beira rail corridor 6, 77
   Benguela 15, 20, 72, 73
   in Benin 42, 47
   Cape-Cairo link 6, 72–73, 74
   Cape-Copperbelt 15, 18
   in Central Asia 102, 106–107, 121, 126
   Cotonou-Parakou 49
   Ethiopia-Djibouti 14, 65–67, 80
   in Iran 121–123
   in Laos 159
   Lagos-Kano line 52
   Lubumbashi-Ilebo 72, 73
   Mafeking-Bulawayo 74
   Malawi-Naccala line 18
   Malvernia 19
   Mashhad-Sarakhs 121
   Matadi-Kinshasa 70, 72, 73
   Marv-Kushk 102
   Mombasa-Kampala link 3, 14, 17
   in Mongolia 8, 140, 144–146
   Naushki-Ulan Bator line 145
   in Niger 47–49, 54
   in Pakistan 85, 124
   Samarkand-Tashkent-Andhijan 102
   in Soviet Union 123

Tanzam-Dar es Salaam 19–20
Tedzhen-Sarakhs 121
Trans-Iranian 3
Transcaspian 102, 104, 105, 106, 124
Trans-Mongolian 134, 143, 145
Trans-Siberian 107, 134, 140, 144, 145,
   146, 148, 149
Turk-Sib 107
Ulan Bator Railway Joint Stock Company
   145
Zamyn-Uud-Ereen link 148
Rao, Narasimha 181
Ras Hotel explosion 59
Rasht 123
*Rassemblement Démocratique Africain* 34
Razi 121
Red Sea 56, 76
Renamo 78
Retief, 76
Rhodes, Cecil 6, 15, 16, 73, 74, 77, 78
Rhodesia 3, 19, 73, 74, 77, 78 *see also*
   Zimbabwe
Rhodesia and Nyasaland Federation 14
Richards Bay 80
Rift valley 58, 59
Riga 123
Romania 125
Roucek, J.S. 91
Royal Lao Government 165, 166
Ruanda-Urundi *see* Rwanda; Burundi
Rubinson, Seven 58
Russia 3, 6, 7, 8, 80, 82, 85, 89–94, 99, 101–
   106, 107, 111, 112, 113, 114, 115, 119,
   123, 126, 127, 134, 136, 137, 138–141,
   146, 147, 148, 151, 207
Russians 101, 138
Rwanda 2, 3, 14, 17, 18, 22, 206, 213

Sabourin, Louis 44
Sacadi tribes 29
Safid Koh *see* Koh Sefid
Sahara 4, 13, 28, 29, 34
Saigon *see* Ho Chi Minh City
Salang Tunnel 86
Samarkand 99, 102
San Marino 2
Sanusi Order 29, 31, 32
Sara 29, 33, 34, 35, 38
Sarakhs 8
Saratov refinery 112
Sarqez 84
Sarra Triangle Dispute 31
Sarup, A 185
Saudi Arabia 62, 65, 119, 124
Savannakhet 164; 166, 167, 168, 169
Sayan mountains 134, 138

Sekong 164
Selenga State Shipping Line 143
Selenge river 136, 143
Selenginsk 139
Semnan 123
Semple's "central countries" syndrome 9
Senegal 19, 22, 210
Senegal River 13
Shaanxi 113
Shaba see Katanga
Shabin Dabaga 138
Shahrud 105, 123
Shangai 118
Shangkun, Yang 147, 149
Sharagal 143
Sharyn Gol 145
Shavinayn Davaa see Shabin Dabaga
Sharif, Nawaz 120
Shir Khan Bandar 86
Shire valley 15
Siberia 101, 112, 136
Siberian Far East Oil Company (Sidanco) 112
Sichuan 113
Siddick, Abba 34
Sierra Leone 12
Sikkim 178
Silk Roads 99, 125
Siltou 30
Singapore 151, 165
Sino-Mongolian agreements 147, 148, 149
Sino-Russian treaties 138, 139, 140
Sino-Russian declarations 141
Sino-Soviet Mongolian agreement 145
Sirindhorn, Crown Princess Mahachakri 169
Sistan 84
Sistema Integrada de Tránsito (SIT) 205, 206
Skobelev, General 102
slavery 4, 29, 42
Slavs 137
Slovakia 2, 207
Slovenia 2
Smith, I.D. 78
Society of Mongolian Sea Lovers 149
Solovyetvsk 144
Somalia 58, 60, 61
Somaliland 75
Songhai 41, 45
South Africa 6, 14, 15, 16, 20, 22, 27, 73, 76, 78–79, 206 see also Nkomati Accord
South African Development Council (SADC) 20, 27, 67
South African Republic see Tranvaal
South Asian Association for Regional Co-operation (SAARC) 206, 207
South China Sea 159, 168

South West Africa 73 see also Namibia
Southern African Development Co-ordination Conference (SADCC) 202, 205, 207
Sovetabad oil field 119
Soviet Union 7, 8, 12, 58, 75, 82, 84, 85, 86, 87, 88, 93, 94, 97, 106, 107, 109, 110, 111, 112, 113, 120, 134, 136, 137, 138, 141, 142, 144, 145, 146, 147, 149, 150, 165, 168, 206–207, 210, 211
break up 1, 120, 125, 126, 153, 207
former Soviet Union republics (FSU) 120, 123, 126, 127
see also Russia
Soviet-Mongolian agreements 142, 144
Spykman, J. 89
St Louis 13
St Lucia Bay 76
St Petersburg 85 see also Leningrad
St Petersburg Convention 90
Stalin, Joseph 146
Stanley, H.M. 70, 72
Stanley Pool 71, 72
Stanleyville see Kisangani
Stanovoy mountains 138
Stellaland 74
Stuart-Fox, M. 158, 159, 161, 165
Suhbaatar 143, 148
Subei see Gansu
Sui 119
Suiyuan 138
Sudan 29, 31, 33, 34, 36, 37, 38, 58, 60
Swazi kingdom 16
Swaziland 2, 6, 12, 16, 17, 22, 27, 77, 78, 79, 200, 204
Switzerland 2, 45, 54, 58, 199, 215
Szentes, Thomas 54

Tabriz 105, 123
Tahoua 45
Taiwan 151
Tajikistan 2, 7, 108, 126
Taklamakan 119
Tambacounda 13
Tamsagbulag 145
Tang-e Gharu 86
Tanzam 18
Tanga 78
Tanganyika 14
Tanganyika, Lake 6, 71, 74
Tangdy-Uula see Tannu-Ola mountains
Tannu-Ola mountains 141
Tanzania 6, 78
Tariat 142
Tarim Basin 118
Tashanta 144

Tashkent 105, 110
Taussig, H.C. 91
Tbilisi 116
Teda 35
Tedaga 28
Tehran 105, 106, 124
Tema 47
Tengiz oil field 97, 114, 115, 116
Tengizchevroil 114
Termez 86
Tes *gol* 141
Tha Deua 163, 167, 169
Thai Express Transport Association 167
Thailand 8–9, 123, 156, 159, 161, 163, 165,
    166, 167, 168, 169, 170, 171
Thakhek 159, 163, 164, 166, 169
Thapa, D.B.S. 185
Thewdros, Emperor 58
Tianjin 8, 134, 140, 148, 149
Tibesti 4, 28, 33, 35 *see also* BET
Tibet 90
Tien Shan 97, 119
Tikhoretsk 116
Tindouf 78
TIR Convention 205
Tobolsk 139
Tomsk 139
Togo 44, 47, 49, 53
Togo-Niger corridor 49
Togolese Presidential Order 47
Tokyo 151
Tombalbaye, François 34, 35
Tongaland 77
Torkham 86
Torghundi 86, 87
Touareg 28, 41, 45
Toundjour 28
Toynbee, Arnold J. 56
Trankell, I.B. 158
Trans-Balkan pipeline 115
Transcaspia 101, 127
Transcaspian region 106 see also Railway,
    Transcaspian
Transcaucasia 1, 7
Transit Treaties 10, 182, 185, 186–191, 198
    *see also* Nepalese treaties
Transneft 115
Transvaal 6, 15, 16, 73, 74, 77, 79
Treaty of Versailles (1919) 5, 46, 74
Trichardt, 76
TRIE Convention 47
Tripolitania 29
Troitskosavsk 139, 144
Tropic of Cancer 30
Tsagaannuur 144
Tsitsihar 138

Tuapse 116
Tubu 28, 29, 33, 35, 36, 37
Tummo oasis 31
Tunisia 32
Turkestan 106, 128
Turkey 7, 115, 116, 118, 120, 127
Turkmen 101, 102
Turkmenbashi 123, 124
Turkmenistan 2, 7, 97, 108, 111, 113, 114,
    115, 118, 119, 121, 123, 124
Tuva 136, 137, 138, 141–142, 150
Tuvans 137
Tyumen 139
Tyva *see* Tuva

Uganda 2, 6, 13, 14, 17, 18, 21, 22, 67, 77,
    198, 200, 201, 206
Uighur *see* Xinjiang Uighur Autonomous
    Region
Ukraine 113, 123, 126
Ukrainians 101
Ulaanbaatar *see* Ulan Bator
Ulan Bator 8, 134, 136, 142, 143, 147
    *see also* Urga
Ulaangom 144
Ulan-Ude 134, 143, 144
Uliassutai 140, 141
Umtali *see* Mutare
*Union Nationale Tchadienne* 34, 35
UNIR movement 36
UNITA 20
United Nations 10, 19, 20, 45, 46, 75, 76,
    147, 151, 165, 178, 197, 200
United Nations African Recovery Program
    60
United Nations Conference on the Law of the
    Sea (UNCLOS III) 10, 181, 190, 198
United Nations Conference on Trade and
    Development (UNCTAD) Code of
    Conduite (1964) 46, 198, 202, 204, 205,
    206
United Nations Development Programme
    (UNDP) 119, 155, 161, 198, 205
United States 14, 36, 37, 62, 75, 75, 82, 86,
    94, 102, 104, 107, 118, 119, 120, 140, 146,
    151, 162, 165, 170, 179, 209
Unocal 119
Upland Lao *see* Lao Soung
Upper Volta *see* Burkina Faso
Urals 114
Urga 138, 140, 141, 142
Urgun 87
Urianhay *see* Tuva
Urumchi 113, 144, 148
Us *trakt* 144
USSR *see* Soviet Union

Ust-Orda 137
Usun-Ser 143
Uvs province 144, 150
Uvs, Lake 141
Uzbeks 139
Uzbekistan 2, 7, 107, 108, 109, 110, 113,
    115, 124, 126

Van Vieng 164
Vasciannie, 182, 184
Vatican City 2
Victoria, Lake 14
Victoria Falls 73
Vienna Convention on the Law of Treaties
    (1969) 181
Vientiane 155, 162, 163, 164, 166, 167, 169
Vietnam 8, 9, 153, 156, 159, 161, 162, 165,
    168, 169, 170, 171
Vinh 166
Vivi 72
Volga river 137, 139
Volgograd refinery 112
Volkstaat 80

Wakhan strip 82, 84
Wiang Chan see Vientiane
Witwatersrand 15
Western Sahara 27, 78
Wilber, D.N. 91
Wolde Mariam, Mesfin 59
World Bank 5, 19, 49, 63, 119, 151, 153, 155
World Trade Organisation 118
World War I 14, 17, 29, 30, 31, 93
World War II 7, 18, 73, 78, 86, 90, 93, 107,
    109, 110, 146, 159, 177, 200

Xieng Khouang 162

Xinkiang 113, 137, 144, 150
Xinjiang Uighur Autonomous region 124,
    137, 138

Yablonovyy chain 134
Yalta conference 146
Yapp, M. 93
Yazd 123
Yellow Sea 124, 134
Yenisey river 140, 141
Yeroo gol 143
Yugoslavia 12, 58, 207, 210
Yumurtalik 116
Yunnan 156, 170, 171

Zaghawa 28, 36, 37
Zahedan 121
Zahir Shah 94
Zaire 1, 5, 70–71, 79, 200, 206, 210 see also
    Congo
Zaire River 70–71 see also Congo River;
    Kinshasa-Matadi corridor
Zambesi River 5, 71, 73, 77
    valley 15
Zambia 2, 3, 14, 15, 17, 18, 19, 22, 73
Zamyn-Uud 134, 145, 146
Zasloff, J.J. 169
Zerma 41, 45
Zimbabwe 2, 6, 14, 15, 17, 20, 21, 22, 78, 80
Zinder 44, 45, 49, 50, 51, 53
Zipfel 73 see also Caprivi Strip
Zululand 77, 79
Zuunbayan 145
Zuwaya 28
Zyuganov, G. 115